Increasing Productivity Through Performance Appraisal

Second Edition

Increasing Productivity Through Performance Appraisal

Second Edition

Gary P. Latham
University of Toronto

Kenneth N. Wexley
Human Resource Decisions, Inc.

ADDISON-WESLEY PUBLISHING COMPANY
*Reading, Massachusetts • Menlo Park, California • New York
Don Mills, Ontario • Wokingham, England • Amsterdam • Bonn
Sydney • Singapore • Tokyo • Madrid • San Juan • Milan • Paris*

0-16   # 2850 4810

Library of Congress Cataloging-in-Publication Data

Latham, Gary P.
    Increasing productivity through performance appraisal / by
Gary P. Latham, Kenneth N. Wexley. -- 2nd ed.
            p.   cm. -- (Addison-Wesley series on managing human
    resources)
    Includes bibliographical references and index.
    ISBN 0-201-51400-1
    1. Employees--Rating of.   2. Labor productivity.   I. Wexley,
Kenneth N., 1943–   .   II. Title.   III. Series.
HF5549.5.R3L367   1993
658.3' 125--dc20   93-26044
                                                                    CIP

This book is in the Addison-Wesley Series on Managing Human
Resources

ISBN 0-201-51400-1
1 2 3 4 5 6 7 8 9 10 BAM 9796959493

To William P. Latham and Helen Wexley
for being models of exemplary performance

The Addison-Wesley Series on Managing Human Resources

Series Editor: John Parcher Wanous, The Ohio State University

Organizational Entry: Recruitment, Selection, Orientation, and Socialization of Newcomers, Second Edition
John Parcher Wanous
1992 (51480)

Merit Pay
Robert L. Heneman
1992 (52504)

Assessment Centers in Human Resource Management
George C. Thornton III
1992 (55403)

Fairness in Selecting Employees, Second Edition
Richard D. Arvey and Robert H. Faley
1988 (00078)

Foreword

This is an exciting time for the Managing Human Resources Series. Originally conceived in 1977, the first six books were published between 1979 and 1982. These books were uniformly well received by academic and business professionals alike. They have been extensively cited by researchers in human resources as state-of-the-art monographs. Moreover, students—both undergraduate and graduate—have found the series books to be both readable and informative.

The series is now in its second phase. *Fairness in Selecting Employees* (1979) by Rich Arvey was revised by Arvey and Robert Faley and published in 1988. This was followed by *Managing Employee Absenteeism* (1990) by Susan Rhodes and Rick Steers. My own book on *Organizational Entry* has been revised and reissued in 1992. Two new titles also appeared in 1992. The first was *Merit Pay* by Rob Heneman, and the second was *Assessment Centers in Human Resource Management* by George Thornton. The commitment from Addison-Wesley to continue and expand the series has been crucial. And now, for 1994 we have the Second Edition of Gary Latham and Kenneth Wexley's *Increasing Productivity Through Performance Appraisal*.

As always, this series is dedicated to the articulation of new solutions to human resources problems. My charge to authors has been to produce books that will summarize and extend cutting-edge knowledge. These authors must be intellectual leaders. In addition, they must make their books readily accessible to college students and human resource professionals alike. Readability need not and must not be sacrificed at the altar of academic scholarship. Both are achieveable, as evidenced by the first books in this series. The recent ones continue this tradition.

John Parcher Wanous
Series Editor

Preface

What are the chances that an employee will get a raise? Land a job in the Chicago or Toronto office? Be promoted to top management?

If a person works for a small company, the answers may depend on a series of informal judgments made by managers who know the employee well. But in a large organization the employee's chances may hinge on something much less personal: an evaluation form completed by a supervisor and then reviewed by another executive, who makes the final decision.

Most organizations are growing more and more dependent on formal performance reviews before making personnel decisions. These companies do not want to rely on informal evaluation systems, because they know that they are better able to avoid conflict with equal employment opportunity laws if they can justify their decisions with valid appraisal standards. More importantly, the companies know that well-developed appraisal systems increase their probability of retaining, motivating, and promoting productive people. Indeed, performance appraisals are crucial to the effective management of an organization's human resources, and the proper management of human resources is a critical variable affecting an employee's productivity.

Purpose of This Book

The purpose of this book is to answer seven questions:

1. How can we respond effectively to legal issues regarding performance appraisal?

2. How should the productivity of an employee be defined?

3. What type of appraisal instrument is not only valid, reliable, and free of bias but also facilitates coaching and developing employees?

4. From whom should data be collected for making appraisal decisions?

5. How do we increase the objectivity and accuracy of appraisers?

6. How do we bring about and sustain effective performance through the use of the performance appraisal?

7. How do we cut a person from the team?

We answer these questions by focusing on empirical research published in scientific journals during the past decade. Thus this book updates our first book (Latham & Wexley, 1981), which examined the literature through 1980 relevant to the first six questions. In this edition we added question 7 because terminations are a reality in organizations today and must be dealt with properly from both psychological and legal perspectives. The result is a book that describes an appraisal system that is valid, satisfies legal requirements, is perceived as fair, and, most importantly, defines and stimulates employee productivity.

Organization of This Book

Chapter 1 provides an overview of performance appraisals and their relationship to productivity. The chapter looks at the role of performance appraisals in the context of the management of an organization's human resource systems.

Performance appraisals have legal standing as tests. Therefore before an organization develops or modifies an appraisal system, it must take into account current laws. Chapter 2 focuses on legal issues in North America prohibiting employment discrimination, the roles of the OFCCP and the EEOC in enforcing those laws in the United States, and court decisions in the United States and Canada regarding performance appraisal. In addition, the 1978 Civil Service Reform Act is discussed because it specifies procedures to be followed in conducting performance appraisals with U.S. government employees and serves as a model for other organizations to follow.

Because performance appraisals must be able to stand up in court, they must be developed and validated carefully. Chapter 3 examines ways of defining and developing measures of an individual's productivity. Special attention is given to job analysis, that is, identifying the critical requirements of a person's job, and with this information developing the performance appraisal instrument. The chapter also considers the meaning of the word *valid* in both the legal and psychometric senses of the word.

Chapter 4 discusses different types of appraisal instruments. Chapter 5 considers sources of appraisals—not only the supervisor but also others—and discusses how they can be used to advantage in providing complete, accurate assessments of an employee's performance.

Regardless of who uses the appraisal instrument, human beings are notoriously poor at recording accurately what they observe. Chapter 6 addresses this topic, describing ways of increasing observer accuracy and objectivity in making performance appraisals.

Chapters 7 and 8 are concerned with increasing employee productivity; if productivity does not increase or remain high, there is little reason from a motivational standpoint to provide the results of a performance appraisal to the employee. Chapter 7 focuses on goal setting and considers the application of goal setting, as well as getting commitment to goals. Chapter 8 describes ways of conducting a formal appraisal interview and suggests ways to appraise and motivate employees on a daily basis, using the principles discussed in Chapter 7.

Inevitably, however, people will sometimes have to be let go. Terminating people with *class* is the subject of Chapter 9. Emphasis is given to ways of fostering and maintaining perceptions of organizational justice on the part of the people who remain on the team. To enhance employee productivity, the coaching staff must both be fair and be perceived as fair.

Acknowledgments

We wish to thank the following people for their comments on one or more preliminary chapters in this book: Dr. Kathryn Bartol,

University of Maryland; Dr. Dennis Dossett, University of Missouri; Dr. Hubert Feild, Auburn University; Dr. Michael Kavanagh, State University of New York, Albany; Dr. Richard Kopelman, City University of New York; Dr. Allen Kraut, City University of New York; Dr. Edward L Levine, University of South Florida; Dr. Steven McShane, Simon Fraser University; Dr. Aharon Tziner, University of Montreal.

We wish to acknowledge the work of Nina Cole and John Sargent for reviewing the literature for Chapter 9. We are particularly indebted to graduate student Daniel Skarlicki, University of Toronto, for his editorial assistance in writing this book, and to John Wanous, our editor, for reviewing this book in its entirety.

Toronto, Ontario   G. P. L.
Okemos, Michigan   K. N. W.

Contents

1

Performance Appraisal: The Key to Increasing Employee Productivity

Introduction

Performance appraisal systems are a lot like seat belts. Most people believe that they are necessary, but they don't like to use them. As a result, appraisal systems are being severely criticized from all sides and are often used reluctantly to satisfy some formal organizational or legal requirement. Managers find performance appraisals troublesome, particularly when they have to criticize an employee's performance and put the criticism in writing, and have become ingenious at finding ways to bypass them. Indeed, top management either ignores appraisals or, more often, goes through the motions but does not abide by the results (Steers & Lee, 1983).

Employees charge that the appraisals are often too subjective, and the federal courts frequently agree with them. Most disappointing of all, many executives themselves realize that existing performance appraisal systems do not bring about a positive change in their employees' behavior. In fact, the reverse is often the case. A seminal article in the *Harvard Business Review* showed that performance typically decreased for up to twelve weeks following an appraisal (Meyer, Kay & French, 1965). This result stems from a tendency for employees to attack the appraisal instrument (e.g., "You aren't measuring me on the right things"), the appraiser (e.g., "If you'd get out of your office more frequently, you would see what I am truly doing for this organization"), or both.

This is unfortunate because performance appraisals are crucial to the effective management of an organization's human resources, and the proper management of human resources is a critical variable affecting an employee's productivity.

Productivity and Human Resources

The productivity of most organizations is a function of the way at least three variables are managed: technology, capital, and human resources. Many organizations have been leaders in realizing dollar opportunities from technological development and capital investment. Many of these same companies, however, have failed to maximize productivity by failing to take full advantage of the abilities of their people.

Increases in performance due to capital or technological investments can be measured in traditional accounting terms (e.g., profits and costs, as measured by output/input). The influence of an individual employee on productivity in most jobs is difficult to measure in traditional cost accounting terms. The influence of an organization's human resources on productivity, however, can be measured in terms of *what people do* on the job. What people do can be appraised in terms of such traditional measures as attendance, accidents, turnover, and grievances. Also, what people do can be measured directly in terms of observations by managers, peers, subordinates, and customers as to the frequency with which employees do those things that are critical to job success. What people do or do not do should be a source of concern to all organizations. Current employee practices, such as coming to work late, stopping work early, and filling work orders incorrectly, cost one of our client companies $80,000,000, which was compounding at 7 percent annually.

Such ineffective employee behavior can and should be changed. Most organizations have little control over cost increases for such items as equipment and energy. But managers *can* influence what people do, to the benefit of their subordinates and the organization that employs them. However, most organizations have not yet totally explored in a systematic manner the development of effective human resource systems.

According to Deming (1986), an industrial engineer who has had a major influence on the quality movement in Japan, the performance appraisal is one of seven deadly sins afflicting managers in North America. He argued forcefully that most appraisals inappropriately attribute variation in performance to the individual employee rather than to problems inherent in the system, which leads managers to make incorrect attributions regarding production shortcomings and concomitantly to create morale problems within the workforce. No employee likes to receive a negative appraisal because of factors beyond his or her control; hence the employee's attack on the appraiser or the appraisal instrument is understandable.

As an industrial engineer, Deming was not aware of the benefit of shifting the appraisal from performance outcomes (e.g., units produced divided by employee hours worked) to employee behaviors that are largely under the person's control. Deming's supporters (e.g., Scholtes, 1987) understand the psychological benefit of using appraisers other than the person's supervisor. Behaviorally based appraisals and nontraditional sources of appraisal are described in detail in Chapters 4 and 5, respectively.

Human Resource Systems: The Key Role of Performance Appraisal

Staffing, performance appraisal, training, and motivation principles are four key systems necessary for ensuring the proper management of an organization's human resources. Of these four systems, performance appraisal is perhaps the most important because it is a prerequisite for establishing the other three.

The efficient use of an organization's human resources begins with *staffing,* namely, choosing the right person for the job. However, before a selection test can be developed for predicting who will be the right person for the job, the word *right* must be defined. To do this, effective on-the-job behavior must be defined. The core of the performance appraisal process is the definition of effective employee behavior. A valid selection test cannot be developed until the organization agrees on an acceptable definition (i.e., measure) of employee behavior. The validity of a test is determined by measuring the performance of people on the test and measuring their performance on the important aspects of the job. If the two measures have a significant correlation, the selection procedure is valid.

Staffing is important for two reasons. A proper staffing procedure can minimize difficulties with U.S. government agencies, such as the Equal Employment Opportunity Commission (EEOC) and the Office of Federal Contract Compliance Programs (OFCCP). More importantly, properly developed staffing techniques increase productivity because they assist organizations in screening out applicants who work at less than acceptable standards. The amount of money saved by effective screening can be enormous. For example, Schmidt et al. (1986) found that the use of validated tests for selecting people in white-collar jobs in the U.S. government results in increases in output worth up to $600 million for each year that the new employees remain employed by the government. The average tenure is thirteen years.

Valid staffing procedures can predict who is likely to be absent, to quit, to be dissatisfied with the job, and to perform the job well. However, if performance appraisals are based on biased or inaccurate observations, no degree of care in the development of selection instruments will improve selection/staffing decisions; the validity of a test is determined by correlating the test scores of individuals with their performance on the job. Therefore to the extent that the performance appraisals are biased, the effectiveness of the selection instruments is reduced.

No approach to staffing is foolproof. Therefore once a person has been selected for a job, the problem becomes one of monitoring and maintaining a high level of performance. Again, this is where performance appraisals play a critical role for both coaching and self-management (see Chapters 3, 4, 7, and 8).

The definition of performance appraisal is not limited to one-on-one situations in which a supervisor discusses with an employee areas deserving recognition and areas needing shifts in behavior. A *performance appraisal* is any personnel decision that affects an employee's retention, termination, promotion, demotion, transfer, salary increase or decrease, or admission into a training program.

A properly developed appraisal instrument serves as a contract between the organization and an employee in that it makes explicit what is required of that individual. Appraising performance is necessary because it serves as an audit for the organization about the effectiveness of each employee. Such a control system, based on key job behaviors that serve as standards, enables a manager to specify what the employee must start, continue, or stop doing. Similarly, such a control system is the crux for self-management on the part of the employee. As noted in Chapter 7, *it is the combination of performance feedback and the setting of specific stretch goals based on this feedback that enables the performance appraisal to fulfill its two most important functions, namely, the counseling (motivation) and development (training) of employees.* These primary purposes of performance appraisal are the basis of decisions made regarding an employee's retention, promotion, demotion, transfer, salary increase, or termination.

During the performance appraisal interview, the supervisor or the employee may determine that the employee is not fulfilling job responsibilities or behaving in a satisfactory manner due to lack of knowledge or skill. In such cases, *training* that brings about a relatively permanent improvement in an employee's behavior is critical for effective human resource development (Wexley & Latham, 1991). The job analysis on which the performance appraisal instrument should be based in order to satisfy legal challenges plays a key role in identifying training content. That is, the job analysis reveals the knowledge and skills in which employees as a group are deficient. In this way the job analysis specifies *what* must be taught in a training program. The performance appraisal identifies *who* should receive the training.

If a person has both the knowledge and skill to do the job but is doing it in an unsatisfactory manner, the problem may be one of *motivation*. The key components of effective motivation strategies include *feedback* as well as *self-monitoring,* which allow an employee to learn how well he or she is doing; *goal setting,* which specifies what the person should be doing; *team building,* which allows the employee to participate with peers and the supervisor in solving problems that impede productivity; and *incentives,* which reward good performance.

Performance appraisal lies at the heart of motivation because it is through the appraisal interview that the employee receives feedback from a manager and others (e.g., peers) regarding job performance. In addition, goals are set in relation to this feedback, problems that surface are resolved through manager-employee discussions, and rewards can be given contingent on satisfactory performance.

In summary, performance appraisal is a fundamental requirement for improving the productivity of an organization's human resources because it is through an appraisal that each individual's productivity is evaluated. An appraisal serves as the basis for counseling and developing an individual in ways that will instill the desire for continuous improvement. Performance appraisal is critical to selection systems because the job analysis on which the appraisal instrument is based enables human resource specialists to hypothesize the selection instruments that are likely to identify effective employees. Once an individual has been hired, it is necessary to determine whether the selection procedure worked. It is the correlation of employee evaluations on a selection instrument with the evaluations on the appraisal instrument that determines whether the selection instrument is a *valid* predictor of performance. After the individual has been on the job, the performance appraisal identifies who is in need of training or motivation.

Viewed in this way, the primary purpose of a performance appraisal system is to provide a measure of job performance that will facilitate ongoing coaching and developing the employee. In addition, at a time when managerial freedom to make personnel decisions is increasingly circumscribed by legal considerations, performance appraisal records should provide the documentation a manager needs if and when these decisions are challenged in court. All too often personnel files yield no more than a succession of undefined "satisfactory," "good," or "outstanding" ratings. As documentation against possible legal challenges or as an aid to improving employee effectiveness, most appraisal systems fall far short.

An Overview of Performance Appraisal

Given the vital role of performance appraisals, organizations need, at a minimum, to check their appraisal systems and the uses of such appraisal systems to determine whether key personnel decisions are affected by employees' age, race, sex, religion, color, national origin, or handicap. If adverse impact is evident, that is, if performance appraisal decisions are significantly different for one group (e.g., women), the organization must either abandon the appraisal system or justify its continued use.

Justifying an appraisal system is not easy. In order to continue using an appraisal system that has been shown to affect one or more groups (e.g., nonwhites, women) adversely, an organization must demonstrate that the system is valid. That is, the organization must show that the appraisal decisions are job related and that the appraisal instrument taps a representative sample of critical job duties.

The appraisal instrument is only as good as the people who use it; an appraiser must accurately observe significant aspects of the employee's job performance. Careful observation is necessary not only for making valid recordings of behavioral measures but also for evaluating the meaning of performance outcomes; in fact, "human judgment enters into every criterion from productivity to salary increases" (Smith, 1976, p. 757). Thus once a valid appraisal instrument has been developed, the decision must be made as to *who* will use the instrument.

There are at least six possible sources of an appraisal. Observations can be made by managers, peers, subordinates, employees themselves, customers, or some combination of the above. Whatever the source of the appraisal, uniformity and objectivity are mandatory for maintaining feelings of equity among employees, particularly when the function of the appraisal is to motivate them through recognition for work accomplishments. Uniformity and objectivity are also a "must" when monetary rewards are tied to performance; a minimum requirement for money to serve as a motivator is for employees to believe that their performance is being recorded objectively by management.

In addition to monetary incentives, goal setting, reinforcement, training in self-management, and team building can function as motivational procedures. These techniques can increase an individual's productivity after the appraisal instrument has been validated and the observers have been trained to record objectively what they have seen an employee do on the job.

Figure 1.1 depicts the activities involved in an appraisal and serves as an outline for this book.

Review Legal Requirements
↓
Conduct Job Analysis
↓
Develop Appraisal Instrument
↓
Select Observers
↓
Train Observers
↓
Measure Performance
↓
Give Employee Feedback
↓
Establish Performance Goals
↓
Praise/Reward Performance
↓
Align Process and Outcome with
Organizational Justice Principles

Figure 1.1
The Performance Appraisal Process

Closing Remarks

That organizations in North America are continuing to attach increasing importance to performance appraisals is evident from a recent survey by Locher and Teel (1988). Whereas 89 percent of organizations in the United States conducted formal performance appraisals in 1977, 94 percent were doing so by 1988. The basis for the importance attached to appraisals can be seen in their myriad purposes (Cleveland, Murphy & Williams, 1989; Lawler, 1988; Mallinger & Cummings, 1986), namely:

1. ensuring mutual understanding of effective performance
2. building confidence between employer and employees

3. clarifying any misunderstandings regarding performance expectations
4. establishing developmental procedures
5. allocating rewards
6. sustaining and enhancing employee motivation
7. career planning
8. fostering communication and feedback

Companies' use of performance appraisals for multiple purposes has increased from 11 percent in 1977 to 30 percent in 1988 (Locher & Teel, 1988). This increase reflects the widespread recognition that performance appraisals that are done effectively increase employee productivity and decrease an organization's costs.

In reflecting on the literature on performance appraisal, one can only marvel at the specific difficult goal that John F. Kennedy set in 1960, namely, to put a man on the moon and bring him back safely within a decade. One can only wonder what would have occurred if the American and Canadian Psychological Associations too had set a similarly difficult goal in 1960 for performance appraisal: "Within this decade we will teach people to appraise others accurately, and we will find ways to create the will within employees to start doing or continue doing things effectively as a result of the appraisal."

The appraisal system we advocate is based in part on three milestones in organizational psychology: the critical incident technique, goal setting, and principles of reinforcement (Dunnette, 1976). Reinforcement refers to making positive consequences the result of engaging in desirable behavior. The book concludes with a discussion of what we believe is another milestone, namely, organizational justice principles that result in employees' perceiving their organization as fair and just.

2

Performance Appraisal and the Law

Introduction

Most organizations do not realize that a performance appraisal is considered a test in the eyes of the law and thus is scrutinized by the courts as closely as selection procedures[1] for adverse impact on members of a protected class (Nathan & Cascio, 1986). Finding ways of minimizing legal challenges to performance appraisals is more a concern to North American organizations than to European ones. In France, for example, legal statutes do not deal directly with the issue of performance appraisal but rather with disciplinary action. The court can annul employer action that appears to be disproportionate to the employee's behavior. A similar situation exists in the Netherlands. In Japan a 1985 law bans sex discrimination and requires companies to offer females the same opportunities available to males, but interestingly, few women choose to apply for career-track jobs (Makihara, 1990).

Legal issues regarding performance appraisal in Canada and the United States arose from the way people historically had been treated on the job because of their heritage (e.g., French), race (e.g., black), age (e.g., over forty), and sex (e.g., female). Thus regardless of the uses for which appraisals are conducted, finding ways to minimize legal challenges to them continues to be a concern for employers in North America as a

---

1. For an extensive treatment of legal issues on recruiting and hiring applicants, see Arvey and Faley (1988).

way of minimizing costs. This is especially true with regard to the outcomes of appraisals, namely, promotions, demotions, transfers, layoffs, and terminations (Martin, Bartol & Levine, 1986) and employees' increasing awareness throughout the past decade of their civil and contractual rights. Moreover, in the 1970s and early 1980s court rulings in more than half the United States were more favorable to employees than to their employers (Weiss, 1988). A study by the Rand Corporation Institute for Civil Justice (1988) revealed that employees are now three times more likely to sue their employers than they were in 1980.

This litigation explosion has put organizations under increasing pressure to ensure that their appraisal procedures are not only supported by sound business practices but also legally defensible. The costs of litigation are high. First, are the quantifiable expenses of attorneys' fees, court costs, expert witness retainers, and, sometimes, settlements or judgments. Second, as Eyres (1989) has noted, are the intangible costs, such as lost management time at depositions and court hearings, disruption to support staff who must probe company records for evidence supporting management action in the performance appraisal process, and negative effects on productivity due to low morale. Together these tangible and intangible expenses emphasize the importance of knowing how to minimize the occurrence of a lawsuit and how to defend the organization when proper decisions result in an unjustified claim by a disgruntled employee who received a negative appraisal. Because of the 1988 Free Trade Act between Canada and the United States, which resulted in a large increase in the number of organizations employing people in both countries, and because the two countries' equal employment laws are similar, these issues are important to most North American employers and employees.[2]

A negative performance appraisal can directly affect an individual's employment status. Frequently such factors as an employee's age, sex, or race may lie behind negative comments couched in objective terms. Therefore, legislative acts and court

---

2. In Canada employment equity issues are usually resolved by human rights tribunals rather than by the courts. The tribunals frequently refer to U.S. case law on performance appraisal systems (Milkovich et al., 1988). A tribunal's decision may be taken to a court of appeal.

decisions have subjected performance appraisals to close scrutiny and rigid requirements to eliminate employment discrimination. Such requirements affect all aspects of human resource systems, including recruiting, hiring, training, upgrading, compensation, demotions, layoffs, and so on. What most managers fail to realize is that their actions may be scrutinized by the courts in Canada and the United States for up to five years after an appraisal decision was made (Eyres, 1989). For example, in *Glass* v. *Petro-tex Chemical Corporation* (1985), the U.S. Fifth Circuit Court ruled that the employee's lack of suspicion that the original denial of her promotion was based on sex discrimination could not prevent her from litigating that denial of promotion five years later in conjunction with a later charge she filed after a second denial of her promotion. The court ruled that originally she might reasonably have given her employer the benefit of the doubt regarding sex discrimination.

The legal requirements for performance appraisal systems are essentially no different from those for any selection test; such systems must be based on a job analysis that facilitates decisions with reliability and validity (Martin, Bartol & Levine, 1986; Nathan & Cascio, 1986). Job analysis refers to a systematic procedure for identifying the behaviors that are central for performing the job well; reliability refers to consistency or dependability in measurement; validity refers to the extent to which a test or appraisal instrument measures what it purports to measure.

This chapter examines important equal employment opportunity laws in North America. We also explain the operation of two U.S. federal agencies whose mandate is to enforce compliance with equal employment opportunity laws. Court cases in Canada and the United States are reviewed with regard to establishing the job relatedness of decisions, especially those dealing with determining who will be admitted to training programs, promoted, laid off, and discharged. The chapter concludes with a discussion of eight ways to minimize legal challenges to performance appraisal.

Legislative Background in the United States and Canada

On July 2, 1964, the U.S. Congress passed the Civil Rights Act, which became effective July 2, 1965. Title VII of that act is concerned with discrimination in all conditions of employment by four major groups—employers, public and private employment agencies, labor organizations, and joint labor-management apprenticeship programs.[3] Any of these four groups found to be discriminating on the basis of race, color, religion, sex, or national origin is in violation of the law. The Equal Employment Opportunity Commission (EEOC) was created as the governmental agency to administer Title VII.

In 1965 the Office of Federal Contract Compliance (OFCC) was established as the administrative body responsible for ensuring that federal contractors and subcontractors conform to Executive Order 11246, which also prohibits employment discrimination on the basis of race, color, religion, and national origin. This order was later amended to include prohibition against sex discrimination. In 1975 the OFCC merged with the Department of Labor and became the Office of Federal Contract Compliance Programs (OFCCP).

On March 24, 1972, Congress passed the Equal Employment Opportunity Act, which extended EEOC coverage to federal, state, and municipal employees, as well as employees of educational institutions. The act also required any organization with fifteen or more employees who work for twenty or more weeks to comply with Title VII. The EEOC was authorized to bring suit in its own name against nongovernmental agencies.

This section concentrates on the OFCCP and the EEOC, for most organizations the most visible agencies in monitoring alleged discrimination in employment.

Office of Federal Contract Compliance Programs (OFCCP)

The OFCCP is concerned with discrimination in hiring, upgrading, demotion, transfer, recruitment and recruitment advertising, layoff or termination, rates of pay or other forms of compensation, and selection for training, including apprenticeship, by any employer with a federal contract of $10,000 or more. The OFCCP requires that all such contracts include special clauses by which a contractor and all subcontractors agree to refrain from engaging in discriminatory practices. If the OFCCP

---

3. The act does not apply to Indian tribes, religious groups, or private clubs that do not receive financial support from the government.

finds that a contractor or a subcontractor has failed to meet the nondiscriminatory requirements of the contract, it can: (1) publish the names of the contractor or the union, (2) cancel the contract, (3) bar noncomplying employers from bidding on future federal contracts until they are in compliance with the law, (4) recommend to the Department of Justice that appropriate action be taken against the contractor or subcontractor when there is an alleged violation of Title VII, and (5) recommend that the Department of Justice bring criminal action against anyone supplying false information to any federal agency or to the Secretary of Labor.

Nearly all manufacturing operations in the country do at least some work as federal contractors or subcontractors and thus are subject to the jurisdiction of the OFCCP. In addition, even if only one facility of a company has a federal contract of $10,000 or more, all facilities of the company are subject to the requirements of the OFCCP. This policy can cause unexpected legal difficulties for some organizations. People at an organization's headquarters are frequently unaware of specific practices at outlying facilities. For example, one multidivisional company had discriminatory practices only in a division that had no federal contracts. Nevertheless the discriminatory practices led the OFCCP to take action against the entire company.[4]

When a large chemical plant had received a complaint from several Mexican-Americans regarding alleged discrimination against them in promotions to supervisory jobs, the OFCCP reviewed all aspects of the plant's employment practices (e.g., promotions, layoffs, hiring procedures, recruiting, training). The OFCCP's recommendations were not restricted solely to the promotional practices of one plant but rather were broad and applied to the entire company.

Complaint Investigations. Any individual may file a complaint alleging discrimination with both the OFCCP and the EEOC. The two agencies, however, try to avoid duplication of

---

4. The EEOC, too, can bring nationwide charges against a firm that engages in discriminatory practices. However, in 1977 the commission decided to no longer do this, because of the difficulty of putting a case together. A major problem with such cases is that the employment practices of a large company, such as Sears, vary across the country. Thus current EEOC policy is to limit job bias charges against a large employer to a specific community.

effort and have agreed that only one of them will usually assume jurisdiction over an individual complaint.

Unlike the EEOC, the OFCCP does not have to defer to a state human rights commission before proceeding with its investigation. The OFCCP is not concerned with a contractor's violation of a local or state law but rather with violations of federal contract compliance requirements.

A sample OFCCP case might proceed as follows: A maintenance supervisor who has been asked to work weekends states that his religion prohibits him from working on Saturdays. As a result, the supervisor receives a poor performance appraisal, is demoted, and is denied an opportunity to attend further training programs. This supervisor may file a complaint with the OFCCP area office within 180 days, alleging employment discrimination on the basis of religion. That area office would then begin an investigation of the employer's practices. The OFCCP can investigate all aspects of employment practices having possible discriminatory consequences. In other words, the agency does not have to confine itself to the specific complaint. If a violation is found, the OFCCP may take any of a number of actions.

Compliance Reviews. An employee complaint is not necessary to trigger an OFCCP compliance review. OFCCP compliance officers can initiate on-site reviews. Two to three weeks advance notice is normally given so that a facility can assemble its employment records.

A local compliance officer has the right to request employment data broken down by race, sex, and national origin of an employer's departments and promotional lines. The officer is likely to inquire about the possible existence of segregated departments or jobs. Another question may involve the promotional history of minorities and women employed by the organization. A compliance officer has the authority to inspect employment records and to inquire into general personnel and employment practices regarding any of these issues.

The OFCCP is concerned particularly with the employment status of women and minorities in six job categories: (1) officials and managers, (2) professionals, (3) technicians, (4) sales workers, (5) office and clerical workers, and (6) skilled craftspeople. Most organizations consider the possibility of contract cancellation so serious that OFCCP field officers frequently are able to exert more influence on the personnel practices of the organizations they review than is justified by their legal authority. This situation is particularly true regarding the soundness or validity of performance appraisal systems. The official position of the OFCCP is that its field officers are to gather evidence about the validity of an organization's appraisal decisions. Any such evidence is to be reviewed by the OFCCP in Washington, D.C., which makes the final decision. The OFCCP has an advisory committee, which includes industrial-organizational psychologists experienced in business, industry, and government, to assist it in examining the soundness or validity of appraisal procedures. An organization confronted with what it regards as a local agency's erroneous negative review should request a review of the evidence by the OFCCP office in Washington.

In general the adoption of race- or sex-conscious quota systems (a fixed percentage) for the transfer, promotion, or admission of employees into training programs is to be avoided unless the organization has been found guilty by the courts of employment discrimination or has job categories in which the employees are predominantly of the same race or sex. To do otherwise is to invite a reverse discrimination suit (alleged discrimination against a nonminority group member, which is also prohibited by Title VII of the Civil Rights Act).

Affirmative action (affording employment and training opportunities to women and minorities) policies do not guarantee that an organization will be free from OFCCP scrutiny. The OFCCP believes that the real measure of an employer's good intentions regarding affirmative action is not a written policy but rather evidence that over a period of time, minority representation has increased at all levels and in all portions of the work force where deficiencies had existed. Thus an organization should not adhere to a specific number of females or minorities who will annually be promoted or admitted to a special training program; rather, it must show that it is increasingly allowing these people access to these employment opportunities. This issue will be discussed further later in the chapter.

Equal Employment Opportunity Commission (EEOC)

The EEOC is an independent federal agency that was created by Section 705 of Title VII of the Civil Rights Act. When the EEOC receives a charge that an alleged violation has occurred, it has the legal power to: (1) subpoena and question witnesses under oath, (2) recommend a conciliation between the complainant and the company, and (3) contact the OFCCP if a federal contractor or subcontractor is involved.

In contrast to the OFCCP, the EEOC does not have the power to order an organization to discontinue a practice that it believes is discriminatory. However, in March 1972 Congress passed legislation giving the EEOC direct access to the courts to present evidence of alleged discrimination. Most court cases involving alleged discrimination stem from charges filed with the EEOC rather than the OFCCP. OFCCP cases are more likely to be settled out of court because a company does not want its contract suspended while waiting for the litigation to end.

The EEOC has the authority to investigate the practices and records of organizations that employ fifteen or more people who work for twenty or more weeks. It can require organizations to maintain records regarding the race (particularly of blacks, native Americans, Hispanics, Asians, and whites), sex, religion, and national origin of all applicants/employees.

Deference to Other Agencies. The EEOC is required to defer to a state's fair employment practice commission (e.g., Washington State Human Rights Commission) before initiating its own investigation. Persons who believe that they have been subjected to discrimination must file a complaint within ninety days with a local agency. Sixty days after the charge has been filed with the local agency for review, the EEOC may begin its own investigation. In conducting its investigation, the EEOC is not bound by the findings of a city or state agency. If the EEOC finds the charge to be substantiated, it provides the complainant with a notice of right to sue. Within ninety days following such notice, the individual must file suit with the court to preserve the claim.[5]

---

5. The EEOC does not have to accept the person's request to withdraw the complaint. It can go ahead on its own and file suit with the court. It is likely to do so if it believes that the individual was threatened or bribed into withdrawing the complaint or if it believes that the likelihood of a similar complaint being filed against the company is high. Likewise, an employee does not have to abide by the EEOC's conclusion that there is no merit to the case. The person may hire an attorney to pursue the case. Because of the EEOC's backlog of cases, many people who feel that their rights under Title VII have been violated bypass the EEOC by hiring their own lawyer.

Investigation of Charges. The EEOC investigates a complaint by first interviewing the complainant and then reviewing the company's employment practices, including hiring, promotion, seniority lists, test files, performance ratings, race identity files, and files on all job openings. It may include information on departments and jobs in addition to those covered by the specific charge. If a finding of probable cause is reached, the EEOC attempts to bring about conciliation; the EEOC's objective is to get the organization to correct the original situation and any other employment practices determined to be in violation of Title VII. Conciliation remedies can include relief for the complainant (e.g., reinstatement, back pay, promotion), relief for other similarly affected individuals, changes in the organization's discriminatory practices, and affirmative action steps involving recruitment of minorities. If conciliation cannot be reached, the EEOC can refer the case to the OFCCP if the organization is a federal contractor or subcontractor, and it can file a legal suit with the court against the organization.

In the United States, managers, supervisors, corporate officers, and in some instances coworkers may be named as defendants and held personally liable for violations of human rights statutes. This is especially likely to occur if the plaintiff made them aware of the complaint and it was subsequently ignored (Munchus, 1989).

An employee can file discrimination charges with two or more agencies (e.g., the EEOC and the OFCCP); thus an employer can be required to conduct a defense with more than one agency at the same time. The employee, however, must ultimately choose the remedy designated by only one agency. In this way employers are not asked to pay twice for one discriminatory action.

Employees who were not involved in the original complaint but who claim similar discrimination as members of the affected class may also join in a suit seeking relief. Employers found guilty in such cases may be required by the court to publish a notice "inviting" members of the class to apply for both jobs and back pay.

Class action suits can result in a finding of discrimination on the part of an organization even if the court finds that the original complainant's claim is without merit. The claim of each class member is considered on its own merits because discriminatory practices may very well have affected others regardless of whether the original complainant was found to have been treated properly.

Currently, Title VII litigation is shifting from getting jobs to keeping jobs (Leonard, 1989). As the workforce ages and the demographic bulge confronts increasingly narrow levels of corporate hierarchies, this trend will continue.

Canadian Legislation

Title VII in the United States has been extended over the years to include marital status and mental and physical disability as protected classes. Paralleling Title VII in Canada is the 1982 Charter of Rights and Freedoms. Section 3 states that race, national or ethnic origin, color, religion, sex, marital status, mental and physical disability, and conviction for which pardon has been granted are prohibited grounds for discrimination. Section 5 states that in devising methods of assessing an individual's job performance, the employer must identify the essential tasks that make up the requirements of the job. Section 10 states that it is a discriminatory practice for an employer, trade union, employer or employee association, or employment agency to enter into an agreement affecting the promotion, training, and apprenticeship or any other matter relating to employment that deprives or inhibits a group of individuals based on prohibited grounds of discrimination. Section 15 allows affirmative action where there is an imbalance in the labor force.[6]

The Canadian Human Rights Act (1978) prohibits companies from paying women less than men for jobs involving equal skills, effort, responsibilities, and conditions, even if different job titles are used. The Federal Employment Equity Act applies to the federal public service and federally regulated companies, such as banks and transportation and communication firms. The act also applies to companies that bid for more than $200,000

---

6. Unlike Title VII, Canada's Charter applies to relations between individuals and government and does not directly control relations between employees, except where the employer is the government. Instead, the Charter prohibits discrimination in the laws governing Canadians. Thus employees have, unsuccessfully, argued that mandatory retirement policies violate the Charter, which prohibits employment discrimination, rather than that the employer violated the Charter.

worth of contracts per year from the federal government. This act affects about one-third of the Canadian workforce.

Whereas U.S. state laws tend to overlap with federal statutes, Canadian jurisdictional lines are relatively clear. The provincial laws cover all employees except those employed by the federal government, crown corporations, and federally regulated industries (e.g., banks, airlines). The Province of Quebec, for example, requires companies with which it has contracts exceeding $100,000 per year to implement employment equity for women, visible minorities (race/color), and native peoples. A separate provincial act requires all employers with more than fifty employees to file hiring plans for people with disabilities. Manitoba and British Columbia state explicitly that employers must be able to show that their hiring, promotion, and termination actions are based on job-related requirements. The 1981 Human Rights Code of Ontario states that every person has a right to equal treatment with respect to employment without discrimination because of race, ancestry, place of origin, color, ethnic origin, citizenship, creed, sex, sexual orientation, age, record of offenses, marital status, or handicap. Age refers to people between eighteen and sixty-five years. Handicap includes physical disability, infirmity, malformation or disfigurement, birth defect, and without limiting the generality of the foregoing, includes diabetes, epilepsy, any degree of paralysis, amputation, visual impairment, speech impediment, or physical reliance on a dog guide or on a wheelchair or other remedial appliance or device. The city of Toronto requires organizations that contract with it to sign a nondiscriminatory declaration regarding race, creed, color, national origin, political affiliation, gender, age, marital status, family relationships, and disability.

Most of these laws also stipulate that employment practices having the effect of excluding target groups, even when there is no intention to discriminate, are also illegal. Thus human rights legislation can be used to enforce both employment and pay equity in workforces not covered by specific legislation.

Areas of Major U.S. Court Decisions

For an indication of how challenges to appraisal practices will be resolved in the future, let us examine major U.S. court decisions concerning performance appraisals. At one time, employers were winning only 5 percent of discrimination cases ending up in court (Mitnick, 1977). In the 1980s, with a relatively conservative Supreme Court, the legal climate began to change in favor of the employer.

Job Relatedness

Griggs v. *Duke Power Company* (1971) was the first U.S. Supreme Court decision involving Title VII.[7] Duke Power had employed only blacks in one department and only whites in the other departments. A high school diploma or a satisfactory score on two standardized pencil-and-paper aptitude tests was required for employment in the four departments in which the whites worked.

The Court's decision made the EEOC Guidelines the law of the land by explicitly endorsing them as "expressing the will of Congress." The Court also ruled that employment criteria (e.g., educational requirements) that adversely affect a class member (e.g., women and nonwhites) must be shown to be job related. Although the specific term *validation* was not used, the Court did endorse the procedures called for by the 1970 guidelines that do require validation. The Court ruled that even though "neutral in intent," employment procedures are not justifiable if they result in discriminatory practices. The Court's opinion suggests that quota systems are contrary to the Civil Rights Act and that it is equally illegal to discriminate against members of nonminority groups. In this regard, the decision reads:

> Congress did not intend by Title VII, to guarantee a job to every person regardless of their qualifications. In short, the Act does not command that a person be hired simply because he was formerly the subject of discrimination or because he is a member of a minority group. Discriminatory preferences for any group, minority or majority, are precisely and only what the Congress has proscribed.

---

7. The adverse-impact principle in *Griggs* was formally accepted in Canada through the 1977 Ontario case *Singh* v. *Security and Investigation Services.*

As a final note, it is appropriate to quote from the closing statement of the Supreme Court's opinion:

> Nothing in the Act precludes the use of testing or measuring procedures; obviously they are useful. What Congress has forbidden is giving these devices and mechanisms controlling force unless they are demonstratably a reasonable measure of performance. Congress has not demanded that the less qualified be preferred over the more qualified simply because of minority origins. Far from disparaging job qualifications as such, Congress has made such qualifications a controlling factor, so that race, religion, nationality, and sex become irrelevant. What Congress has commanded is that any test used must measure the person for the job, not the person in the abstract.

Job Analysis and the Appraisal System

Several court decisions were focused on the job analysis and the appraisal instrument on which the appraisal was or should have been based. A job analysis should serve as the basis for constructing the appraisal instrument because the job analysis identifies the criteria that are important for determining whether a person is performing the job effectively (see Chapters 3 and 4). The job analysis makes clear to people what must be done to be successful and must be in writing so that there is a record. The record must allow others who follow the same steps in the job to obtain replicable results. In other words, two or more people (interobserver reliability) must be able to repeatedly (test-retest reliability) reach the same conclusion or outcome as to the important criteria for evaluating job performance. Equally important, a job analysis shows whether the appraisal instrument is content valid; it reveals the extent to which the person is evaluated only on job-related factors. Thus performance appraisals are viewed by the courts as tests in the same vein that selection procedures are viewed as tests. Information on job analysis links job content with the content of the appraisal instrument (Nathan & Cascio, 1986).

In *Brito* v. *Zia Company* (1973) Zia was found to be in violation of Title VII when a disproportionate number of protected group members were laid off on the basis of low performance appraisal scores. In its findings the Court commented that the performance appraisal system Zia used in determining layoffs was, in fact, an employment test. Moreover, the Court stated that the company had not shown that its performance appraisal instrument was valid, that is, related to *important* elements of work behavior in the jobs in which the employees were being evaluated. Rather, the Court found, the evaluations were based on the best judgments and opinions of supervisors "... but not on any identifiable criteria based on quality or quantity of work on specific performance that were supported by some kind of record."

In *EEOC* v. *Sandia Corporation* (1980) the appeals court supported a lower court finding that the engineering firm had engaged in age discrimination in its reduction-in-force policy. The court found the appraisal instrument to be "extremely subjective, to be unvalidated, and to contain built-in bias against the protected age group" (Martin, Bartol & Levine, 1986, p. 389). The trial court stated that "the evaluations were based on best judgments and opinion of evaluators, but were not based on any definite identifiable criteria based on quality or quantity of work of specific performance that were supported by some kind of record." This wording is nearly identical to that used in *Brito*. Not surprisingly, the courts were unimpressed by the company's efforts to reconstruct performance ratings after the fact by attempting to base them on objective criteria and reclassifications by supervisors who were already aware of the subjective ratings the plaintiffs had received.

In *Wade* v. *Mississippi Cooperative Extension Service* (1974) black employees alleged that the evaluation instrument used to appraise their performance discriminated against them as a class. The Court held that the Extension Service had the burden of demonstrating that the appraisal instrument was job related (i.e., valid) and served a legitimate employment need.

In finding the Extension Service guilty, the Court noted that what the company called an "objective appraisal of job performance" was in fact based on supervisory ratings of such general characteristics as leadership, public acceptance, attitude toward people, appearance, grooming, personal conduct, outlook on life, ethical habits, resourcefulness, capacity for growth, mental alertness, and loyalty to the organization:

> As may be readily observed, these are traits which are susceptible to partiality and to the personal taste, whim,

or fancy of the evaluator. We must then view these factors as presently utilized to be patently subjective in form and obviously susceptible to completely subjective treatment.

The limitations of trait scales are discussed further in Chapter 4.

Some people (e.g., Barrett & Kernan, 1987) have argued that because of the subjectivity inherent in a performance appraisal, it should not be examined by the courts in the same way as relatively objectively scored multiple-choice tests that are used for selection purposes. Indeed, this was the position taken by the trial court in *Watson* v. *Fort Worth Bank and Trust Company* (1988). Clara Watson, a black employee, had been rejected four times for a promotion to supervisor. The bank used its rating scales, as well as interviews and experience require-ments—so called "subjective evaluation devices"—to make its promotion decisions. The appellate court affirmed the lower court's finding that the bank was not racially discriminatory, despite Watson's claim that the bank relied on subjectively administered, unvalidated performance evaluations.

The American Psychological Association (APA) filed an *amicus curiae* brief with the Supreme Court, in which it cited empirical research generated by industrial-organizational psy-chologists (e.g., Latham, Wexley & Pursell, 1975, described in Chapter 6) to argue that subjective-assessment devices are, in fact, amenable to the same psychometric scrutiny as are so-called objective assessment devices, such as written tests (Bersoff, 1988). The Supreme Court agreed with the APA's posi-tion, stating that its decision in *Griggs* could be largely nullified if it were to conclude otherwise. Employers would be encouraged to abandon standardized validated tests in favor of unvalidated subjective devices. Thus the Supreme Court stated:

> We are . . . persuaded that disparate impact analysis is in principle no less applicable to subjective employment cri-teria than to objective or standardized tests. In either case, a facially neutral practice, adopted without discrimi-natory intent, may have effects that are undistinguish-able from intentionally discriminatory practices. . . . If an employer's . . . subjective decision making has precisely the same effects as a system pervaded by impermissible intentional discrimination, it is difficult to see why Title

VII's proscription against discriminatory activities should not apply. (p. 2786)

The Supreme Court ruled in favor of Watson.

In *Albermarle Paper Company* v. *Moody* (1975), the performance appraisals were not criticized as a test but rather as the *criteria,* or performance measures, against which the selection tests for hiring purposes had been validated.[8] The Supreme Court ruled that in the process of validating its tests, the company had not conducted a *job analysis* to identify the critical requirements of jobs. Instead, the selection tests had been validated against supervisory rankings that did not define the basis of the employee performance rankings. Furthermore, employees were ranked against one another without regard for the fact that they were doing different jobs. The Court concluded that ". . . there is no way of knowing precisely what criteria of job performance that supervisors were considering, whether each supervisor was considering the same criteria—or whether, indeed, any of the supervisors actually applied a focused and stable body of criteria of any kind."

Admission into Training Programs

Appraisal of people's performance usually determines who will receive training in a given area. Completing the training in a satisfactory manner usually leads to a positive appraisal of their subsequent performance. Hence the Court's interest in admission into training programs.

In a case involving admission into a university (*Bakke* v. *Regents of the University of California,* 1978) the Supreme Court decided that explicit quotas for minorities were wrong. (Sixteen seats in the medical school had been reserved for nonwhites.) Justice Powell wrote: "The guarantee of equal protection cannot mean one thing when applied to one individual and something

---

8. As noted in Chapter 1, the first step in validating a selection instrument is to define how performance will be measured, which should be done through a systematic job analysis. Second, on the basis of the knowledge gained from the job analysis, psychologists develop tests that should predict who will do well on the performance measures. Third, people are measured on how well they do on the test and on the job performance measures. If the correlation between the two sets of measures is significant, the test is considered valid. In *Albermarle* the correlation was significant, but the Court did not like the performance measures against which the test was validated.

else when applied to a person of another color." However, the Court did make clear that preferential-treatment programs are appropriate when they remedy past instances of discrimination against minorities. There was no history of past discrimination at the university where Bakke had applied for admission. Thus the Court decided in Bakke's favor.

This decision set the stage for a suit filed by Brian Weber against Kaiser Aluminum and Chemical Corporation and the Steelworkers Union. Kaiser and the union had agreed to establish an affirmative action training program. Blacks accounted for less than 2 percent of the 273 craftspeople at the plant but constituted 39 percent of the local workforce. To close the gap, the company and the union decided to accept whites and blacks into the program on a one-to-one basis. When Weber was rejected from the program, he sued both his employer and his union, charging that he had been illegally excluded from a skilled-craft training program that would have made him eligible for higher-paying jobs. Weber had more seniority than two blacks who had been admitted into the program. Seniority is protected under Title VII.

By a 5-to-2 vote, the Supreme Court ruled that employers can indeed give blacks special preference for jobs that were traditionally held by whites. Moreover, the Court stated that whether or not the company had discriminatory job practices in the past, it could use affirmative action programs to remedy a "manifest racial imbalance" in employment without fear of being challenged for its efforts in the courts.

This latter statement is important for employers; it means that companies and unions can establish affirmative action plans under similar conditions without fear of losing lawsuits on the basis of a charge of reverse discrimination. Equally crucial for organizations is the provision that organizations that set up affirmative action programs are not required to admit to discriminatory practices in the past. Admission of past discrimination could create costly lawsuits.

Thus goals are acceptable if they deal with job categories that have traditionally been segregated and if they are *temporary* in nature. Justice Brennan noted that when the percentage of black skilled workers at the Kaiser plant approximates the percentage of skilled blacks in the local labor force, the program will end.

The Supreme Court reached similar conclusions in *Johnson* v. *Santa Clara County Transportation Agency* (1987) and in *United States* v. *Paradise* (1987). In the former case the Court ruled that the county did not violate Title VII by promoting a female employee over a male who had been originally selected for the position prior to the county's consideration of a voluntary affirmative action plan. The Court noted that the male did not have significantly higher test scores or experience than Johnson and that the county had applied the Weber standards correctly by acting to remedy a "manifest imbalance" in its workforce caused by "traditionally segregated job classifications." None of the 238 employees in skilled craft positions was female. In the second case the Court supported a promotion order of one black state trooper for every white trooper until a 25 percent black quota had been reached at the corporal officer level, because there were so few nonwhite officers in the force.

Promotion

The burden of proof before the courts with regard to a promotion decision shifts responsibilities in the following way. If the plaintiff establishes a *prima facie* case of employment discrimination, the burden shifts to the organization to show that there was a legitimate nondiscriminatory reason for the action taken. The organization must then provide performance appraisals and any other evidence that supports its action (Martin, Bartol & Levine, 1986). The plaintiff is then given an opportunity to show that the organization's explanation for its decision is in fact a pretext for what is in reality discriminatory behavior.

Promotion decisions are often difficult for an organization to defend successfully in the courtroom (Goddard, 1989); the organization must be able to justify what is essentially a prediction that the plaintiff would not be the best choice for a particular higher-level job. To successfully defend itself, the organization should be able to show one or more of the following to be true (Martin, Bartol & Levine, 1986).

First, the company must show that the plaintiff had performance shortcomings in areas of the present job that are also important aspects of the higher-level job. In *Jackson* v. *Gulf Oil Corp.* (1981) the company showed successfully that the transfer of and failure to promote the plaintiff did not constitute either race or sex discrimination. The woman's appraisals showed that although she met the minimum job requirements, she needed extra time to complete her assigned duties and had difficulty performing analytical work. Moreover, the appraisals indicated that she was uncooperative. Five supervisors (note the interobserver reliability) supported this assessment of her.

Second, the company should be able to show that the employee failed to obtain the appropriate credentials necessary to perform the higher-level job effectively. In *Casas* v. *First American Bank* (1983) the bank showed that a minority female had indeed received "competent" and "commendable" ratings, but her appraisals also indicated that she had been advised repeatedly that she would not be promotable until she became knowledgeable about the bank's literature on its money market funds. Moreover, she had twice declined an opportunity to gain needed managerial experience by becoming a supervisor in a subdepartment, she had dropped out of the bank's career development program, and she did not take outside courses that had been recommended to her. The Court concluded that the bank had not discriminated on the basis of race, sex, or national origin.

Third, the company should be able to show that the employee who received the promotion was the person with the superior credentials. In *Chaves* v. *Thomas* (1984) a Hispanic male employee, an attorney for the EEOC, argued that his credentials were superior to those of a promoted black male. But the performance appraisals revealed that the person who had been promoted had extensive experience in the new job area and had received four "outstanding" ratings, whereas the plaintiff had received none. The Court ruled in favor of the EEOC.

Fourth, the organization must be able to show that the plaintiff performed poorly when given key responsibilities that are part of the higher-level job. This was done effectively by Camelot Inn (*McCarther* v. *Camelot Inn of Little Rock*, 1981). McCarther, who had been doing well in his job, was given the opportunity to be the temporary head of the purchasing department while his supervisor was on vacation for two weeks. The general manager returned to find a shortage of $1700 in the storeroom. He learned that McCarther had been frequently away from his post and that the storeroom had been left unlocked; these issues were discussed with McCarther. Nevertheless, he sued the company when another person got the promotion, asserting that he was more qualified and had more experience than the person who received the promotion. The Court ruled that comparisons with the person who received the promotion were unimportant because the plaintiff had demonstrated his inability to perform adequately in the position when given an opportunity to do so.

Layoffs

In layoff situations employee comparisons are a crucial issue. In *Coburn* v. *Pan American World Airlines, Inc.* (1982) the forty-three-year-old plaintiff's appraisals showed that he had been a satisfactory employee. But Pan American showed that one of the retained supervisors was older than Coburn and that Coburn was terminated only after the airline had conducted a peer-group analysis comparing other supervisors in the same area having the same responsibilities. The Court sided with Pan American. (The effectiveness of peer appraisals is discussed in Chapter 5.)

In layoff situations seniority needs to be taken into account with unionized workforces because seniority is protected under Title VII. *Wygant* v. *Jackson Board of Education* (1986) reaffirmed that stance by ruling against a collective bargaining agreement in which the ratio of black to white schoolteachers was to be maintained during layoffs. Specifically, the Supreme Court ruled that there must be strong evidence of prior discrimination within the organization before a voluntary plan can be put into effect that results in preferential treatment for members of a particular racial class. Thus only where an employer or labor union has engaged in persistent or egregious discrimination is such a voluntary plan acceptable (Redeker, 1986).

Discharges

The basic issue in discharges is the employee's inability to function effectively on the job. The focus is on comparing the performance of the discharged employee against the employer's minimal standards, not the performance of other employees (Martin, Bartol & Levine, 1986). Comparative issues become important only when the discharged employee argues that other individuals were not dismissed for similar infractions or shortcomings. Effective discharge strategies that employers can use include those that show that: (1) the employee had exhibited a consistent pattern of unsatisfactory performance, (2) previously satisfactory performance had deteriorated, or (3) the employee had exhibited a previously unnoticed shortcoming.

A frequent cause of litigation is failure to give the employee a reasonable timeframe in which to correct poor performance. In fact, employees often report they were never even informed that their performance was unsatisfactory. Managers must provide candid feedback even, and most importantly, when it is negative. Many managers are reluctant to hurt an employee's feelings; when they do state that the person's performance is inadequate, they often resort to vague generalities, such as "You are just not cutting it" (Eyres, 1989). The courts generally find such vagueness not supportable and rule in favor of the terminated employee.

A personality conflict can be grounds for discharging an employee; a company has the right to set performance standards and to discharge employees who do not meet them. But the employee must be told explicitly that his or her job is in danger and be given a reasonable time period to correct the situation. In *Chamberlain* v. *Bissell, Inc.* (1982) the employer was found negligent for failing to inform the employee during the appraisal review that discharge was being considered unless the employee made a quick and significant improvement in his performance.

In *Howard* v. *Miller Brewing Co.* (1983) performance appraisals showed that Howard was "marginal in all respects" during his first year of employment and "nearly satisfactory" during the second year. The Court attributed a great deal of credibility to a person who had been a peer shift-supervisor and who was now Howard's immediate supervisor. This testimony corroborated documentation that the plaintiff was not punctual, failed to communicate and coordinate his activities with other supervisors, and made costly errors despite efforts of peers and supervisors to help him perform the job. The performance appraisal data led the Court to dismiss the plaintiff's claim that he had been discharged on the basis of his color and race.

In *Palmer Coking Coal Company* v. *Director, O.W.C.P.* (1983) the Office of Personnel Management (OPM) provided evidence that it had informed a discharged minority male employee verbally and in writing of his performance shortcomings, that he had been given unsatisfactory appraisal ratings, and that he had even been suspended before OPM resorted to a discharge. The ruling, in favor of OPM, commented that not only was there no evidence of racial discrimination but also that OPM had "exercised great patience in tolerating the plaintiff's ineptitude. . . ."

Performance deterioration that results in a discharge can be problematic when the person has been employed with the organization for a considerable period of time. Several years of employment in the organization implies that the person's performance must be satisfactory or the discharge would have occurred earlier. Performance appraisal documentation, however, resulted in the court's ruling in favor of the company in *Erwin* v. *Bank of Mississippi* (1981). The appraisals included comments that Erwin, a fifty-year-old employee who had been with the bank for six years, needed to take the initiative in developing his banking skills and in building an effective training program. He was finally discharged for his inability to obtain cooperation from other bank officers and his failure to make the requested improvements in the training program.

In *Grant* v. *Gannett Co., Inc.* (1982) a fifty-nine-year-old advertising manager who had worked for the company for thirty-two years was dismissed because his performance did not conform to the management style that Gannett desired when it took over the company. The testimony of witnesses corroborated that Grant did not cooperate fully with the implementation of equal opportunity programs in his unit, properly conduct performance appraisals of his people, or hold monthly meetings. Grant's failure to meet the newspaper's expectations were discussed with him several times prior to his discharge. The court ruled that the plaintiff failed to prove by a preponderance of evidence that age was the determining factor in his dismissal.

A male record clerk in *Martinez* v. *El Paso County* (1983) won his case on the basis of sex discrimination by showing that his dismissal occurred without warning for undocumented deficiencies in typing skills. The inadequacy of the county's standards against which Martinez's work was evaluated was revealed when it was shown that a female with lesser skills and seniority was retained.

Even when an employee has performed well on most of the job criteria, the person can be discharged if there is a "serious shortcoming." In *Everitt et al.* v. *City of Marshall, Texas et al.* (1983) a black female police dispatcher was discharged for failing to check for warrants on file, when such checks were required by police personnel working in the field. Even though

Everitt had "extremely favorable" performance evaluations, the court acknowledged that failure to check for warrants could endanger the lives of officers, and thus there were adequate grounds for her dismissal.

Can a company suffering financial hardship replace a person in an age-protected class with a younger person who is willing and able to perform the job equally well at significantly less pay? In *Metz* v. *Transit Mix, Inc.* (1987) the company, which was suffering financial problems, discharged Metz, a fifty-four-year-old employee of twenty-seven years and replaced him with a forty-three-year-old with seventeen years' experience who was willing to take the job for approximately half of Metz's salary. The Seventh Circuit Court ruled that Metz, a satisfactory performer, was indeed protected under Title VII. Employers cannot justify as age-neutral their selections for workforce reduction, based on tenure status for cost-saving purposes, which has the effect of eliminating older employees who have built up, through the years of satisfactory service, higher salaries than their younger counterparts (Kandel, 1988).

How should an organization deal with religious beliefs that affect an employee's willingness to come to work? In *Ansonia Board of Education* v. *Philbrook* (1986) the superior court held that once an employer offers a reasonable accommodation, it has satisfied its duties and need not accept other proposed accommodations even if they are without undue hardship. In *Hudson* v. *Western Airlines, Inc.* (1988) Hudson claimed that the airline violated Title VII when it discharged her for refusing to work a flight assignment on her Sabbath. The Court ruled in favor of the company because she failed to avail herself of a reasonable option, namely, a collective bargaining agreement that allows flight attendants to trade flight assignments as well as days off.

How should a person's physical or mental handicap be taken into account before a discharge is considered warranted? The ruling in *Jasany* v. *United States Postal Service* (1985) was that one is not handicapped unless the physical or mental impairment affects a range of jobs. Thus people would not be considered handicapped simply because they are short or are suffering from eye strain.

In *Ratheon Co.* v. *FEHC* (1988) the Court ruled that employee fear that might hurt morale was an insufficient basis for preventing an AIDS victim from coming to work. The same opinion was reached in *Chalk* v. *United States District Court* (1988).

Is firing someone for his or her appearance necessarily a violation of Title VII? Among the more interesting cases is *Craft* v. *Metromedia, Inc.* (1985), in which the Court found no violation of Title VII when a television studio removed anchorwoman Craft because of concerns over her appearance. Craft alleged that this was stereotypical sex discrimination because standards for on-the-air personnel were stricter for women than for men. But the evidence showed only that the television studio was extremely concerned about viewer reaction.

With regard to sex discrimination, Vinson (*Meritor Savings Bank* v. *Vinson,* 1986) claimed that she submitted to sexual demands but never reported the incident, out of fear of losing her job. The district court ruled that the sexual relationship was voluntary and the bank not liable, because of "no notice." But the Supreme Court found absolute liability without notice and rejected the bank's argument that Congress was concerned only with tangible loss of an economic character and not psychological aspects of the workplace. The Court stated that a plaintiff can establish a violation of Title VII by proving that discrimination based on sex created a hostile or abusive work environment. Arguing that the complainant was not found to participate against her will is not a defense, the Court ruled, because the sexual advances were unwelcome. The bank's contention that the harassee's failure to notify it should insulate it from liability "might be substantially stronger if its procedures were better calculated to encourage victims of harassment to come forward."

Tribunal and Court Rulings in Canada

The Canadian Supreme Court has not yet made any rulings regarding performance appraisal violations under the 1984 Canadian Human Rights Act. Lower court rulings, however, have made clear that performance appraisals can be used as a basis for demotion and termination (e.g., *Trotter* v. *Chesley Town,* 1990).

A growing number of human rights tribunals have questioned the validity and objectivity of the appraisal system

(Milkovich et al., 1988). In a case similar to *Albermarle,* Ontario Hydro was found to have discriminated when it used a ranking procedure with no explicit performance criteria to lay off employees. The ranking had an adverse effect on black employees. Another Ontario Human Rights Commission tribunal ruled that a poorly designed evaluation system was further evidence of the employer's tendency to use discriminatory practices. Another tribunal ruled against the company for failing to properly communicate performance requirements to the employees (*Reid* v. *Russel Steel Ltd.,* 1981).

In his review of legal decisions, McShane (1989) found that the Canadian courts take the following factors into account when reaching a decision: cause of poor performance, effect of poor performance on the employer, job duties relevant to performance standards, provision of feedback and warnings, the credibility of the source of the appraisal, and whether the appraisal was contrived.[9]

Cause of Poor Performance. Both Deming's adherents and industrial psychologists should applaud the fact that the courts examine the cause of poor performance before deciding against an employee. If the cause of poor behavior is due to factors beyond the employee's control, an employer cannot argue just cause for a dismissal. In *MacEachern* v. *Nova Scotia Attorney General* (1987), the court ruled that there was wrongful dismissal because of external factors, including interference by senior administrators, beyond the supervisor's control.

In *Benson* v. *Co-Op Atlantic* (1985) the court ruled in favor of the employee because she had been on the job for only four days and had not received adequate training. Moreover, power disturbances during that week had affected the operation of the computers on which she was being trained.

It is noteworthy that an organization is likely to win a just-cause argument if it can show that the employee's performance did not reach a satisfactory level subsequent to training (*Scott* v. *Domtar Sonoco Containers Inc.,* 1987). But the organization is not required to provide training for employees who lack

---

9. These cases deal with common-law wrongful job dismissals; in the United States the employment-at-will doctrine is still being scrutinized, and the courts have been concerned primarily with violation of Title VII.

the skills they claimed to have at the time of hire (*Cornell* v. *Rogers Cablesystems Inc.,* 1987). Rather, the employer needs to show only that it provided an orientation to the work setting and normal supervisory support (*Manners* v. *Fraser Survey Docks Ltd.,* 1981).

Effect of Poor Performance on the Employer. Evidence that the employee's performance hurt the organization in some tangible fashion may be required. In *Roscoe* v. *McGavin Foods* (1983) Roscoe, a regional manager, was dismissed for having a "bad attitude" toward his work. The court ruled that there was no evidence that his attitude had a detrimental effect on the company. Moreover, there was no evidence that the company's performance improved after Roscoe's dismissal.

When evidence exists that the person's performance is hurting the organization, the organization must give the person a reasonable opportunity and resources to improve performance (*Robson* v. *General Motors of Canada,* 1982). Evidence of improvement, even if not up to standard, may result in a decision in favor of the employee (*Tabone* v. *Midas Canada Inc.,* 1986).

Job Duties and Performance Standards. To prove just cause for dismissing an employee, Canadian courts will require evidence of one or more of the following regarding the person's job duties:

1. The company must show that the tasks the employee was performing poorly were *relevant.* In the MacEachern case, for example, the supervisor was in fact warned of the need to improve her interpersonal skills in dealing with subordinates. Nevertheless, the court ruled in her favor because the job description did not include interpersonal skills as a job requirement.

2. As in the United States, the employee must be evaluated against *specific,* relatively objective criteria (*Ibrahim* v. *Association of Professional Engineers, Geologists and Geophysicists of Alberta,* 1985).

3. The relative importance of the evaluation criteria must be made explicit to the employee (*Vorvis* v. *Insurance Corporation of British Columbia,* 1984).

4. The criteria must be *reasonable* in terms of the time frame to attain them, external conditions affecting them, and the level of performance expected (*Tabone*).

5. Consistency or uniformity in application will be examined. If comparable performance of others is accepted by the organization, the court will reject a just-cause argument (*Gray* v. *Electrolux Canada,* 1986).

6. The court will examine "promises" made or implied by the organization when the employee was hired. Thus an employer cannot raise its performance criteria and then dismiss a semiqualified employee if the employer agreed to hire the employee at the lower performance standard (*Markou* v. *Water Refining Company Limited,* 1980).

Feedback and Warnings. As in the United States, the Canadian courts insist that timely, specific, and consistent feedback be given to an employee before an organization can mount a convincing argument of dismissal for just cause. Management may appear to condone the person's poor performance if the feedback is not timely (*Stein* v. *B.C. Housing Management Commission,* 1989). The feedback must also address specific areas of performance weakness (*Cole* v. *Dresser Canada Ltd.,* 1983) and must make clear that the employee's job is in jeopardy (*Tremblett* v. *Aardvark Pest Control, Ltd.,* 1987).

Credibility of Appraisal Source. The court is likely to rule in favor of the organization when the evaluator is seen as "balanced and detached" (*Kraft* v. *Wine Rope Industries,* 1985). The court is likely to rule in favor of the employee if there appears to be ill-feeling by the evaluator toward the employee (*Paitich* v. *Clarke Institute of Psychiatry,* 1988) or if other employees have complained about the evaluator (*Waite* v. *LaRonge Child Care Co-operative,* 1985).

Contrived Appraisals. The court takes a dim view of appraisals that are prepared primarily to document an employee's poor performance. For example, the court ruled in favor of the employee (*Wallace* v. *Toronto Dominion Bank,* 1981) because a management memo requested that the next appraisal contain negative comments about the employee. Similarly, it ruled in favor of the employee (*Roberts* v. *Versatile Farm Equipment et al.,* 1987) because the company did not have formal appraisals but developed one in order to justify the employee's demotion.

The Shifting U.S. Legal Climate

In recent years the legal climate began shifting in favor of the employer rather than the employee. In *Watson* v. *Fort Worth Bank and Trust Company* (1988) the U.S. Supreme Court required the employee to identify the specific employment practices allegedly responsible for any observed statistical disparity. Moreover, any such statistical evidence must be sufficiently substantial to prove that the practice in question caused the exclusion of promotion-eligible employees because of their membership in a protected group.

Further evidence in this shift occurred in *Price Waterhouse* v. *Hopkins* (1989). Written appraisals of Hopkins by her supervisors suggested strongly that her gender played a part in the decision to deny her a promotion. However, the court ruled that an employer may avoid a finding of liability by providing a preponderance of evidence that the organization would have made the same decision even if it had not taken the employee's gender into account (Blumrosen, 1989; Dwyer, 1989).

Ward's Cove v. *Antonio* (1989) went even further in creating a favorable legal climate for employers. The Court concluded that simply showing that an employer has a higher proportion of minorities in low-level jobs is insufficient to prove employment discrimination. Thus comparative statistics within an organization or industry are now irrelevant. The proper comparison, the Court ruled, is with the percentage of qualified women and minorities in the surrounding workforce.

In *Cygnar* v. *Chicago* (1989) the Seventh Circuit Court ruled against the city when a police official transferred most of the white males to another division and replaced them with blacks. The court stated that the city's actions were based on the city official's perception of racial imbalance rather than on a comparison with the relevant labor pool. The city was required to pay each transferred police officer $50,000.

The Supreme Court has ruled that the cumulative outcome of a company's multiple employment practices will not be examined. Instead, the employee must show that each employment practice being challenged causes a disparate impact. This decision is consistent with the ruling in *Watson.*

The Court now requires the employee to show that there is an alternative employment practice that equally serves the employer's interest in productivity. The employer then must subsequently refuse to use it before the employee can win a charge of employment discrimination.

These court cases served as the impetus for the revision of the 1964 Civil Rights Act (CRA). The stated purpose of the CRA of 1991 is to restore the strength of federal antidiscrimination laws that had been weakened by recent Supreme Court decisions. The act also extends Title VII coverage to extraterritorial employment.

With regard to *Ward's Cove,* the terms "business necessity" and "job related" were restored to reflect the concepts envisioned in the *Griggs* case. The revised CRA requires that the company show that the practice in dispute is significantly more likely to produce an effective workforce than other, less discriminatory alternatives.

The 1991 CRA also states that if the complaining party can demonstrate that the elements of an employer's decision cannot be separated for analysis, the selection process may be analyzed as one employment practice. The CRA also makes clear that employers are liable for any reliance on prejudice in making employment decisions. Thus a complaining party may establish that an employment practice is unlawful by demonstrating that a characteristic protected by Title VII was a "motivating factor" in the decision, even though other factors also motivated the decision.

The amount of compensatory damages that may now be awarded for future pecuniary losses, emotional pain, suffering, inconvenience, mental anguish, loss of enjoyment of life, and other nonpecuniary losses, and the amount of awardable punitive damages, is limited to:

- $50,000 for covered employers with more than 14 and fewer than 101 employees in each of 20 or more calendar weeks in the current or preceding calendar year;
- $100,000 for covered employers having more than 100 and fewer than 201 employees during the relevant periods;

- $200,000 for covered employers having more than 200 and fewer than 501 employees during the relevant periods; and

- $300,000 for covered employers having more than 500 employees during the relevant periods. (Act § 102)

Minimizing Legal Challenges

Civil Service Reform Act of 1978

The Civil Service Reform Act of 1978 is important because of its attention to performance appraisals. It thus provides a model for organizations to follow. Section 430 of the act deals specifically with the establishment of performance appraisal systems for all U.S. federal employees except those in the Central Intelligence Agency, the Foreign Service, and the General Accounting Office, as well as judges, physicians, dentists, nurses, and individuals appointed by the President. The act serves as a sound, straightforward model to performance appraisal for the private sector as well. Adherence to the act should minimize successful legal challenges to a performance appraisal.

In brief the act states that each agency shall develop one or more appraisal systems that encourage *employee participation* in establishing performance standards based on *critical* elements of the job. The method or procedure (e.g., job analysis) by which such critical elements are established must be recorded in writing. The employee must be advised of these critical requirements *before* the appraisal. Most important, an employee's appraisal must be based solely on an evaluation of performance of the critical requirements of the job. "An appraisal system must not include any controls, such as a requirement to rate on a bell curve, that prevent fair appraisals of performance in relation to the performance standards" (*Federal Register,* 1979, p. 3448). In short, appraisals must be based solely on how well the job is being performed.

The appraisals are to be conducted and recorded in writing at least once a year. The results of the appraisal must yield information that can be used for making decisions regarding the "training, rewarding, reassigning, promoting, reducing in grade, retaining, and removing employees" (Public Law 95–454, 1978, 92STAT., p. 1132). Thus rewards should be tied directly to performance. An employee designated to receive a reduction in grade or termination must receive thirty days advance written notice of the proposed action, with identification of the critical elements of the employee's job involved in each instance of unacceptable performance. The employee must be allowed to respond to the charge orally and in writing.

Because of the importance of performance appraisals in rewarding and punishing (e.g., terminating) an employee, each federal agency is required to provide training to those individuals who conduct appraisals (see Chapters 6 and 8 for approaches to training). In addition, each agency must establish procedures for conducting periodic evaluations of the effectiveness of its appraisal system and use the evaluation data to refine, alter, or improve the system. The Office of Personnel Management is responsible for determining whether an agency is fulfilling the requirements of the act, and it has the authority to direct an agency to implement or to revise a system to meet the requirements of this act.

Other Preventive Measures

Organizations in Canada and the United States need to take several other steps to minimize successful legal challenges (Burchett & DeMeuse, 1985; Goddard, 1989; Metz, 1989; Weiss, 1988). First, the race or sex of an employee should not be taken into account when promoting, transferring, laying off, or terminating people unless an imbalance in the organization needs to be corrected. This imbalance must be based on the percentage of women and members of minority groups in the organization versus those who are qualified in the area labor market.

Second, the organization should conduct a job analysis to determine those characteristics necessary for successful performance. For example, Ackerman, an equipment installer with asthma, filed suit against Western Electric after she was dismissed. The court (*Ackerman* v. *Western Electric Co., Inc.,* 1988) looked at how much time she spent on tasks that might interfere with her asthma and found that they took only about 12 percent of her time. Thus the court ruled in her favor, concluding that these tasks were too insignificant and infrequent to be considered an essential function of her position.

Third, the critical requirements for effective performance should be incorporated within a behaviorally based rating instrument. Fourth, appraisers should be trained to use the rating instrument. Fifth, the organization must ensure that job-related performance and promotion standards are applied consistently.

Sixth, the appraisals should be documented. The Ward's Cove case mandated employers to keep records that reflect the cumulative effect of its decisions, as well as the individual impact of its separate procedures. Failure to do so may be considered an admission of guilt.

Seventh, employees should be coached on ways to correct identified deficiencies in their performance. Finally, employers should develop and encourage the use of procedures employees can use to challenge appraisals perceived to be unfair. These eight steps underlie the discussion in the remainder of this book.

Closing Remarks

The following list identifies key legal considerations affecting performance appraisals:

1. The courts have ruled that any decision-making processes, from background checks to supervisory performance ratings, that affect an employee's status in an organization are tests and thus are subject to scrutiny for adverse impact.

2. Employers sometimes attempt to distinguish among a hiring, a promotion, or a performance appraisal decision. They sometimes assert that there are no lines of progression within the organization and that a transfer should not be regarded as a promotion. However, the courts generally find such distinctions irrelevant. It is the employment practices that are subject to challenge, and the question is whether the organization's practices are discriminatory (*Domingo* v. *New England Fish Co.*, 1977).

3. An employee who files an action under Title VII has the burden of establishing the existence of employment discrimination. The employee may use statistical proof, although proof of specific instances of discrimination is sometimes required. Then, as ruled in the *Albermarle* case, the organization has the burden of

proving that its appraisal decisions were made on a nondiscriminatory basis.

4. Establishing a violation of Title VII does not require proof that the defendant *intentionally discriminated* against one or more people. According to the *Griggs* case, "Congress directed the thrust of the Act to the consequences of employment practices, not simply the motivation." The inquiry must therefore be directed to the impact of an allegedly discriminatory personnel practice or performance criterion (the *Domingo* case). However, the courts do distinguish between adverse impact and disparate treatment. A plaintiff can claim that a superficially neutral practice has an adverse impact on nonwhites. The issue is then characterized as an adverse-impact case, and intent becomes irrelevant. Alternatively, the plaintiff can claim that there is disparate treatment, as when a nonwhite is reprimanded or dismissed for something a white can allegedly do with impunity. Here intent is an issue.

The crux of statistical proof in discrimination cases is the presentation of percentage differences between majority and minority groups sufficiently substantial to support an inference that such differences would not exist in the absence of discrimination. The burden then shifts to the company to dispel the inference. If it is unsuccessful, the court may proceed as if discrimination explains the observed differences, even in the absence of *direct* evidence of discrimination, as in the *Domingo* case.

The numerical methods used to assess the adverse impact of performance appraisals depends, according to Edwards (1976), on the nature of the personnel decision it supports. If the decision is to retain or to lay off, a direct comparison of proportions of minority and majority persons assigned the same status should be made. If the performance appraisal results in assigning employees to rating categories, such as excellent, above average, average, and below average, statistical comparisons of the frequencies of minorities and nonminorities in each category should be made.

If a numerical score is assigned to individuals, as in behaviorally anchored rating scales, the averages for minority and nonminority groups should be statistically compared. If the sample is large enough to be statistically significant and if the odds of observed differences occurring by chance alone are less than 1 in 20, the courts are likely to determine that the statistics suggest an inference of discrimination (Edwards, 1976).

6. Where demographic statistics are ruled admissible, employers often contend that the labor market can be defined only in terms of the geographic area where the employer hires its employees. But in cases such as *Domingo,* the courts have ruled that this limitation is improper, especially if the employer seeks to use an area other than that surrounding the place of business. The courts consider the area where an organization chooses not to hire its employees as relevant as the areas where it does hire. The courts have not adhered to one formula in defining the relevant labor market but rather have treated the issue as a question of fact to be legally determined.

7. The courts have developed a deep skepticism of appraisal techniques involving supervisory judgments that depend almost entirely on subjective evaluation (*Rowe* v. *General Motors,* 1972). The courts have specifically condemned procedures based on trait scales (*James* v. *Stockham Valves and Fittings Co.,* 1978). Trait scales, discussed in Chapter 3, consist of vague terms, such as "commitment," "initiative," and "aggressiveness," that are not defined in terms of overt observable behavior.

8. The best defense against a charge of adverse impact in performance appraisal is a properly validated appraisal system. In order to show that a measure is valid, "there must be a proper job analysis to determine appropriate measures of job performance. These job analyses are required so that the study's author may select the most important behaviors or measures of job performance for correlation to the test results"

(*Dickerson* v. *U.S. Steel Corp.,* 1978). As noted in *Albermarle,* "Without a job analysis to define the knowledge, skills, or behavior required on the job, and a description of how the appraisal instrument samples critical and/or frequent components of a job, a claim of validity cannot be substantiated." In *United States* v. *City of Chicago* (1976) the appellate court rejected a study that had no job analysis in it. In short, the performance appraisal system must be shown to be job related if adverse impact is shown. Job analysis, described in detail in Chapters 3 and 4, identifies the important tasks, duties, and responsibilities of a job.

9. In short, organizations can minimize legal challenges in appraisals by taking certain steps. First, race, sex, or ethnic group should not be taken into account when promoting, transferring, laying off, or discharging employees. Second, a job analysis should be conducted to identify critical aspects of employees' jobs. Third, the critical requirements for effective performance need to be incorporated into rating instruments. Fourth, appraisers who use these instruments need to be trained in making sound ratings. Fifth, the use of these ratings for personnel decisions must be applied consistently across employees. Sixth, all appraisals must be carefully documented. Seventh, the appraisals should be used to coach employees to improve their job performance. Eighth, mechanisms need to be established by which employees can challenge an appraisal they feel is unfair.

3

The Development and Validation of Appraisal Systems

The primary purpose of performance appraisal is to counsel and develop employees on ways to increase their productivity. The first step in this process is to define employee productivity; the second step is to develop ways of measuring it. In this chapter we discuss productivity, the importance of job analysis for defining it, and the concepts of reliability and validity in measuring it. In Chapter 4 the relative advantages of different appraisal instruments are assessed.

Productivity

During the past twenty years, the rate of productivity growth in leading Western nations has declined. There has been a negative growth rate, however, in only the United States and Canada (Tuttle, 1983).

The quest for productivity in these two countries will continue to frustrate people if they try to treat it primarily as a problem in capital investment. Productivity comes not from machines but from people—employees who design, maintain, and operate the equipment or manage the work flow. This statement should be self-evident, but the issue is rarely addressed when productivity concerns are tackled. This is unfortunate because regardless of the total investment in technology or equipment, the fact remains that the individual employee is key to productivity. Thus a critical question for management is: Do people know what they are supposed to do in job X? Making certain that the answer is yes is the first and foremost step to improving an employee's performance.

Whose job is it to get the answers to this question? A blithe response would be that it is everyone's, just as it is everyone's responsibility to be concerned with employee safety, product quality, cost reduction, and so on. But just as the engineering department has primary responsibility for designing equipment, the maintenance department has primary responsibility for maintaining and repairing it, and the operations people have primary responsibility for running the equipment at optimal efficiency and effectiveness. Similarly, the human resource department has primary responsibility for helping determine what employees in their respective jobs must do to design, maintain, and operate the equipment effectively.

Senior management has the duty of developing a clear corporate vision and setting specific, challenging goals relative to this vision. The human resource department has primary responsibility for ensuring that every employee knows what to do to implement the strategy necessary to achieve the vision. It is not sufficient for human resource departments to be concerned solely with traditional personnel functions, such as recruitment, compensation, and benefits. It is their charge to ensure that the fundamental step is taken for employee productivity, namely, that employees are informed about what they must do to be maximally productive on the job. To do this, human resource specialists need to develop a means of measuring an employee's performance.

Human resource departments have typically shied away from measuring the performance of the individual employee. Typically, they have viewed productivity as strictly an output/input ratio expressed on an economic scale. They sometimes measure input in terms of attendance, punctuality, or hours on the job. Output frequently is not measured at all; for most jobs it is extremely difficult, if not impossible, to obtain an objective performance measure (e.g., number of trees cut down, vehicles sold, patients treated, etc.) for each employee throughout the organization. This is true in engineering, maintenance, and operations, as well as for staff positions. Even when such a measure does exist, it almost always fails to provide a comprehensive measure of an employee's productivity. For example, a secretary may type 100 error-free words per minute but may also take forty-five-minute coffee breaks, interrupt the work of peers, and use equipment improperly. It would be naive to evaluate that secretary's productivity solely in terms of typing speed. Furthermore, economic measures (e.g., sales) are almost always affected, both positively and negatively, by factors over which the individual has minimal, if any, control. Thus an employee can be rewarded or penalized erroneously. Consequently, human resource departments—if they do so at all—usually measure employee performance through either trait scales or cost-related outcomes.

Trait Scales

The most frequent approach to measuring an employee's performance is to use traits, e.g., "loyal," "dependable," "decisive," and "self-managing." One advantage of this approach to measurement is that the same appraisal scale, with slight modifications, can be used for all employees, ranging from the CEO to the company's entry-level positions. Everyone wants people to be loyal, dependable, decisive, and self-managing, regardless of their job title. Tables 3.1 and 3.2 are examples of trait scales that have been used by organizations.

A second advantage of trait scales is that they can be developed quickly. It does not take considerable time or imagination to brainstorm a set of adjectives that are considered positive, complimentary, and necessary for all employees (e.g., "creative," "teamplayer," "tactful"). Hence the entire organization can get by with only one appraisal form. But the advantages of *ease* in developing only *one* instrument are illusory. Feedback and goal setting must be specific if they are to bring about a relatively permanent change in an employee's behavior (Wexley & Latham, 1991). Further, the feedback and goal setting must be related to critical or important aspects of the job if they are going to meaningfully affect an employee's performance (Tziner & Kopelman, 1988). What is critical or important in one job is not necessarily critical or important in other jobs. Appraisal instruments must be designed for the job or job family in question if the appraisal process is to be effective.

Traits such as commitment, creativity, loyalty, initiative, and the like are words surrounded by ambiguity. Telling a person to be a better listener or to show more initiative may be good

Table 3.1

A Trait-oriented Performance Appraisal Rating

Name:	
Department: Section: Position: Reporting Period:	
a = superior b = above average c = average d = below average e = unsatisfactory	
1. Ability to Adapt: a c e b d	9. Practical Talent: a c e b d
2. Diligence and Application: a c e b d	10. Potential: a c e b d
3. Cooperation with Others: a c e b d	11. Communication Skills: a c e b d
4. Quality of Work: a c e b d	12. Planning: a c e b d
5. Making Decisions: a c e b d	13. Capacity: a c e b d
6. Manner and Appearance: a c e b d	14. Leadership: a c e b d
7. Job Contribution: a c e b d	15. Calmness: a c e b d
8. Initiative: a c e b d	16. Personal Conduct: a c e b d

advice, but it doesn't tell the individual *what to do*. These words must be defined explicitly for the employee.

For example, a director of research and development was told by the vice-president to work on her communication skills. Because she was from a foreign country and felt ill at ease speaking before a large group, she enrolled in an intensive three-day course to improve her oral skills at a cost to the organization of $3000 a day. At her next performance appraisal interview six months later, the vice-president repeated the same criticism to the employee. She became highly irritated and explained to the vice-president the value of the course she had taken to improve her skills. Astonished, the vice-president

Table 3.2

A Trait-oriented Performance Appraisal Rating

Name		PLC/CO	Class		Date	Situation		
S = Sufficient D = Deficient								
	S D			S D			S D	
Bearing		Integrity			Initiative			
Enthusiasm		Decisiveness			Judgment			
Justice		Endurance			Dependability			
Physical Courage		Knowledge			Unselfishness			
Tact		Loyalty			Moral Courage			
Remarks: Comment on all weaknesses. Unobserved traits will not be marked.								
					Overall Evaluation (Circle One)			
(Use reverse, if necessary)		Satisfactory		Unsatisfactory			Marginal	
Plt. Ldr		Rank		Card Initials				

replied that all he wanted was for her to send him copies of memos she sent to a rival vice-president!

As another illustration of problems with trait-oriented appraisal instruments, ask ten people to write a description of an aggressive employee. Many people will write a positive description; others will describe the person using such words as "obnoxious," "pushy," or "inconsiderate." As Peter Drucker (1973, pp. 424–425) argued so cogently:

> An employer has no business with a man's personality. Employment is a specific contract calling for specific per-

formance, and for nothing else. Any attempt of an employer to go beyond this is usurpation. It is immoral as well as illegal intrusion of privacy. It is abuse of power. An employee owes no "loyalty," he owes no "love," and no "attitudes"—he owes performance and nothing else . . . . Management and manager development should concern themselves with changes in behavior likely to make a man more effective.

Finally, as pointed out in Chapter 2, a trait-oriented appraisal instrument is likely to be frowned on by the courts because traits are so vague. Consequently there is often little agreement among raters when a person is evaluated on traits (Austin & Villanova, 1992). As Borman (1979) concluded, traits refer at best to potential predictors of performance rather than to performance itself. Thus they may be appropriate to use on a selection test, but they are poor from the standpoint of feedback to and goal setting with the employee on ways to maintain or improve performance. (The pivotal role of goal setting in motivation is the subject of Chapter 7.) When traits are evaluated, the feedback is usually too limited because appraisers are reluctant to give an employee a low rating on traits that implicate personal qualities (Austin & Villanova, 1992).

Cost-related Outcomes

A second approach to measuring an employee's performance is to supplement the use of traits with measures of cost-related outcomes or to use the latter alone. This approach usually finds favor with senior-level managers, stockholders, and consumers because of their concern with the economic health of the organization. That is, they are concerned with quantitative measures or performance outcomes, such as profits, costs, and returns on investment, which should be a major responsibility of a manager. Therefore it could be argued that an appraisal document should measure the manager, if not individual subordinates, on the extent to which these measures are satisfactory. Such measures usually serve as excellent indicators of an organization's effectiveness.

A survey of Fortune 100 companies revealed that management by objectives (MBO) is the preferred method of assessing an employee's contribution to the organization's bottom line

(Bretz & Milkovich, 1989). MBO advocates emphasize the principles of goal setting and feedback (Drucker, 1973; Odiorne, 1970). But these two principles are not unique to MBO. What is unique is its emphasis on the "bottom line." Were X, Y, and Z activities completed? Were they completed on time? Was the quality satisfactory? In short, was the goal(s) attained? Thus issues concerning an employee's personality, which are dominant in the use of trait scales, are avoided.

When MBO is done optimally, the effect cascades throughout the organization. Senior-level managers set specific, challenging goals relating to the attainment of the organization's mission. They then set specific stretch goals with their subordinates, who in turn repeat the process with their subordinates, and so on. The setting of specific difficult but attainable goals has been shown to be one of the most robust motivational techniques in the psychological literature for increasing employee performance (Locke & Latham, 1990). But as Donald Petersen, the former president of Ford Motor Company has noted, this emphasis on goal attainment is also a weakness of MBO. When receiving a "good" appraisal is contingent on goal attainment, an employee is often motivated to set easy goals and find ingenious ways to make them appear difficult to the boss.

For example, a high-level manager in the start-up operation of a paper products company set stringent targets to "shoot for" regarding start-up costs. Due to the inefficiencies of outside contractors, the targets were not attained. The manager was severely penalized at Christmas bonus time and again the following February at his annual performance review. He then vowed that he would not repeat the same mistake. Rather than correct the mistake in terms of tighter controls on contractors, he defined it in terms of setting specific, relatively easy goals. And those whom he now manages have learned the same "lesson." The problem was that the manager and his confidants believed that tight controls had been in place to no avail. Today this manager is a senior vice-president in his organization.

For similar reasons, LTV, the giant conglomerate in Texas, has abandoned bottom-line measures as an index of an individual's managerial effectiveness. One president of an LTV company may be downgraded for exceeding a goal, while another company president is rewarded handsomely even though the goal was not achieved. The reason for this seemingly bizarre inequity is that the president who failed to achieve the goal may have been judged to have done exceedingly well in spite of his product mix, the geography in which he was operating, and the overall economy—in other words, factors over which he had minimal control—whereas the other person did exceedingly well because of different factors beyond her control. LTV believes that a sole reliance on bottom-line measures can lead to erroneous performance appraisals. The emphasis at LTV is to identify the kind of behaviors required to accomplish short- and long-term goals of the organization, to focus attention on assessing *how* an executive performs or behaves in the present organization, and to assess the environment in which the results were achieved—problem by problem—company by company—individual by individual.

The quality of the results or outcomes of a person's behavior, LTV realizes, is largely a function of the environment which existed during the period. To some extent the environment can and should be predictable, but unexpected problems and opportunities to overcome or seize, as the case may be, will arise and affect results (Meyer, 1981).

Cost-related outcomes are generally inadequate indicators of an individual employee's job effectiveness, for the following six reasons:

1. Cost-related measures are almost always deficient in that they often omit important factors for which a person should be held accountable (e.g., teamplaying as defined by a superintendent in one district loaning equipment to a superintendent in another district). This deficiency is a major criticism of MBO. Emphasis is placed primarily on tangible results that are perceived to be easily measurable. Consequently many employees feel that there is an overemphasis on quantitative goals and that they are neither measured on nor given credit for important nonquantitative aspects of their jobs (Ivancevich, Donnelly & Lyon, 1970). For example, a marketing manager might specify that a major objective for the forthcoming year is to increase the number of accounts by 10 percent in the Toronto area. A human resources manager, however, would have difficulty expressing the desired end results of a

new career development program in percentage figures. This problem has caused much frustration and anxiety among MBO participants (Ivancevich, Donnelly & Lyon, 1970).

MBO proponents argue that the objectivity gained by using concrete, tangible measures eliminates errors in observation and judgment that often occur when ratings are used. However, careful observation is still a necessity for evaluating the meaning of any so-called objective performance criterion, such as tardiness, absences, and accidents, as well as for making valid ratings on so-called soft measures. "Human judgment enters into every criterion . . ." (Smith, 1976, p. 757).

2. Cost-related measures are difficult to obtain on employees in many jobs. For example, a cost-related measure of a logging cutter's effectiveness might be the number of trees cut divided by the number of hours worked. But what cost-related measures exist for a human resource manager, an engineer, or a teacher?

   Even when such measures can be obtained, they are usually applicable only for the work group as a whole, because no one worker has substantial control over the output measured. Employee performance is usually affected by the performance of others; if they do poorly, the employee does poorly. Work groups should be evaluated, but performance appraisal is concerned with the individual employee.

3. Cost-related measures often take into account factors for which the individual is not responsible. This, Deming (1986) argued, is one of the "sins" that managers commit with their people. Tools and equipment, materials and supplies, budgetary support, time availability, and the work environment—noise, heat, and light levels—are all examples of such situational factors. To the extent that they constrain performance, the motivation level of employees is reduced because their belief that their effort will lead to good performance is decreased (O'Connor et al., 1984). Thus to the extent that only performance outcomes are measured

and situational constraints affect them adversely, the employee may choose to either quit the job or lower commitment to those goals for which situational variables inhibit goal accomplishment (O'Connor et al., 1984). Employees with high levels of ability and motivation are especially likely to do so. Situational inhibitors obviously have a minimum effect on the potential performance of persons with little ability or motivation. The consequence can be an organization populated by the latter group of people.

Cummings and Schwab (1973) argued that it is particularly unfair to distribute organizational rewards on the basis of these cost-related measures unless the employee has substantial control over the output measured. However, they pointed out that group productivity data may be useful for evaluating the manager of the work group. We would argue that even here the evidence (e.g., Curtis, Smith & Smoll, 1979; Likert, 1967) suggests that this is not always appropriate, because the performance of work groups is usually affected by other work groups with which they are linked. Moreover, the leader's performance is often directly affected by the performance of subordinates whom he or she may lack the authority to reprimand or replace. Further, the performance of groups can be affected by the same situational constraints that affect the individual employee.

4. Reliance on "bottom line" measures can encourage a "results-at-all costs mentality" that can run counter to both corporate ethics policies and legal requirements, as well as to the overall productivity of the organization. For example, lending a truck to a fellow superintendent may hurt the monthly cost sheet of the lender but may significantly increase the profits of the organization as a whole. Nevertheless, the person whose appraisal is based primarily on minimizing costs is unlikely to loan the truck unless pressured to do so.

5. Economic measures or performance outcomes by themselves do not inform employees what they need to do to

maintain or increase productivity. Thus they should be downplayed for counseling and development purposes unless the critical behaviors that an employee can engage in to influence them are defined explicitly. Cost-related measures may indicate whether an employee is or is not influencing the "bottom line" positively, but the answers to the questions of how or why can remain elusive.

For example, telling a baseball player that he just struck out will not come as a surprise to him. What the player needs to know, and what a good appraiser-counselor should be able to tell him, is exactly what he must do (strategies, tactics) to at least get on first base and possibly hit a home run. Long before Deming, therefore, many industrial psychologists (e.g., Campbell et al., 1970; Guion, 1961; Otis, 1952) were vocal about the need to measure and evaluate an employee in terms of *observable job behaviors* that are critical to job success or failure. As Wernimont and Campbell (1968, p. 373) noted: "The applied psychologist should reaffirm his mandate and return to the measurement of behavior. Only then will one learn by what means and to what extent, an individual has influenced his rate of promotion, salary increases, or work group's production."

In an Iowa government survey, two-thirds of the employees indicated that MBO was of little help in planning for and receiving training and development activities (Daley, 1987). Their dissatisfaction with the training aspect of the MBO process was so high that it eroded their belief in the fairness of the entire appraisal process.

Consistent with the anecdotal evidence obtained by Deming's supporters (e.g., Scholtes, 1987), organizational psychologists have conducted systematic research showing that:

> . . . the perception of causes of poor performance may lead to inaccurate appraisals and points of conflict . . . . the data suggest that supervisors make

attributions and responses partly as a function of the seriousness of the outcome. In work settings these outcomes may be completely out of the subordinate's control (e.g., whether a patient falls out of bed when the railing is down) . . . . supervisors would be more efficient if they concentrated on trying to change the behavior that caused the incident rather than focusing on the outcome. What our analysis suggests is that when poor performance occurs but the outcome is not serious, the supervisor is more likely to overlook the problem. This strategy can lead to serious negative consequences at some later time and is clearly not an effective means of feedback. To change behavior we must focus on the behavior, not the outcome. (Mitchell & Wood, 1980, p. 138)

6. As noted by Feild and Holley (1982), emphasizing cost-related measures could be contrary to the legal emphasis on giving feedback to the employee. It is one thing to tell an employee whether he or she is doing well or poorly on the job; it is quite another to counsel him or her on what he or she can start doing, stop doing, or consider doing differently as a result of an unfavorable outcome measure. Only behavioral criteria permit the latter. Thus the problem is not in looking at outcome measures but rather the failure to conduct a job analysis to identify the critical behaviors over which the individual has control and that in turn will affect those outcomes.

So, what is productivity? The Japanese Productivity Center, citing the European Productivity Center, argued that above all else, productivity is an attitude of mind. It is mentality of progress of the constant improvement of that which exists. It is the certainty of being able to do better today than yesterday and less well than tomorrow. It is the will to improve on the present situation no matter how good it may seem, no matter how good it may really be. It is the constant adaptation of economic and social life to changing conditions; it is the continual effort to apply new techniques and new methods; it is the faith in human progress.

This statement shows that North American psychologists are not alone in eschewing economic output/input ratios in defining an individual's productivity. One difficulty with this statement, however, is that it is filled with trait-oriented variables, such as "faith in human progress" and "will to improve." A job analysis is required to identify how these terms can be demonstrated in observable behavior so that reliable and valid appraisals can take place. The productivity of the individual is best measured in terms of the frequency with which critical behaviors are emitted.

Behavioral Criteria

Before reviewing the research on job analysis and the development of behaviorally based appraisal scales, let us discuss the philosophy underlying them.

In his 1964 presidential address to the Division of Industrial Organizational Psychology of the American Psychological Association, Rains Wallace (1965) warned against compromising "our goal of reliability and freedom from bias in order to maintain criteria which are clearly relevant to management's ultimate goals" (p. 414). He was referring to the limitations of cost-related measures. In his 1952 presidential address to that same body, Jay Otis (1952) stated that we need to "educate management so that significant job behavior can be substituted for those judged to be less desirable" (p. 80). Our interest needs to be "directed toward what workers do" (p. 81). There needs to be "a continuing search for job behavior that leads to success" (p. 83). "Our purpose is the identification of behavioral areas which may be used to serve as indexes of excellence" (p. 85).

Behaviorally based appraisal measures can account for far more job complexity; they can be related more directly to what the employee does, and they are more likely to minimize irrelevant factors not under the control of the employee than can trait or cost-related measures. Behavioral criteria developed from a systematic job analysis make explicit what one must do to be productive. Examples of behavioral measures for supervisors are shown in Table 3.3. If a supervisor is suddenly doing poorly on the job, the manager along with the supervisor can use the appraisal instrument to diagnose what this employee must do to improve performance. Good cost-related outcomes (e.g., profits) rarely come about serendipitously. Someone must do

Table 3.3
Example of Behavioral Measures for Evaluating Supervisors

1. Explains job requirements to new employees in a clear manner (e.g., talks slowly; shows them how to do it).

   Almost Never   0   1   2   3   4   Almost Always

2. Tells workers that if they have questions or problems to feel free to come and talk to him or her.

   Almost Never   0   1   2   3   4   Almost Always

3. Distributes overtime equally, taking into account seniority.

   Almost Never   0   1   2   3   4   Almost Always

---

something to make them good. Behavioral measures based on a job analysis indicate precisely what is being done by an individual to warrant recognition, discipline, transfer, promotion, demotion, or termination.

Certainly traits or "bottom-line" cost-related outcomes should not be ignored; rather, they must be defined in terms of the behaviors that affect the bottom line. For example, in baseball, coming to work, striking out, and hitting a home run are all bottom-line measures. Similarly, reducing costs by 10 percent, selling fifty-two cars in a month, and turning a report in on time are performance outcomes. What makes behavioral criteria more comprehensive than economic measures by themselves is that behavioral measures not only measure the individuals on factors over which they have control but also specify what the person must do or not do to attain these outcomes (e.g., swinging level of bat, stepping into the ball, swinging late).

In summary, a well-constructed appraisal instrument includes the behavioral strategies necessary for employees to affect the desired outcomes. The bottom line defined in cost-related terms is a primary measure of an organization's effectiveness. The purpose of the appraisal instrument is to specify what each employee needs to do to influence that bottom line. The appraisal instrument will do this to the extent that the behavioral criteria are based on a systematic job analysis and the instrument is reliable and valid.

Minimum Standards for Appraisal Instruments

There is general agreement in the psychological literature as to the characteristics of a good appraisal instrument. This agreement is compatible with court cases that cite the presence of three characteristics as essential issues to be examined when appraisal systems are challenged on the basis of such factors as race, sex, or age discrimination. These same three characteristics are necessary if behavioral criteria are to serve as indicators of cost-related outcomes. These three characteristics are a *job analysis* that yields a *reliable* and *valid* appraisal instrument.

Job Analysis

Industrial engineers perform job analyses to identify optimal work methods, facilities, and environments. Human resource specialists conduct job analyses to identify the behaviors necessary for performing optimally in specific jobs. Job analysis can be defined as the process of obtaining information on what employees do in the job; it is the search for job behaviors that lead to success; it is the identification of behavioral areas that serve as indicators of excellence (Otis, 1952). In short, the basic question of job analysis, as practiced by human resource specialists, is: "What is the nature of the behaviors called for by the job or the employment situation" (Guion, 1961, p. 145).

A primary benefit of job analysis is that it enables human resource specialists to develop appraisal scales that truly assist people in evaluating the productivity of themselves and others. This approach to productivity is an excellent way of reducing costs. Another way that human resource departments can control costs is to minimize legal conflicts over performance appraisals.

A job analysis is a legal requirement for performance appraisal instruments. The 1978 *Uniform Guidelines* make this explicit: "There shall be a job analysis which includes an analysis of the important work behaviors required for successful performance.... Any job analysis should focus on work behavior(s) and the tasks associated with them." [See 14.C.2]

This position was endorsed in *Kirkland* v. *New York Department of Correctional Services* (1974), which struck down the claim of validity for the appraisal instrument even though the instrument had been evaluated favorably by six subject-matter experts. Specifically, the court did not agree that the experts "had in their heads a job analysis sufficient to satisfy legal and professional requirements." In *Greenspan* v. *Automobile Club of Michigan* (1980) the judge stated: "The criteria actually employed by the Defendants were not developed by professional consultants, but rather were adapted from a commercially available method of job analysis from which Defendants borrowed what they believed to be pertinent to their needs."

In an analysis of sixty-six legal cases involving charges of discrimination resulting from performance appraisal, Feild and Holley (1982) identified six variables that since 1976 have resulted in an organization's winning its case. In particular, the employer must be certain that the content of the performance appraisal system is based on job analysis, and that performance measures are job related, specific work behaviors and not based on general traits that lend themselves to opinions, subjective judgment, and rater bias.[1] In a review of the literature on legal standards for job analysis, Thompson and Thompson (1982) concluded that the results of the job analysis must be in writing; the data must be collected by an expert in job analysis from up-to-date sources, such as job incumbents, supervisors, and training manuals; and on-the-job performance must be observed by the analyst.

Legal issues aside, employees frequently do not understand why their production rate is good or bad. "I don't know what I'm doing right, but I hope my luck continues" is a statement voiced much too often in organizations. A job analysis that defines production rate in terms of job behaviors critical to affecting it removes the mystery for employees. The issue is to choose the job analysis method that will facilitate this understanding.

---

1. Measures of the results or outcomes of work behaviors such as production rate or error rate may be used without a full job analysis where a review of information about the job shows that these criteria are important to the employment situation of the user. Similarly, measures such as absenteeism and tardiness, or turnover, may be used without a full job analysis if these behaviors are shown by a review of information about the job to be important in the specific situation (EEOC, 1979, p. 2319).

A number of acceptable procedures exist for conducting a job analysis, each differing in terms of its possible contribution to the objectives of management. One way of classifying job analysis techniques is through the use of either: (1) task or activity statements that culminate in a definition of the job-oriented content of the job(s), or (2) behavioral statements that culminate in the worker-oriented content of the job(s). Techniques of the first type, which aim at uncovering the things a worker does on the job, include the critical-incident technique and task analysis. Techniques of the second type, which identify the characteristics of the successful employee in the job, include position-analysis questionnaire, ability-requirements scales, and threshold trait analysis (Wright & Wexley, 1985).

Human resource specialists agree that there is no one best way to do a job analysis (Levine, Ash & Bennett, 1980), although one method may be superior to another for a specific application. Levine et al. (1980) compared four methods of job analysis: the critical incident technique, job elements, the position-analysis questionnaire, and task analysis. The analysts, human resource specialists, found the position-analysis questionnaire (PAQ) to be the least favorable approach for providing information to develop a performance appraisal instrument or for establishing content validity. (Content validity is concerned with the degree to which items on the rating scale are a representative sample of all important items that could have been included in the scale (Bernardin, Morgan & Winne, 1980).) The critical incident technique (CIT) was the method most favored for providing adequate information to develop content-valid appraisal measures.

In a second study Levine et al. (1983) compared the CIT with those three methods plus four more: ability requirement scales, functional job analysis, task inventory, and threshold trait analysis. Again, the CIT was rated higher than the other methods for developing an appraisal scale, although the difference between the ratings for the CIT and functional job analysis was not statistically significant.

In an exhaustive review of the job analysis literature, McCormick (1979) reached a similar conclusion regarding the CIT: It is ideal for the development of performance appraisal measures. Similarly, Austin and Villanova (1992) concluded that the CIT is a cornerstone of behavior-based performance measurement systems.

According to Flanagan (1954), the CIT requires observers who are aware of the aims and objectives of a given job and who see people perform the job on a frequent basis (e.g., daily) to describe to a job analyst incidents of effective and ineffective job behavior that they have observed over the past six to twelve months. Thus supervisors, peers, subordinates, and clients may be interviewed about their observations of the *critical requirements* of the job.

The specific steps in conducting a job analysis based on the critical incident technique are as follows:

1. *(Introduction):* I am conducting a job analysis to determine what makes the difference between an effective and an ineffective (e.g., supervisor, dentist, secretary). By effective performance I mean the type of behavior that, when you saw it occur, you wished all employees would do the same thing under similar circumstances. By ineffective performance I mean behavior that, if it occurred repeatedly or even once under certain circumstances, would make you doubt the competency of the individual.

   I am talking with you because you are aware of the aims and objectives of the job, you frequently observe people in this job, and you are able to discern competent from incompetent performance. Please do not tell me the names of any individual to whom you are referring. (Note: Job incumbents are not interviewed concerning their own behavior, as they are usually objective in describing their *effective* but not their *ineffective* behavior (Vroom & Maier, 1961).

2. *(Interview):* I would like you to think back over the past six to twelve months of specific incidents that you have seen occur. (The emphasis on the past twelve months is to ensure that the information is currently applicable. For example, behaviors that were critical for a salesperson in the 1950s may no longer be critical in the 1990s. Moreover, memory loss may distort the facts if the analysis is not restricted to recent incidents. The requirement that the interviewer report

only first-hand information maximizes the objectivity or factual nature of the information to be reported.)

Can you think of an incident? (If the answer is no, the following comments may stimulate recall.)

- Write down the five key things that an employee *must* be good at in this job. What is the first thing you wrote? Can you think of an employee who within the past year demonstrated that point? What was the second thing you wrote? The third, etc.?

- Tell me the first initial (in order to maintain anonymity) of the most effective person you know in this job. Suppose I could argue that this person is ineffective. What incidents can you cite to change my opinion?

You have thought of an incident. Good. For each incident you recall, I am going to ask you three questions:

- What were the circumstances surrounding this incident? In other words, what was the background? What was the situation? (This question is important because it establishes *when* a given behavior is appropriate.)

- What exactly did the individual *do* that was either effective or ineffective? (Generally, effective incidents are requested before ineffective incidents. Although there is no empirical evidence to support this practice, our experience indicates that when effective incidents are requested first, the interviewee does not feel that the information is being obtained for a witch hunt. The purpose of this second question is to elicit information concerning specific *observable* behavior.)

- How is the incident you described an example of effective or ineffective behavior? In other words, how did this affect the task(s) that the individual was performing?

Generally, an interviewee is asked to report five effective and five ineffective incidents. Attention is given to both types of incidents because an effective incident is not necessarily the opposite of an ineffective incident. For example, setting a specific goal was found to be effective for increasing the productivity of loggers, but not setting goals by no means led to bankruptcy (Latham, 1969).

Ten incidents are collected because they can usually be collected within one hour, the maximum time period that many employees can be away from the job without disrupting their work day. No more than ten incidents are collected from any one individual so that the data are not biased by talkative people. In order to obtain a comprehensive sample of incidents, at least thirty people should be interviewed.

The interviewer must be skilled in collecting information describing *observable* behaviors. If the interviewee says, "...the employee really showed initiative in solving the problem," the interviewer must probe, "What exactly did the individual *do* that demonstrated initiative?"

Because the crux of the critical incident technique is obtaining examples of behavior, a brief quiz follows. Examine these statements and determine which ones describe observable behavior. The answers are given at the end of this chapter.

1. She looked sloppy in public.
2. He wore pants covered with grease.
3. She asked who owned the wallet.
4. He was an honest man.
5. The engineer could handle any emergency, as shown by her behavior last Christmas.
6. When the landing flaps failed to work, the engineer replaced the cable over the drum.
7. The radar observer was weak on scope interpretation.
8. She was afraid of heights but overcame her reluctance and became proficient in all phases of flying.
9. On the previous biology exam, the student received an A. The student got a "big head" and made a poor score on the next quiz.

The people from whom the critical incidents are collected should be subject matter experts (SMEs)—people who are aware of the aims and objectives of the job, who frequently observe people performing the job, and who are able to determine whether the performance is competent or incompetent when they see it occur. Moreover, SMEs should comprise a representative sample of people in terms of age, race, sex, and experience (Landy & Vasey, 1991; Mullins & Kimborough, 1988).

The CIT is not without its criticism, however. Flanagan (1949) argued: "This procedure has considerable efficiency because of the use of only the extremes of behavior. It is well known that extremes can be more accurately identified than behavior which is more nearly average in character" (p. 423). Blum and Naylor (1968) retorted that this limits the use of the technique for extracting material for job descriptions because so much information is, by definition, deleted. Our response to this argument is that a job description and an appraisal instrument are not necessarily the same. One criterion for evaluating the effectiveness of an appraisal instrument is whether it can discriminate between effective and ineffective performers. To the extent that an appraisal instrument contains behaviors that are exhibited by everyone, the instrument would not differentiate effective from ineffective performances.

A second criticism of the CIT is that it is time consuming (Levine et al., 1980). Literally hundreds of incidents must be collected to ensure that the appraisal instrument is content valid. Additional time is needed to categorize the incidents and to develop the appraisal scale.

An approach that does not violate the intent of the CIT but removes the criticism regarding the focus on "extreme behavior" is to define the words "effective or competent" and "ineffective or incompetent" and then focus on the word "do." "What have you observed a person *do* to demonstrate that he or she is effective or ineffective?" If the respondent talks in terms of traits, the question can be rephrased by asking what the person did to demonstrate that he or she is lazy, industrious, creative, mediocre, and so on.

A procedure that gets around the criticism regarding length of time as well as the focus on extreme behavior has been described in detail by Drauden and Peterson (1977). In brief, six to eight SMEs follow the rules of brainstorming to list behaviors that are important to the job in question. They then group similar behaviors together to develop a performance criterion. The performance criteria and the behaviors that define them are listed on a questionnaire and sent to supervisors and job incumbents, who rate each behavior in terms of importance and the amount of time the behavior is necessary on the job.

Reliability and Validity

In addition to being based on a job analysis, the appraisal instrument should facilitate performance measurement that is both reliable and valid (Austin & Villanova, 1992). Reliability affects validity in that a performance measure that is extremely unreliable cannot be valid.[2] For example, if a supervisor rates employees solely in terms of their moods on a particular day, the scores may not be consistent (reliable) from one time period to the next. Furthermore, the performance appraisal instrument will not be measuring the employees' performance but rather their mood swings. Thus the measure is not valid. A valid measure should yield consistent (reliable) data about what it is concerned with, regardless of when the measures are taken and who takes them.

The following methods can be used to determine the reliability of a performance appraisal system. Each is designed to answer a different issue.

1. The *test-retest* method assesses the reliability of a performance measure in terms of its stability from one time period to another. This assumes, of course, that the employee's level of performance is expected to remain constant over a period of time. Thus it provides a measure of the extent to which the appraisal measure is *free from* time-sampling errors, such as random fluctuations in the rater's standards or in the operation of the machinery or equipment. This requires measuring the performance of the same employees (e.g., thirty or more) on two or more occasions with the same performance appraisal instrument. The degree of similarity from time to time is the measure of reliability.

   Perfect reliability yields a correlation coefficient of 1.0. A correlation coefficient can vary between +1.00 and −1.00. A positive correlation means that employees

---

2. Reliability is an attribute of one factor, e.g., a job performance rating. Validity is the relationship between two factors, e.g., how a performance rating correlates with another independent measure of performance.

who perform highly at one point in time are likely to perform highly at a later point. Conversely, a negative correlation means that employees with high performance at Time 1 are likely to have low performance at Time 2.

When the correlation coefficient is 0.00, no relationship exists between the two time periods. However, a test-retest reliability coefficient will never be 1.0, because individuals will vary in their performance due to knowledge and skill acquired over time. The reliability measure, however, should ideally be 0.70 or higher. To the extent that the performance measures are unstable, they may reflect nothing more than random fluctuations over time due to such things as fatigue level or mood swings. When behavioral criteria are used, the random fluctuation in work or fatigue may be indigenous to the rater instead of, or in addition to, the employee. For this reason, calculating interobserver reliability is useful for determining the reliability of an appraisal.

2. Interobserver reliability is assessed by determining the agreement (consistency) between two or more raters in evaluating an employee *independently*. The last word in this sentence is key. Consider the following example:

> Pat, I am considering Sam for the position of V.P. of Sales. I think she is fantastic. You have worked with her. What do you think?

Intentionally or unintentionally, there is an attempt by the speaker to bias Pat's appraisal. Hence even if there is agreement between the appraisers, there is no evidence of interobserver reliability because the assessments were not made independently.

Assessing interobserver reliability is analogous to comparing a number of photographs of an employee that were taken at the same point in time, but by two or more photographers working independently. Perfect interobserver reliability (i.e., 1.0) is rarely obtained because two or more observers seldom see an employee at the same points in time or in the same way. However, the correlation among different raters should be at least 0.60 (Osburn & Manese, 1972). When the agreement is less than 0.60, when the raters have had opportunities to observe the employee, and when they are capable of discerning competent from incompetent performance, it is likely that the appraisal is not measuring the employee's performance, but rather the different attitudes and biases of the appraisers. Breaking down an appraisal decision into a series of straightforward judgments is one way of increasing interobserver reliability (Jako & Murphy, 1990).

3. Another measure of an appraisal scale's reliability is its *internal consistency,* which provides an indication of the homogeneity, or "sameness," of the items that comprise that scale. It answers the question of whether all the items on a scale are assessing the same dimension (e.g., concern for quality). Thus it provides a measure of the extent to which the scale is free of content sampling error. For example, if one appraisal scale is designed to assess concern for quality, items that assess concern for increasing market share would not correlate with quality and hence would be discarded from that particular scale.

Internal consistency is determined by correlating the odd- and even-numbered items on a rating scale. Ideally, the correlation should be at least 0.80. This number is higher than that for test-retest and interobserver reliability because both the source of the ratings and the timing of the ratings are held constant. Moreover, statistical procedures exist for developing an internally consistent scale, whereas the person who develops the appraisal scales has no control over the behavior of the employees who are being appraised or the opportunities of the people who observe and record the behavior of employees.

As previously noted, the reliability of a performance appraisal criterion is important because, in general, it sets the upper limit on validity (Ryan & Smith, 1954). However, an appraisal measure may be reliable but not valid in that the measure may be consistently measuring the wrong thing (e.g., it reflects the prejudices of two or more supervisors year after year rather than the employee behavior). Moreover, the instrument may yield consistent ratings of the employee's behavior, but if the observations are being used to make judgments about the employee's potential for other jobs, the appraisal may not be valid if the requirements for those other jobs are vastly different.

A discussion on validity is meaningful only in terms of the specific uses for which the appraisal will be used. An appraisal may be valid for one purpose and invalid for another. To be useful for the organization, the appraisal system must be both reliable and valid for every purpose for which it is being used.

The validity of an appraisal instrument can be assessed in three primary ways. First, the appraisal instrument must be *content valid.*

Second, if one purpose of the appraisal instrument is to predict future performance of employees on a different job, *predictive validity* should be shown. Performance appraisal scores obtained on individuals in the present job are correlated with performance measures of the same individuals in a subsequent job. Predictive validity, however, is seldom used by organizations, because the validation sample requires the collection of performance measures on thirty or more people.[3] Unfortunately, there are seldom that many job openings in an organization for a given position above the entry level.

Construct validity, a third approach for establishing the job-relatedness, or validity, of an appraisal system, may be used when predictive validity is not technically possible. It is used to *infer* the degree to which the persons being evaluated possess some quality or construct (i.e., employee worth to the organization) presumed to be reflected in the performance measure (Blum & Naylor, 1968). The general procedure for determining construct validity involves gathering several different performance measures that logically appear to measure the same con-

---

3. Arvey and Faley (1988) describe procedures for obtaining large sample sizes. First, two or more jobs that are substantially similar (e.g., clerical and secretarial jobs) might be treated as one job. Second, a job analysis can be conducted to isolate dimensions of behaviors that are common to several jobs, and the sample in those jobs can be used to validate appraisal decisions for those behavioral dimensions. This procedure is known as *synthetic validity.*

struct (e.g., administrative skill) and then observing the relationship among these appraisal measures. A high intercorrelation is an indication of construct validity.

The use of different observers can also be used in a multitrait/multirater framework (Lawler, 1967) to assess the construct validity of appraisal decisions. The use of the word "trait" here simply refers to the use of multiple criterion dimensions (e.g., technical competence, interpersonal skill, administrative ability). "Multiple raters" refers to the use of different raters, such as supervisors, peers, and subordinates, in making appraisals of the employee. To show construct validity of the appraisals, there should be agreement among knowledgeable observers of the employee's performance on each individual criterion. However, how employees are evaluated on one criterion (e.g., technical competence) should not necessarily correlate highly with how they are evaluated on another criterion (e.g., interpersonal skill). A high correlation among the different criteria is traditionally interpreted as evidence of halo error (see Chapter 6). That is, it is presumed that the raters are making one overall global rating without taking into account how each employee is truly doing on the different aspects or dimensions of the job. The assumption underlying this argument is that it is unrealistic to think that everyone who is outstanding on one criterion measure is equally good on all aspects of the job. People have different strengths and weaknesses. A performance appraisal system with construct validity should reflect these individual strengths and weaknesses.

It is the requirement of a low correlation between different aspects of job performance (e.g., mechanical skill versus verbal skill) that differentiates this approach to measuring construct validity from the method of assessing interobserver reliability. However, in practice, it is fallacious to assume that high intercorrelations among the different performance criteria are always indicative of halo error. Most organizations, including universities, strive for homogeneity by discharging individuals who perform poorly in one or more areas. Moreover, the criteria used to evaluate performance are often logically related. For example, university students are evaluated on their cognitive skills. Thus we would expect their performance in one class to be similar to their performance in another class. In the population at large, interpersonal skill and mechanical skill do not correlate with each other. But within an organization the correlation may be quite high if only those people who are high on both dimensions were hired and if those who subsequently slipped on either one of these dimensions were discharged.

In closing this discussion on reliability and validity, it is important to understand that neither reliability nor validity refers to a specific procedure but rather to the inferences that are made from the use of one or more of these procedures. The key consideration in reliability and validity is whether these inferences are appropriate. Further, the categories of content validity, predictive validity, and construct validity are three inseparable aspects of validity, not discrete types of validity. The classification is made for convenience and clarity for discussion purposes only. For example, we emphasized that the appraisal instrument must contain a representative sampling of critical job behaviors if it is to be considered content valid. But what good is this requirement if the recorded observations of people fulfilling these requirements are biased or incomplete? "The emphasis, therefore, should be on validation as a total process of investigation, leading to information bearing on the appropriateness of inferences about individuals" (Industrial-Organizational Psychology Division of the American Psychological Association, 1980, p. 3).

Practicality and Standardization

Related to the issue of validity are the issues of practicality and standardization. An appraisal instrument must be understandable, plausible, and acceptable to those who will be using it (Smith, 1976). If the users perceive the instrument as difficult and cumbersome to administer, it cannot serve the purposes for which it was established. This requirement from an organization's standpoint is obvious, but it relates to legal requirements as well.

If an appraisal system is shown to be affected by the race or sex of employees, the courts may require that its continued use be justified by its *business necessity*. That is, an organization would have to show that the system is essential to the safe and efficient conduct of the business. A system that is not practical cannot be serving important organizational purposes. The danger here, of course, is that in attempting to be practical, organizations are often very impractical in trying to develop a simple, easily administered appraisal system based on traits (see Figs. 3.1 and 3.2) that can be used for all employees.

Standardization refers to minimizing differences in administering and scoring the appraisal instrument. Standardization is important because appraisal data are used to compare employees who may or may not be in the same unit of the organization. A system that is not standardized in its administration—that uses different procedures from place to place or time to time—raises the probability that at least some differences in the performance measures of different employees are in fact the result of the appraisal system and its administration rather than of real differences in employee performance (Lazer & Wikstrom, 1977).

Composite Versus Multiple Criteria

The controversy over composite versus multiple criterion measures is a recurrent topic in developing appraisal instruments. This controversy concerns when and how to combine various measures of an employee's performance. Advocates of the composite position believe that the method for combining criteria (e.g., appraisals of technical competency versus administrative ability versus teamplaying) should be specified prior to implementing the appraisal system in the organization. At least three different methods can be used to combine job performance measures.

First, each criterion measure can be weighted equally. This practice assumes that each criterion is equally important for defining overall success on the job. Although this assumption may be erroneous, the argument can be made that in the long run we can only guess at the correct weighting anyway. Consequently we will make less error if all the criteria are treated as equally important.

Second, the criteria can be subjectively weighted (Toops, 1944; Nagle, 1953; Schmidt & Kaplan, 1971) by "experts" (e.g., supervisors or job incumbents). The problem with this approach is that the experts frequently disagree with one another.

Third, the criteria can be weighted in terms of their dollar value for the organization (Brogden & Taylor, 1950). The problem here is that most measures of job effectiveness are not expressible in monetary terms for each individual worker (Skarlicki, Latham & Whyte, 1993).

Advocates of the use of multiple criteria argue that most measures of job performance (e.g., manual dexterity, ability to make oral presentations, budget preparation) are relatively independent of one another (e.g., Ghiselli, 1956). Thus there is no way to combine the scores on the different measures into a single value, unless a dollar value can be calculated. If criterion elements display low or zero correlations with one another, they are obviously measuring different variables, and weighting them into a composite results in scores that are so ambiguous as to be uninterpretable. Nevertheless, a decision often needs to be made regarding the status of an employee for such purposes as pay raises and promotions. Guion (1965) argued that the decision makers should refrain from combining the scores until a decision is necessary. The scores should then be subjectively weighted to take into account the prevailing needs and market conditions of the organization.

Closing Remarks

Guidelines for developing and using performance appraisal instruments can be followed on the basis of the 1980 Principles of Validation and Use of Personnel Selection Procedures prepared by Division 14 (Society for Industrial-Organizational Psychology) of the American Psychological Association and the 1978 Civil Service Reform Act.

1. The appraisal instrument must be based on a systematic examination of the job and the context in which it is performed.

2. The job analysis should be conducted when the job is reasonably stable and not in a period of rapid evolution. The logic of the job analysis is that it is undertaken under conditions as comparable as possible to those that will exist when the appraisal instrument will be used.

3. The job analysis information should be obtained from a sample of individuals who are representative of the populations of people and jobs to which the results are to be generalized.

4. The appraisal instrument should contain criteria that represent important work behaviors or behavioral outcomes as indicated by the job analysis. There is little value in measuring ability to handle trivial aspects of work.

5. The possibility of bias or other contamination should be considered. For example, economic measures may be excessive or deficient. Behavioral measures may be affected adversely by rater biases or an inadequate opportunity to observe the individual on the job.

6. The criterion measures must be reliable. Low reliability can place a ceiling on validity.

7. If several criteria or scales that make up the appraisal instrument are to be combined to obtain a single score, there should be a rationale to support the rules of combination.

8. The appraisal criteria should be subjected to pretesting and an analysis of the procedures in terms of the means, variances, and intercorrelations of its parts. Parts that do not contribute to the total variance should be eliminated. The appraisal instrument should enable the appraiser to differentiate good from poor performers.

9. Concerns over high intercorrelations among criteria on the appraisal form should be dealt with judiciously. Extreme redundancy of measurement should be avoided. However, a certain amount of redundancy provides adequate reliability of measurement. Discarding different items with high intercorrelations may reduce accountability and control by the organization and impede feedback to and development of the individual. For example, just because the grades university students receive often intercorrelate highly, that is no reason to suggest that they should be graded in only one class.

10. Persons who provide the appraisal information must be clearly qualified to do so; they must have thorough knowledge of the job, ample opportunity to see the individual on the job, and expertise in interpretation of what is seen. Furthermore, individuals who con-

duct appraisals should be thoroughly trained with regard to recording accurately what is seen and in reporting what was seen to the employee.

11. Reports on the appraisal system should enable a person competent in personnel assessment to know precisely what was done. The reports should be worded to communicate as clearly and accurately as possible the information readers need to know to complete appraisal forms completely and faithfully.

12. The appraisal instruments should be reviewed periodically and revised as needed. New appraisal instruments may be necessary whenever there is a substantial change in the organization's goals, technology, procedures, or workflow.

13. Reports should be written that warn readers against common misuses of appraisal information (e.g., using present assessments for determining managerial potential in the absence of valid data). The appraisal system must be valid for every purpose for which it is being used.

14. The procedures manual for persons who conduct appraisals should specify the procedures to be followed and emphasize the necessity for standardization of scoring and interpretation.

15. People should be evaluated on the extent to which they fulfill the requirements of the job rather than on how well they perform relative to other employees.

Answers to Quiz

1. No. What is meant by "sloppy"?
2. Yes.
3. Yes.
4. No. Explain what was done to indicate honesty.
5. No. Describe the emergency. Describe the behavior.
6. Almost. Specify the type of cable and the drum.
7. No. Define weak. Define scope interpretation.
8. No. Define reluctance, proficient, and "all phases."
9. No. Define "big head" and poor score.

4

Types of Appraisal
Instruments

The instrument used to appraise employees lies at the core of the appraisal system. As the diagnostic tool the appraiser uses to coach employees, the appraisal instrument is the basis for setting goals, which in turn directly affect an employee's motivation (Locke & Latham, 1990). In this chapter various appraisal instruments are reviewed against the criteria described in Chapter 3, namely, validity, reliability, freedom from bias, and practicality, especially user preference. The chapter concludes with a discussion of the appraisal in the context of "organizational fit."

The North American courts do not wish to recommend a particular type of appraisal instrument but rather require only that it be used in a manner free from bias and discrimination (Barrett & Kernan, 1987). Consequently, industrial-organizational psychologists have focused on the reliability and validity of appraisals. In addition, users' reactions to different types of appraisal forms have been studied because the objective characteristics of an appraisal instrument affect perceptions of fairness and hence how well the appraisal is accepted (Lawler, 1967). Moreover, as Murphy (1991) has argued, "an appraisal system that was moderately accurate, but which satisfied important organizational goals (e.g., motivating employees, providing useful feedback) would surely be preferable to one that provided completely accurate ratings at the expense of achieving important goals" (p. 49).

The appraisal instrument, like any measurement tool, is limited in its accuracy to the extent that the user may abuse it. The validity of an appraisal is frequently attenuated by the rating errors described in detail in Chapter 6. Rating errors may be defined technically as a difference between the output of a human judgment process and that of an objective, accurate assessment uncolored by bias, prejudice, or other subjective, extraneous influences (Feldman, 1981). Two examples of rater error are halo and leniency.

Halo error is the exaggeration of the homogeneity of a person's behavior. A senior manager who is observed doing very well on one criterion (e.g., reducing costs) may be rated erroneously as doing well on all criteria (e.g., developing a vision). Leniency error occurs when people receive a higher rating than they deserve. The prevalence of rating errors on the part of appraisers led to the development of forced-choice scales.

Forced-Choice Scales

This method of appraisal was developed by the U.S. Army after World War II (Sisson, 1948; Cozan, 1955). Its unique feature is that the rater is forced to choose, from several sets of four behaviors (tetrads), which behavior best describes the employee and which is least descriptive. The appraiser does not know which item "counts." That is, the rater does not know which item has a mathematical relationship to an important outcome. In this way an objective rating is facilitated, and subjective judgment is minimized. An example of a forced-choice item for appraising the performance of a professor is:

1. Publishes research in scientific journals each year
2. Obtains high teacher ratings
3. Refuses to speak to the dean
4. Refuses to serve on university committees

Two of these items describe positive behaviors, and the other two describe undesirable behaviors. The rater is required to check one behavior that is most descriptive and one behavior that is least descriptive of the employee.

In this way the rater's ability to exhibit bias or favoritism is reduced, there is a good distribution of ratings rather than a pile-up at one end of the scale (leniency), and the rating is not influenced by the job title of the employee, because the appraiser does not know which two of the four behaviors in a tetrad "count" for the employee. Only the human resource department has this information.

The assumptions underlying the scale are as follows:

1. Any real differences that exist among employees in competence can be described in terms of objective, observable behavior.

2. Behavioral items differ in their degree of general favorableness and raters' tendency to use them. This tendency can be determined statistically.

3. Behavioral items differ in the extent to which they characterize employees at both extremes of job performance. This discriminative value can also be determined statistically.

4. Pairs of job behavioral items can be selected that are equal in preference value but differ in discriminative value. An appraiser who is forced to choose which item is most or least descriptive of an employee is thus unable to bias the appraisal (for or against) because the preference values are equal.

A typical forced-choice scale contains from fifteen to fifty tetrads, depending on the level of the job being evaluated and the complexity of its duties. A drawback is that it requires a willingness by the appraisers to rate their employees when they cannot tell whether they are giving one person a more favorable rating than another. Another drawback is that it does not allow self-monitoring by the employee. In other words, by not knowing the discriminative value of the behavioral items, an employee cannot provide him- or herself with feedback regarding job performance.

In 1950 the Army abandoned this system. The raters found it so unacceptable to rate without knowledge of how this rating affected the final outcome that they concentrated on finding ways to beat the system (Rogers, 1960). This is understandable. A primary purpose of performance appraisal is to counsel and develop an employee in order to bring about and sustain effective on-the-job behavior. This objective is impossible with a forced-choice scale.

Behaviorally Anchored Rating Scales (BARS)

Smith and Kendall (1963) felt that most rating errors are not due to deliberate misrepresentation on the part of the rater.

Rather, they argued, the problem to overcome when making appraisal decisions is the lack of standardization among appraisers. An employee's work might be considered "outstanding" by one superior and only "acceptable" by another. The solution to the problem, they stated, is to use behavioral descriptions exemplifying various degrees (e.g., excellent, average, or poor) of each performance criterion (e.g., technical proficiency). Each behavioral description is called an "anchor"; hence the term behaviorally anchored rating scales (BARS) makes explicit to the rater what constitutes a given level of performance (e.g., excellent, satisfactory, below satisfactory, or unacceptable).

Another acronym for BARS is BES, or behavioral expectation scales, which refers to the fact that each behavioral example, or anchor, is worded in the form of an expectation: "Could be expected to explain the logic behind an organizational policy." Each anchor illustrates to the rater what is meant by excellent, satisfactory, or below adequate performance. Thus an employee does not need to engage literally in the specific behavior that was chosen to illustrate a 7 (i.e., outstanding behavior) in order to be rated as a 7.

The format allows the rater to document the basis for each rating on each performance criterion (e.g., development of subordinates) with notes about the employee's behavior. Thus the rater infers from a diary regarding the employee's behavior the rating that the employee should receive. This inference about a numerical rating is relatively standardized across raters through the use of the behavioral anchors. If the employer or employee suspects that standardization is not occurring, a third party (e.g., human resource manager) can read the diary notes to see if they do in fact support the numerical rating. Smith and Kendall argued that the rater's awareness that this could very well occur should facilitate honest, conscientious ratings.

To make them "user friendly," BARS are presented in the form of graphic rating scales arranged vertically.[1] The behavioral anchors are printed beside each horizontal bar at different

---

[1] A graphic rating scale per se provides little structure for an appraiser in that it does not define what the employee is being evaluated on. An example is: Self-Management:

	1	2	3	4	5	
	very poor			very good		

levels along a vertical line according to their scale position (e.g., 7, 5, 3, etc). "This format was chosen as a means of combining the relevance to direct observation of critical incidents and similar techniques, with the acceptability to raters of graphic rating scales" (Smith & Kendall, 1963, p. 150). An example of a BARS is shown in Table 4.1.

The procedure for developing BARS is straightforward. First, job experts, such as supervisors and job incumbents, brainstorm the performance criteria on which the employees in a given position should be appraised. The criteria mentioned most frequently are selected. Content validity is ensured by determining whether the results of a job analysis (e.g., the critical incident technique) yield the same performance criteria considered to be important as did the brainstorming sessions. A key part of this step is the emphasis on using the rater's own terminology rather than that of human resource specialists in labeling both the performance criteria and the behavioral anchors.

Second, the job experts brainstorm observable behaviors that illustrate high, acceptable, and low performance on each criterion (e.g., technical proficiency, interaction with subordinates, budget forecasting). Alternatively, critical incidents from the job analysis are classified as examples of high, acceptable, or low performance. Third, these behaviors are edited into the form of expectations of specific behavior.

Table 4.1
Example of a Behavioral Expectation Scale for Work Habits

┼	7	Could be expected to come to work 5 days a week
┼	6	
┼	5	Could be expected to inform supervisor in the event of
┼	4	an absenteeism or late arrival
┼	3	Could be expected to miss 2–3 days of work per month
┼	2	
┼	1	Could be expected to come to work on what appears to be a random schedule

Record notes throughout the appraisal period before making a rating.

Fourth, judges—people who will subsequently use the scale for performance appraisals—indicate independently what performance criterion identified in the first step is illustrated by each behavioral example. Examples or incidents from step 2 are eliminated if there is little agreement as to the performance criterion to which each behavior or incident belongs. A performance criterion is eliminated if behaviors are not consistently reassigned to their original category.

Fifth, each vertical scale for appraising an employee on one performance criterion (e.g., technical proficiency), along with the behavioral expectations, is presented to still another group of judges, who rate each behavioral expectation according to the desirability of the behavior illustrated. Behaviors are eliminated if the dispersion of judgments is large or if the distribution is multimodal. The remaining behaviors are assigned a numerical value on the scale.

Several variations of this procedure for developing BARS exist. Regardless of the variation used, the following advantages are said to occur: (1) the scales are developed by the rater/ratee for the rater/ratee, (2) the terminology of the rater/ratee is retained, (3) each performance criterion is defined explicitly by critical behaviors/incidents that are scaled (e.g., by raters/ratees), and (4) conceptually independent performance criteria are generated (Bernardin & Boetcher, 1978).

The importance of these four points was stressed by Smith and Kendall (1963):

> We believe that most rating errors are not due to deliberate faking. Moreover, no rating scale is really proof against distortion by a rater who wants to do so. Better ratings can be obtained, in our opinion, not by trying to trick the rater (as in forced-choice scales) but by helping him to rate. We should ask him questions which he can honestly answer about the behaviors which he can observe. We should reassure him that his answers will not be misinterpreted, and we should provide a basis by which he and others can check his answers. (p. 151)

This statement is important from a historical perspective. Because of the rater error that had occurred with trait-based scales and because of raters' dissatisfaction with the attempt to "fool" them by using a forced-choice scale, Smith and Kendall emphasized one primary criterion for evaluating the worth of BARS, namely, resistance to rater error. This explains why subsequent research has focused so heavily on rater error rather than on the use of BARS as an instrument for counseling and developing the employee and on the training that appraisers need to do so effectively. Any instrument in medicine, physics, and engineering, let alone human resource management, is only as good as the person who is trained to use it. A primary advantage of BARS as an appraisal instrument is that underneath each scale, the appraiser is asked to record critical incidents throughout the appraisal period to substantiate the assigned rating. This documentation is crucial for a valid rating, effective discussion, and legal defensibility.

BES have at least two additional advantages. First, because the anchors are behavioral and are expressed in the raters' own terminology, much of the ambiguity of trait-based rating scales is eliminated. Second, these scales may lend themselves to employee counseling/motivation by providing the employee with specific feedback on strengths and areas in need of improvement. This is true to the extent that the supervisor has had the self-discipline to systematically record a representative sample of incidents describing the employee's behavior throughout the appraisal period.

Despite their many advantages, however, BES/BARS have several limitations, one of which is the fact that a substantial number of critical incidents generated in the job analysis are discarded. That is, if seven job categories or performance criteria are identified as critical for appraisal purposes, the maximum number of incidents that can be used as anchors is only fortynine out of a possible total of literally hundreds of different incidents that were reported in the critical incident job analysis.

> If one assumes that the original pool of incidents generated in any BARS study all represent behavior that an evaluator may see and assess in an applied setting, instruments defined and anchored by relatively few examples would create at least two problems. First, the evaluator may have difficulty assigning observed behaviors to specific dimensions. Second, the evaluator may have difficulty deciding the scale value of effectiveness of the

observed behavior against the examples provided. (Schwab, Heneman & DeCotiis, 1975, p. 558)

A second problem, cited by the same authors, is that the subjective process used in developing the instrument, namely, judges categorizing the incidents, may result in criterion categories that are not independent. Independent categories are important for minimizing redundancy in the instrument's measurement. If the differences between rating categories are not distinct enough, the rater will tend to give the same (or almost the same) rating to an employee across categories when this is not warranted.

A third problem, pointed out by Borman (1979), is that raters sometimes have difficulty discerning any behavioral similarity between a ratee's performance and the highly specific behavioral examples used to anchor the scales; they are unable to match observed job behavior directly with the scale anchors. In some cases they cannot even infer the overall performance dimension or criterion on which to rate the specific incidents that they have recorded.

A fourth problem is that for BES to be used properly for counseling and development purposes, the supervisor must keep a diary of each employee's behavior throughout the appraisal period. Most people lack the discipline and time to do this. BES advocates acknowledge this point and recommend that each superior's manager police each subordinate manager on the extent to which a diary is kept on each employee (Bernardin & Buckley, 1981). Keeping an up-to-date diary on each employee is, in fact, critical with BARS because the behavioral anchors are simply illustrations or cues for the rater as to what constitutes high, average, or poor performance. Thus, the ". . . observed incidents will be more important in the ultimate ratings than the anchors" (Bernardin, Morgan & Winne, 1980). The diary illustrates each employee's performance. In essence, the diary is critical for determining which anchor best describes or illustrates to the employee the context in which the rater's observations took place. However, if interpretations of the observed incidents differ substantially from one rater to the next, rater error will still be potent, and interobserver reliability will be low regardless of format. A procedure that overcomes these and other limitations of

BES/BARS but retains their advantages is called *behavioral observation scales* (BOS) (Latham & Wexley, 1977).

Behavioral Observation Scales (BOS)

Although BARS exist for a wide variety of jobs, probably no profession has been studied as thoroughly for BARS development as the nursing profession. The same statement can be made for the logging profession with regard to the development of BOS.

In 1968 the research arm of the American Pulpwood Association initiated a series of studies to determine what differentiates the performance of loggers. This research was of considerable practical importance because paper companies, such as the Union Camp Corporation, Container Corporation of America, Owens Illinois, Inc., and the International Paper Company, were dependent on the pulpwood producer, an independent businessperson, to supply them with their primary raw material—wood. Objective records of a producer's cords-per-employee-hour existed. However, because of differences in type of equipment, terrain, wood species, weather, and so on, this measure was not considered satisfactory to determine whose operation should be upgraded, financed, allowed access to cut private timber, and so forth. The key question was what job behavior correlated significantly with cords-per-employee-hour.

In developing the *behaviorally summated rating scales*, we developed criteria by (1) analyzing the job, (2) developing measures of the behavior, (3) identifying the criterion dimensions by factor analysis, and (4) developing reliable measures with construct validity. Thus in developing BOS, (1) a job analysis was conducted using the critical incident technique, (2) from this job analysis behavioral items were discerned, (3) a factor analysis was conducted using a five-point Likert scale on the frequency with which each behavior was observed, and (4) the summated scores on each behavioral criterion were correlated with cords-per-employee-hour. Interobserver reliability, test-retest reliability, and the internal consistency of the behaviors comprising each criterion were shown to be satisfactory, and the significant correlations between the behavioral criteria with the bottom-line measures were evidence of construct (employee effectiveness) validity (Latham & Wexley, 1977; Latham, Wexley & Rand, 1975; Ronan & Latham, 1974). An example of a BOS is shown in Table 4.2.

Table 4.2

Example of One BOS Criterion, or Performance Dimension, for Evaluating Managers

I.   Overcoming Resistance to Change*

    (1) Describes the details of the change to subordinates.

        Almost Never 1 2 3 4 5 Almost Always

    (2) Explains why the change is necessary.

        Almost Never 1 2 3 4 5 Almost Always

    (3) Discusses how the change will affect the employee.

        Almost Never 1 2 3 4 5 Almost Always

    (4) Listens to the employee's concerns.

        Almost Never 1 2 3 4 5 Almost Always

    (5) Asks the employee for help in making the change work.

        Almost Never 1 2 3 4 5 Almost Always

    (6) If necessary, specifies the date for a follow-up meeting to respond to the employee's concerns.

        Almost Never 1 2 3 4 5 Almost Always

Total = _____

Below Adequate	Adequate	Full	Excellent	Superior
6–10	11–15	16–20	21–25	26–30

*Scores are set by management

The primary difference between BES and BOS is essentially the same as that differentiating the Thurstone (1928) and Likert (1932) approaches to the development of attitude scales. The development of the BES is similar to the Thurstone approach in that judges numerically rate incidents obtained in the job analysis in terms of the extent to which each incident represents effective job behavior.

The BOS is similar to the Likert method in that, as noted above: (1) a large number of behavioral statements related to the object in question (e.g., costs) are collected; (2) employees are observed and rated on a five-point scale as to the frequency with which each of them has been observed engaging in each of the behaviors (hence the term observation scales); (3) a total score for each employee is determined by summing the observer's responses to all the behavioral items; and (4) a statistical analysis is conducted to identify those behaviors that most clearly differentiate effective from ineffective performers. The use of statistical analysis (e.g., factor analysis or item analysis) to select items for building an appraisal instrument most clearly distinguishes the Likert/BOS methods from the Thurstone/BES methods.

This difference between BOS and BARS can be crucial. A five-point Likert scale (ranging from "almost never" to "almost always") was used in the research on loggers because of the forest products industry's need for a behavioral inventory of the pulpwood producer. Such an inventory would not only facilitate appraisal decisions by company officials but would also facilitate self-management (goal setting, feedback, and self-reinforcement of effective behavior) on the part of the individual logger. Thus the behavioral inventory, based on the CIT, was key to improving productivity. It told both the appraiser and the employee what to look for if productivity is a desirable goal. It helped each logger to "self-observe/self-remember/self-regulate."

A complete appraisal instrument for evaluating employees is shown in the Appendix. The BOS are nothing more than behaviorally summated rating scales; the appraiser simply adds (sums) the numbers (ratings) indicative of the frequency with which an employee has been observed engaging in specific behaviors. The term BOS, used to divert attention from the "E" in BES, connotes the necessity of both supervisors and subordinates knowing explicitly prior to an appraisal period what the employee is to do on the job and what the supervisor should look for (observe) to coach, counsel, and develop that employee.

Development of BOS

A number of specific steps are required for developing BOS.

1. Critical incidents that are similar or identical in context are grouped together to form one behavioral item. For example, Latham, Fay, and Saari (1979) used two or more incidents concerning a supervisor who compli-

ments or rewards employees for doing a good job to write the item "Praises and/or rewards subordinates for specific things they do well."

2. Behavioral items that are similar are grouped together by job incumbents or analysts to form one BOS criterion. For example, the behavioral item above was grouped together with similar items (e.g., counsels employees on personal problems) to form the criterion "interactions with subordinates."

It should be noted that using job analysts to categorize the incidents takes less time than training job incumbents how to write behavioral items that are observable and clustering them into meaningful criteria. The advantage of having job incumbents rather than the researchers categorize the incidents and develop the appraisal instruments, although appealing intuitively, has yet to be justified empirically.

Some people have interpreted the results of two studies (Friedman & Cornelius, 1976; Warmke & Billings, 1979) as suggesting that user participation in developing an appraisal scale leads to a reduction in rating errors (see Chapter 6) when the scale is subsequently used to appraise people. Neither study, however, provided an adequate test of the participation hypothesis because none of the researchers addressed the issue of the value of job analysts versus job incumbents' developing the appraisal instrument. Before one considers conducting such a test, we would like to point out that the requirement for every rater to physically participate in the construction of all phases of a rating scale is not technically feasible in all but very small organizations. Even there, the extent to which there is a changing workforce would make the procedure impractical.

We believe that the contribution of information by raters as part of the job analysis is necessary to ensure that a representative sample of critical job behaviors is included on the instrument. Moreover, the job behaviors must be written in a form that is clear and unambiguous to the raters. To do this, only a representative sample of users of the rating scale needs to contribute this information for the job analysis, not every single rater who will use the scale. This procedure, we believe, meets the spirit and intent of the 1978 Civil Service Reform Act, which requires that employees have a say in the areas on which they will be evaluated.

3. Interjudge agreement is assessed to determine whether another individual or group of individuals would have developed the same behavioral criteria from the critical incidents obtained in the job analysis. This step is similar to the reallocation step (Smith & Kendall, 1963) followed by BES advocates.

   The incidents are placed in random order and given to a second individual or group, who reclassifies them according to the categorization system established in step 1. The ratio of interjudge agreement is calculated by counting the number of incidents that both groups agree should be placed in a given criterion, divided by the combined number of incidents both groups placed in that criterion. Thus if one group of judges classified incidents 4, 7, 8, 9, and 17 under the same criterion and a second group classified incidents 7, 8, and 9 under that category, the interjudge agreement would be 0.60.

$$\left[\frac{(7, 8, 9)}{4, 7, 8, 9, 17} = \frac{3}{5} = 0.60 \right].$$

   A decision is usually made that the ratio must be 0.80 or higher for a behavioral criterion to be acceptable. If the ratio is below 0.80, the items under the criterion are reexamined for possible reclassification or rewriting of the criteria to increase specificity.

4. The BOS criteria (e.g., interactions with peers, safety, technical competency) are examined for their relevance, or content validity (Nagle, 1953). Relevance or content validity is concerned with the systematic evaluation of appraisal instruments, by people who are intimately familiar with the job, to see if the instrument includes a representative sample of the behavioral items of interest (Anastasi, 1976).

One way to test for content validity is to set aside 10 percent of the incidents prior to the categorization of the critical incidents. After the categorization is completed in step 1, these incidents are examined to see if any of them describe behaviors that have not yet appeared. If this examination necessitates the development of a new behavioral criterion or the formation of two or more behavioral items under an existing criterion, the assumption that a sufficient number of incidents has been collected is rejected.

A second test of content validity involves recording the increase in the number of behavioral items with the increase in the number of incidents classified. If 90 percent of the items appear after 75 percent of the incidents have been categorized, the content validity of the BOS is considered satisfactory.

5. The appraisal instrument is developed by attaching a five-point Likert scale to each behavioral item. Only five numbers are placed under each behavioral item because research has shown that there is little utility in adding additional scale values beyond 5 (Jenkins & Taber, 1977; Lissitz & Green, 1975).

Observers (e.g., peers, supervisors) are asked to indicate the frequency with which they have observed a job incumbent engage in each behavior. An example of one behavioral item follows.

Immediately informs supervisor of people who need ear plugs.

Almost Never   0   1   2   3   4   Almost Always

Employees receive a 0 if they have been observed engaging in a behavior 0–64 percent of the time, 1 for 65–74 percent of the time, 2 for 75–84 percent of the time, 3 for 85–94 percent of the time, and 4 for 95–100 percent of the time.[2] These percentages, corresponding to the five points on the Likert scale, can change

---

[2] Other percentages can be used. For example, some authors have used intervals of 20 percent for the five numbers (e.g., Latham, Mitchell & Dossett, 1978). The percentages are usually chosen by the clients.

depending on the job and organization involved.[3] In some cases the behavioral items are stated in terms of ineffective behavior if that is the way the incidents were described by the interviewees during the job analysis.

6. Many items on the BOS, although critical in terms of defining highly effective or ineffective performance, occur either so frequently or infrequently that they do not differentiate good from poor job incumbents. For example, of ninety supervisors rated on "Has the smell of liquor on his/her breath," Latham, Fay & Saari (1979) reported that eighty-five received 4 (Almost never), four received 3 (Seldom), and one person received a 2 (Sometimes). A major purpose of a performance appraisal instrument is to differentiate between good and poor performers. The item above does not meet this requirement, since almost every supervisor received the same rating. Therefore, these types of items are eliminated by conducting an item analysis. This statistical procedure involves correlating the scores on each behavioral item with the sum of the remaining items so that each section on the appraisal instrument is unambiguous to the appraiser.

7. If there are approximately three to five times as many individuals to be rated as there are behavioral items, a factor analysis can be conducted. A factor analysis groups behavioral items together on the extent to which they correlate with one another to form different behavioral criteria (e.g., interaction with peers, organizational commitment). This grouping removes the need for two groups of judges to categorize the incidents into overall categories and is one reason why factor analysis rather than judges should be used to

---

[3] The degree to which observers can distinguish between 0–64 percent of the time, 75–84 percent of the time, and the like is sometimes questioned. Judgment obviously affects these ratings, as it does any criterion measure. Therefore we strongly recommend teaching skills in observing and recording job behaviors (see Chapter 6). However, adequate measures of reliability and validity have been obtained with this procedure in the absence of rater training (e.g., Latham & Wexley, 1977; Latham, Wexley & Rand, 1975).

group the items into behavioral categories. It saves time. Further, it ensures that the different behavioral criteria will be independent of one another and thus contain the minimum number of items on which the employee should be evaluated.[4]

Since each BOS criterion contains a different number of behavioral items, the question of weighting the scales may need to be considered. Many BOS users adopt a grade-point average (GPA) analogy. For example, college students are graded from 0.0 to 4.0; a grade-point average (overall performance rating) is usually computed by averaging across all courses regardless of the number of exams (items) used in each course (criterion). That is, each course grade is weighted equally. The score received on each BOS criterion can be used to compute the "GPA" for each job incumbent. Giving each criterion equal weight is compatible with research in selection (Lawshe, 1959; Trattner, 1963) showing that the sophisticated weighting of predictors (e.g., using multiple regression) seldom yields higher validities than simply adding the individual predictor scores. Moreover, refraining from using a statistical weighting procedure allows the supervisor to use his or her own "expert judgment" to take into account prevailing conditions (e.g., the general economy, an organization's competitive position in the market, distribution of present skills within the organization) when a decision based on an overall evaluation of the employee (e.g., promote, lay off, transfer) is required (Guion, 1961).

---

[4] The primary concern here is the ability of behavioral items to discriminate between effective and ineffective job performance. Having independent criteria is an ideal goal for statisticians, but "it is unlikely to occur for real behaviors" (Smith, personal communication, 1979), because the criteria are often logically related. For example, BOS may tap different aspects of supervisory behavior as opposed to skills that are logically unrelated (e.g., physical versus cognitive abilities). Multidimensional criteria are necessary because the measures seldom overlap one another completely, and, more importantly, they facilitate accountability and control by the organization, as well as feedback and development for the individual.

Advantages of BOS

The advantages of using BOS for conducting performance appraisals include the following:

1. BOS, like BES, are developed from a systematic job analysis supplied by employees for employees, thereby facilitating understanding of and commitment to the use of the appraisal instrument. The frequently heard complaints from both managers and subordinates that the items on the appraisal instrument are either sufficiently vague to defy understanding or completely inappropriate for the individual's appraisal are minimized. Thus both approaches satisfy the requirement of the 1978 Civil Service Reform Act to allow employees to participate in identifying the critical requirements of their jobs.

2. BOS can either serve alone or as a supplement to existing job descriptions in that they make explicit what behaviors are required of an employee in a given job. As a job description, BOS can also be used as a "job preview" for potential job candidates by showing them what they will be expected to do. Job previews are an effective means of reducing employee turnover and job dissatisfaction (Wanous, 1989). They can assist candidates in deciding whether they would want to consistently demonstrate the behaviors described on the BOS.

3. BOS, unlike BES, are content valid in the sense that the behaviors differentiating the successful from the unsuccessful performer are included on the instrument. Appraisers are forced to make a thorough evaluation of an employee rather than emphasizing only what they can recall at the time of the appraisal. Again, it must be stressed that a major limitation of BES is that it requires the appraiser to have the discipline to record daily, in brief essay form, employee performance incidents. The typical supervisor simply does not have time to record systematically instances of adequate and inadequate behavior. Thus the behaviors that are recorded, both effective and ineffective, are

unlikely to be a representative sample of the employee's behavior (Feldman, 1979). The BOS approach specifies to both the supervisor and the employee "exactly what must be observed."

4. BOS facilitate explicit performance feedback in that they encourage meaningful discussions between the supervisor and the employee of the latter's strengths and weaknesses. Generalities are avoided in favor of specific overt behaviors for which the employee is praised or is encouraged to demonstrate on the job.

   Explicit performance feedback using BOS combined with the setting of specific goals has been shown repeatedly to be an effective means for bringing about or maintaining a positive behavior change (Dossett, Latham, & Mitchell, 1979; Latham & Yukl, 1975; Latham, Mitchell & Dossett, 1978). BES can facilitate feedback to the extent that the supervisor has the discipline to record a representative sampling of incidents describing the employee's behavior during the appraisal period. BOS procedures also request the supervisor to record incidents describing the employee's behavior. We have found, however, that supervisors often ignore this request and base their feedback on the numbers that they have circled under each behavioral item. The behavioral items not only focus the supervisor's attention on what to look for during an appraisal period but also facilitate recall in discussing the results of the appraisal with the employee.

5. BOS can satisfy EEOC guidelines in terms of validity (relevance) and reliability. After reviewing sixty-six employment discrimination cases, Feild and Holley (1982) recommended the use of BOS for performance appraisals because the content validity, interjudge agreement of the categorization system, and the internal consistency of the criteria are usually found to be satisfactory. In previous studies (Latham & Wexley, 1977; Latham, Wexley & Rand, 1975; Ronan & Latham, 1974) the test-retest and interobserver reliability, as well as the validity of the BOS in indicating

employee attendance and productivity, were demonstrated. Rater bias is minimized because observers do not have to extrapolate from what they have observed to the placement of a checkmark beside an example on the scale that may or may not be appropriate.

6. Among the highlights of research conducted in the 1980s on performance appraisal was the rediscovery of an unpublished manuscript by Wherry on a theory of rating (Wherry & Bartlett, 1982). The theory states that an accurate rating is a function of the ratee's performance, the rater's observations, and the rater's recall of those observations. The resulting theorems and corollaries support the use of BOS. For example, rating accuracy will occur to the extent that scales have as their behavioral referents tasks controlled mainly by the ratee. Rating accuracy increases to the extent that the behaviors are observable. Of particular relevance to BOS is the theorem that accuracy increases when the rater is forewarned as to what to look for, since this focuses attention on pertinent behaviors. Thus the rater knows what he or she is to try to remember. Also, longer objective descriptive statements will be more effective than single phrases in increasing accuracy. Of relevance to both BES and BOS is the theorem that keeping a written record between rating periods of specifically observed critical incidents will improve objectivity of recall.

The use of BOS avoids the following problems with BES that were listed by Atkin and Conlon (1978).

1. Endorsement of an incident above the neutral point of BES implies endorsement of all other incidents between the incident checked and the neutral point. This endorsement, which may be unwarranted, is avoided with BOS because the rater is allowed to evaluate an individual on each and every item. Making several ratings, as is done with BOS, rather than one per dimension, as is done using BES, may increase the reliability of each BOS dimension score for the same reasons that adding items to a test generally increases

the test's reliability—it reduces content sampling error (Borman, 1979).

2. The subjective definition of "critical" is minimized in the generation of the behavioral items for BOS. Rather, emphasis is placed on developing an inventory of behaviors, rating employees on the frequency with which they demonstrate each behavior, and conducting an item or a factor analysis for determining the items that should comprise each criterion on the final rating instrument.

3. In using BES, standard or normal behaviors may not be remembered in the same way as unusual or unique behaviors. Hence at the time of the rating, raters may not have enough information about the performance of standard behaviors to use them in the BES context unless the raters had recorded the incidents when they occurred. The BOS, however, serve as a checklist for both the rater and the ratee to take into account in their respective day-to-day job functions. That is, the rater knows what he or she should be alert to in observing an employee, and the employee knows explicitly what the rater is looking for. Thus a smaller cognitive load is placed on the rater and the behaviors to be rated are more salient than is the case with BES.

4. Consistent with problems surrounding the use of judges to develop Thurstone scales, Atkin and Conlon (1978) suggested that to the degree to which supervisors believe that a particular dimension is substantially more important than others, they will define a relatively narrow range of acceptable behaviors, a relatively broad set of unacceptable behaviors, and virtually a null set of neutral behaviors. With the BOS, raters need only indicate the frequency with which they observe the behavior; the behaviors to be observed are listed on the scale.

Essentially, the choice of BOS versus BES can be reduced to a preference for Likert versus Thurstone scales. Empirical comparisons of these two scales in the area of attitude measurement have demonstrated the superiority of the Likert scale in terms of reliability (Seiler & Hough, 1970). It is unlikely that a substantially different conclusion will be reached in the area of performance appraisal.

Criticisms of BOS

If diary keeping with BARS is objectionable on practical grounds, BOS can be criticized with regard to the difficulty inherent in an appraiser's observing employees on an exhaustive inventory of items. This objection can be countered on three points. First, the instrument needs to contain a representative sample of all the behavioral items that could have been included if it is to satisfy the purpose for which it was developed—counseling and developing employees. Second, showing the content validity of the appraisal scales will be necessary if the appraisals are challenged in a legal proceeding. Third, it is neither necessary nor desirable for the supervisor alone to make appraisals. As noted in the next chapter, peers are an excellent source of valid appraisals.

A second criticism of BOS is that the five-point frequency scale is not truly a ratio scale in practice. It is not realistic to require a rater to be held accountable for ascertaining whether a person literally did something 95 percent of the time versus 94 percent of the time.

Related to this criticism is that each behavior is rated on the same basis. Kane and Bernardin (1982) have argued that this is not a tenable practice. In a police detective's job a 74–85 percent occurrence rate may constitute superior performance in obtaining arrest warrants within three months in homicide cases but abysmal performance in being vindicated by the internal review board in instances of having used lethal force.

This problem has at least three solutions. First, don't rate each behavior on the same basis. The frequency with which a behavior must be exhibited to get a numerical rating of 0–4 can be determined by the user. There is nothing to prevent the client from changing the interval to fit the item. Second, it is not necessary for an appraisal scale to list every dysfunctional behavior. Nevertheless, decisions regarding performance can still be made. For example, a police officer with a perfect record over five years might still be discharged if only once he or she physically assaulted the chief of police. The discharge could occur even though no item on the BOS referred to a physical assault on an officer. As Bernardin, Morgan, and Winne (1980) stated, content validity is concerned with the degree to which the rating scale items are a representative sample of all important items that could have been included in the scale. Thus the scale does not have to include every single important item.

A third criticism of BOS concerns the use of statistical procedures for identifying the criterion dimensions and the behaviors that comprise them. Most companies employ a small number of employees, making it virtually impossible to conduct a factor analysis. When item analysis is used, Kane and Bernardin have warned against the danger of capitalizing on sampling error with regard to calculating the reliability of an appraisal scale. Specifically, they argued that the sample of employees who are appraised to determine the reliability of the appraisal instrument must not be the same group of employees who were involved in the process of developing items for the appraisal instrument.

The basis for these concerns is threefold. First, the original group may not be representative of the subject population. Moreover, the data may have been collected when the working conditions were not representative of those to be found in subsequent periods during which the appraisal instrument is to be used. Third, as Kane and Bernardin argued, the raters who participated in the development of the items on the appraisal instrument must be different from the raters who are used to determine the scale's reliability, in order to avoid capitalizing on chance factors that might inflate the reliability estimate.

Because the legal profession devours the literature on job analysis and performance appraisal and because these people often have difficulty judging the merits of conceptual arguments in a scientific forum, three additional empirical studies were conducted to test Kane and Bernardin's concerns. These studies were necessary because if Kane and Bernardin were correct, satisfying their concerns would prove an awesome burden from a legal standpoint due to the small ratio of raters to ratees available in most organizations, making it virtually impossible to conduct a satisfactory test of the internal consistency of an appraisal scale.

In the first of three studies the internal consistency of the same BOS in the same forest-products company for which

Latham, Fay, and Saari (1979) had developed BOS two years previously was calculated. Thirty-four employees were evaluated for this study by eleven managers. These raters and ratees were relatively new to their jobs and thus had not been included in previous research studies.

The second study involved ten employees who had used the BOS to appraise one another's performance. The employees worked for a forest-products company other than the one on which the BOS was originally used. In the third study nineteen part-time employees from nineteen different companies rated their respective supervisors on the same BOS.

The internal consistency of the BOS in each of the three studies is comparable to the original reliabilities obtained by Latham, Fay, and Saari, where the same people who had developed the appraisal instrument had also been used to assess its reliability. Such findings show that calculating the internal consistency of an appraisal instrument subsequent to an item analysis is not affected appreciably by error variance due to the ratees who are assessed, or by influences on the ratings resulting from different time periods. In addition, capitalization on error resulting from the use of the same raters when calculating internal consistency measures of behavioral criteria is minuscule.

Mixed Standard Scales (MSS)

Similar to the forced-choice scale, the MSS, developed by Blanz and Ghiselli (1972), does not allow the appraiser to know what performance criterion is being evaluated. The appraiser simply responds to behavioral items in terms of whether an employee's performance is better than (+), equal to (=), or worse than (–) the behavioral item. The primary purpose of this instrument is to reduce rating errors such as halo and leniency.

In a study of government employees, Hughes and Prien (1986) evaluated three scoring methods for MSS. No significant differences among them were found with regard to variance in score distribution, interobserver reliability, or validity. Prien and Hughes (1987) concluded that MSS can be used to identify and minimize rating errors of halo and leniency.

Research Comparing Appraisal Instruments

Raters must be trained in order to reduce rating errors regardless of the appraisal scale that is used. The reason is that human judgment enters into interpretation of performance on any criterion, regardless of whether the performance measure consists of cost-related variables, traits, BES, or BOS. As noted earlier, rating error may be defined technically as a difference between the output of a human judgment process and that of an objective, accurate assessment unclouded by bias, prejudice, or other subjective extraneous factors.

A job analysis can specify training content. That is, it can reveal what an observer does that allows him or her to be more accurate than another observer. Thus a training program can teach people to recognize the multidimensionality of an employee's performance, the importance of recording factually what is seen, and the development of specific examples of effective and ineffective behaviors.

Using this approach to training, Fay and Latham (1982) found that rating errors are made regardless of whether BOS, BES, or trait scales are used. However, once raters are trained, the rating scale is in fact important. BOS and BES were shown to be superior to trait scales in resistance to rater error. There was no significant difference between BOS and BES in this regard.

A criticism of BOS, not mentioned earlier, is aimed at the very essence of these scales. BOS attempts to bypass general impressions and judgments by dealing strictly with the appraiser's observations of the ratee's behaviors. This assertion has been challenged on the basis that raters using BOS must rely on their memory to estimate the frequency with which employees demonstrated specific work behaviors during an appraisal period. The results of a laboratory study by Murphy, Martin, and Garcia (1982) showed that a rater's memory for actual behaviors fades, and the task of recalling the frequency with which a behavior occurred shifts from an observation task to an inferential one.

Hoffman, Fredricks, and Doverspike (1983) compared BOS, BARS, and trait scales. Test-retest reliabilities for the three scales were 0.65 (BOS), 0.59 (BES), and 0.49 (trait scales). The researchers concluded that neither BOS nor BARS reflect only the observations of the appraiser. Both instruments have an evaluative component to the extent that once a traitlike representation of a ratee's performance has been formed by the rater, it affects behavioral recall because the general impression affects the appraiser's attention, encoding, and storage.

McKenna and Golz (1983) pointed out that the information available to an appraiser is influenced by at least three variables: (1) the emotional interest or involvement of the appraiser in the ratee's behavior, (2) the "concreteness" of the behaviors to be recalled, and (3) the temporal, spatial, and sensory proximity of the appraiser to the employee's behavior. They questioned Murphy's methodology on each of these factors. First, Murphy's student raters had no real emotional or personal stake in the behavior of the person shown on the videotape. By contrast, a supervisor's job depends in part on the behavior of subordinates. This clearly increases the emotional significance of behavioral observations for the supervisor and therefore the availability of the information for later recall.

A second criticism of the Murphy study is that the items on their scales were not behaviorally specific. The two BOS, however, were subjected to factor analysis and were highly reliable. Unfortunately, little or no detail about the steps taken to develop their BOS had been provided. Consequently, McKenna and Golz conducted a field study in which BOS and trait scales were constructed.

Their study focused on faculty advisors in a small undergraduate liberal arts college where their performance in this area is a key factor affecting their promotion, tenure, and salary. The BOS were constructed using factor analysis. Following the same statistical procedures used by Murphy, Martin, and Garcia, the authors showed that delayed recall did not result in BOS-trait convergence. McKenna and Golz concluded that for supervisors who have regular, relevant contact with subordinates, memories of such behaviors should be highly available for recall, even after significant time delays.

In reviewing this literature we contend that human beings are imperfect observers and scorers of information. This has been shown again and again in the work of Loftus (1983) with regard to eyewitness testimony. Nevertheless, no one would recommend that the use of eyewitnesses be disregarded. Similarly, we remain supportive of behavioral criteria. The BOS, as McKenna and Golz pointed out, focus the appraiser's attention on the occurrence of specific critical job behaviors and thus try to shorten, albeit not bypass, the chain of inferences leading to a performance appraisal. Because any appraisal instrument is susceptible to traitlike judgments, the issue becomes one of training raters to increase their objectivity.

No rating scale in itself should be expected to be free of rating error. For the performance appraisal process to perform any organizational function effectively, clear relationships between desired performance behavior and rewards must be established. The questions to ask here include the following: Do the scales facilitate this perception among appraisees as well as appraisers? Do the scales facilitate recognition of individual employee strengths and weaknesses as related to work performance? Do the scales help members of a team perceive a clear relationship between their job behavior and subsequent performance ratings? Do the scales facilitate self-management on the part of the employee? For the appraisal process to function effectively, employees must be presented with explicit information linking desired behavior and organizational rewards. If the appraisal instrument defines productivity behaviorally and if employees who engage in these behaviors are reinforced, commitment to the appraisal process is likely to occur on the part of both the supervisor and the subordinate.

User Reactions to Appraisal Instruments

A sole emphasis on the reliability and validity of an appraisal instrument can prove to be a mistake. In too many instances psychometrically sound instruments either are not used or are soon abandoned because of researchers' failure to take into account user perceptions (Dreher & Sackett, 1983). If appraisers perceive the instrument to be difficult and cumbersome to use, it probably will not be used properly, if at all. Thus focusing on user reactions to appraisal instruments is critical for application.

Bernardin, Morgan, and Winne (1980) had seventy-six police officers rate different appraisal formats on their usefulness for evaluation procedures. Both officers and supervisors were most impressed with the potential fairness inherent in the forced-choice system. Based on the results of the attitudinal questionnaire and the subsequent discussions with numerous officers and supervisory personnel, a forced-choice system of evaluation and summated rating scales based on specific critical incidents were developed. After the police officers reviewed examples of BARS, a decision was made not to use them.

The researchers concluded that BES leave something to be desired with regard to interrater reliability, convergent and discriminant validity, as well as the external validity of ratings. They concluded that the forced-choice technique has received the most empirical support in the form of a normal distribution of ratings and high interobserver reliability. With regard to practicality, they cited several authors who reported strong support for the use of these scales in law enforcement. This review also indicated that behaviorally based summated scales were generally supported by both empirical research and anecdotal, attitudinal data.

Due to cost considerations (practicality), forced-choice scales were developed only for patrol-level positions. But based on the published literature, questionnaire data, and small-group discussions with the police concerning different appraisal formats, Bernardin developed BOS for all ranks and positions within the police department.

In these BOS, the rater was required to judge the frequency with which the statement of behavior was observed. Each response category was then weighted according to the desirability of the stated behavior, with "always" getting the highest point total and "never" getting the lowest point totals. Following the procedures recommended by Latham, Fay, and Saari (1979), the scales were developed by: (1) performing job analysis of each position to determine the critical elements that should be assessed; (2) constructing behavioral statements based on the information derived from the job analysis; (3) testing the longer forms to determine the reliabilities of each scale; (4) conducting item analysis on the scales to identify those items that did not contribute to the internal consistency of each scale; and (5) selecting a smaller number of reliable and valid items.

The content validity of the resulting BOS was defined as the degree to which the rating scale items are a representative sample of all important items that could have been included in the scale. Through small-group discussions, consensus was reached that each of the rating scales had acceptable content validity. The internal reliability estimates ranged from 0.84 to 0.96.

This research suggests that BOS are superior to BARS; on the basis of work by Latham and his colleagues, it appears that both BOS and BES are better than trait scales when the appraiser has been trained to overcome rating errors. Forced-choice scales are of considerable merit with regard to psychometric considerations. The chief drawback of forced-choice scales is that they do not permit the counseling and developing of employees. Moreover, they do not permit self-management on the part of the employees. The fact that employees in the Bernardin study liked them suggests that employees do not necessarily see the value in being counseled by their supervisors. To the extent that this finding is generalizable to other occupational groups, it may reflect the fact that supervisors are not adequately trained in how to effectively develop their employees.

Fay and Latham (1982) used a twelve-item questionnaire to examine the practicality of BOS, BES, and trait scales. The questions focused on the user's judgment of content validity (e.g., the appraisal scale forces me to rate things that don't seem relevant; the appraisal scale omits relevant items) as well as their reactions to the ease and convenience of using the scale for personnel decisions (e.g., the scale is a helpful tool in counseling an employee on how to improve performance; the scale makes it easy to differentiate high, average, and low performance; the scale makes it easy to explain to an individual how a decision was made). Users of BOS rated the scale significantly higher than did users of BES or trait scales. There was no significant difference between users of BES and trait scales on their respective judgments of practicality.

Wiersma and Latham (1986) examined the practicality of BOS, BARs, and trait scales in terms of user preference in the securities field. They found that managers and employees preferred BOS to BARS in all cases; in all but two cases BOS were preferred to trait scales. They also found that attorneys who specialize in U.S. Title VII litigation preferred BOS to the two alternatives in terms of defensibility in the courtroom. Thus it is not surprising that such organizations as the U.S. Drug Enforcement Administration use BOS (Musicante, Pajer & Goldstein, 1988). After reviewing sixty-six employment discrimination cases, Feild and Holley (1982) recommended the use of BOS for performance appraisal purposes.

Wiersma, van den Berg, and Latham (1992) replicated the Wiersma and Latham (1986) study in the Netherlands. The data were collected from supervisors and peers who had appraised people using BOS, BARS, and trait scales. The results showed that BOS were preferred over the other two methods for providing feedback, differentiating among performers, determining training needs, setting goals, objectivity, and overall ease of use. The trait scale was viewed as good or slightly better than the BARS. Thus it would appear that the practicality of BOS is not culture bound.

In a well-controlled laboratory experiment, Rothstein and Chooi (1990) examined the comparative benefits of feedback based on BARS and BOS on subsequent attitudes toward the appraisal process. College students were randomly assigned to either the BARS or BOS appraisal condition. The two appraisal instruments, consisting of the same performance dimensions, were those that had been developed for clerical employees in a public utility corporation.

The students performed an in-basket exercise and held a group discussion. The appraisers were blind to the hypotheses of the study. The results showed that people who received feedback based on the BOS evaluated the appraisal more favorably than did those who received feedback via BARS, regardless of whether they were high, medium, or low performers. The authors concluded that the specificity of the feedback from BOS enables individuals to understand exactly what they need to do to improve their performance. In addition, the feedback is seen as nonevaluative. If an employee receives a low score on the BOS, it does not suggest that the individual is somehow inadequate; instead, it indicates that specific behaviors are not being observed.

Tziner and Kopelman (1988) examined BOS and graphic rating scales on three goal-setting dimensions: goal clarity, goal acceptance, and goal commitment. The employees' scores on each of these dimensions were higher when BOS were used. These results were due to the behavioral specificity provided by the BOS.

In a study of employees at the Israel Airport Authority, Tziner and Latham (1989) found that appraisals using BOS resulted in higher subsequent job satisfaction and organizational commitment than did appraisals in which graphic scales or no scales were used. The specificity of BOS strengthened the employees' feelings of control over their work and dissipated feelings of ambiguity about expectations and requirements. Similarly, Tziner, Kopelman, and Livneh (1992), in a study involving a large hospital complex, found that appraisals based on BOS resulted in high levels of goal clarity and goal commitment, as well as employer satisfaction with the process.

Dickinson and Zellinger (1980) found that raters prefer BARS to MSS. Because MSS do not facilitate communication between raters and ratees, further research in this area would appear to be unwarranted.

Closing Remarks

Performance Appraisal and Organizational Fit

Latham and Fry (1988) have argued that human resource specialists typically ignore macrovariables, such as an organization's strategy, technology, structure, and design when developing performance appraisal systems. In addition, they often fail to take a contingency perspective regarding the congruence, or fit, between the organization and its environment, subunits within the organization as a whole, and the performance of the employees within those subunits. Only when there is congruence can the organization and the employee perform at optimal levels.

Table 4.3 shows the process that effective organizations typically follow in order to achieve congruence between macro- and microvariables. The sequence can start anywhere and loop backward or forward, depending on the circumstances unique to the organization. Important organizational variables include its strategy, design, technology, and structure.

Strategy

Strategy formulation answers such questions as: What businesses should we be in? How do we compete in those businesses? The answers identify not only the organization's mission but also environmental factors, such as customers, markets, regulatory bodies, and competitors that must be managed if the organization is to be effective.

Strategy implementation results in a hierarchy of goals and plans that span the organization from top to bottom so that the performance of an employee is aligned with the mission of the organization. The need for this macro- and microcongruence

Table 4.3
Relationships Among Macro- and Micro-Organizational Variables

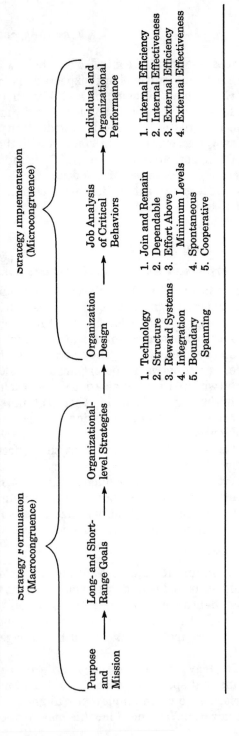

Strategy Formulation
(Macrocongruence)

Strategy Implementation
(Microcongruence)

Purpose and Mission	→	Long- and Short-Range Goals	→	Organizational-level Strategies	→	Organization Design	→	Job Analysis of Critical Behaviors	→	Individual and Organizational Performance
						1. Technology		1. Join and Remain		1. Internal Efficiency
						2. Structure		2. Dependable		2. Internal Effectiveness
						3. Reward Systems		3. Effort Above Minimum Levels		3. External Efficiency
						4. Integration		4. Spontaneous		4. External Effectiveness
						5. Boundary Spanning		5. Cooperative		

must be taken into account when conducting the job analysis so that the organization's mission serves as the cornerstone of the performance appraisal system. Otherwise, strategy formulation may be reduced to rhetoric, and the organization's effectiveness will be severely reduced.

As noted earlier, a job analysis is based on the informed judgment of job experts. This judgment can be considered informed only if it reflects knowledge of the organization's mission and strategy. As the mission and strategy change, the job analysis must be redone. For example, the job analysis performed on executive positions in Scott Paper Company's Northwest Division was completely redone two years later when the mission and the strategy to attain it were reformulated as a result of changes in environmental conditions (competition, economic recession, and threat of a hostile takeover). If the people from whom the job analysis information was collected were not aware of these changes, the BOS would have been left unchanged, with possible unfortunate consequences for the employees. If the people from whom information was collected regarding the role of middle management were not aware of these changes, the BOS would also have been left unaltered. This is also true for Scott Paper's first-line supervisors and hourly employees. The result would have been "business as usual" that could very well have led to "no business at all."

When conducting a job analysis for developing an appraisal instrument, human resource specialists should identify observable behavior on the part of an employee that falls into categories labeled by Kilmann and Herden (1976) as external effectiveness, internal effectiveness, external efficiency, and internal efficiency. External effectiveness refers to the behavior of job incumbents necessary for satisfying regulatory groups, consumer groups, and environmentalists (e.g., meets yearly with OFCCP compliance officers). Internal effectiveness focuses on behavior necessary for the establishment of a positive climate within the organization, such as high employee motivation and commitment (e.g., leaves work area neat and clean for employee on the following shift). External efficiency refers to employee behaviors necessary for maximizing the organization's bargaining position in environmental exchanges. Included under this dimension are behaviors critical to the distribution of products and services (e.g., conducts cold calls on at least twenty potential customers per week). Internal efficiency takes into account behavior critical for maximizing output to input and return on investment (e.g., makes periodic suggestions that improve the plant's effectiveness and efficiency).

To be of value, a performance appraisal instrument must reflect the relative weights of these four dimensions in the organization where each employee works to achieve both macro- and microcongruence. For example, the nuclear power industry places great weight on external effectiveness at the expense of internal efficiency because environmental groups pose a serious threat to its very existence. If the people from whom the job analysis information is collected were unaware of this fact, inappropriate criteria could be used for evaluating employees. If powerful forces suddenly provided support to the industry, its strategy would likely change in emphasis, and the appraisal instrument should reflect this change.

Organization Design

Contingency theory (Galbraith, 1977) is based on the proposition that there is no one best way to design an organization. An optimal design takes into account the level of uncertainty faced by the organization.

When the external environment is stable and predictable (mechanistic), tasks should be broken down into specialized elements, the hierarchy should be well defined, and decision making should be centralized. But when the environment is uncertain (organic), tasks should be constantly adjusted and redefined, decision making should be decentralized, and there should be few formalized rules and procedures.

Table 4.4 contrasts mechanistic and organic variables. A job analysis must take into account the behaviors critical on the part of job incumbents who work in these different environments. For example, Lawrence and Lorsch (1967) found that research and development, production, and marketing subunits faced different degrees of uncertainty in different industries and thus should be structured differently (either more organic or mechanistic), depending on the level of uncertainty in their subenvironments. These authors coined the term "differentiation" for differences in the behavior required of managers in different departments in order to be effective. Lawrence and Lorsch also found that the greater the degree of differentiation, the

Table 4.4

Differences in Organizational Design Variables for Organic and Mechanistic Subunits

Subunit Context Variables	Organic Subunits	Mechanistic Subunits
1. Technology		
a. Exceptions	Many	Few
b. Search	Unanalyzable	Analyzable
c. Interdependence (within group)	High	Low
2. Structure		
a. Centralization	Low	High
b. Formalization	Low	High
c. Specialization	High	Low
3. Integration (between-unit interdependence)	High importance	Low importance
4. Boundary spanning Environmental interdependence)	High importance	Low importance
5. Reward system	Goal identification Task involvement	Rule compliance Individual and group rewards
6. Critical job behaviors	Effort above minimum Spontaneous Cooperative	Join and remain Dependable Effort above minimum
7. Major performace dimensions	Internal and external effectiveness External efficiency	Internal efficiency

greater the need for integration; namely, the greater the need for collaboration among departments in order to achieve unity of effort. The job analysis should define those behaviors necessary for collaborative effort.

Technology and Structure

Technology and structure covary with uncertainty to affect performance. Organic units face high levels of uncertainty; they have imperfect knowledge of the transformation process, and they encounter many exceptions requiring unsystematic, unanalyzable search behavior. Thus they have highly interdependent workgroup members. The appropriate structure is one of informal, decentralized decision making by highly educated, professional specialists. Mechanistic units, because of near-perfect knowledge of the transformation process, can be designed with prespecified technology and structure. For example, an assembly-line technology is characterized by few exceptions, analyzable search, and low subunit interdependence with highly formalized and centralized decision making. Assembly-line workers are usually not professionals and require little specialized education and training. A job analysis must focus on these differences if the resulting appraisal instrument is to be of value in different organizations and subunits within the organization. It is virtually impossible for the same appraisal instrument to be applicable across all organizations or all subunits within one organization, because behavior that is critical under one set of circumstances may be inappropriate under another. This is another reason why the critical incident technique, with its focus on the context in which the behavior occurs, is ideal for developing performance appraisal instruments.

Mechanistic subunits require behaviors that are in compliance with written rules and procedures. Organic subunits require behavior that is spontaneous, creative, and cooperative. Because of high task uncertainty, written rules and procedures are difficult to specify with any degree of validity. Self-management on the part of employees becomes critical. It is the purpose of the job analysis to define these terms in the form of observable behavior (e.g., delegates responsibility commensurate with the knowledge of subordinates; solicits divergence of thinking on issues; identifies problems not previously considered; exposes important issues for which there may be no immediate answer; invites input of people on issues that will directly affect them before making a decision).

5

Nontraditional Sources of Appraisals

Once an appraisal instrument has been developed that is *reliable, valid,* relatively *free of bias,* and *practical,* attention must be given to who is qualified to use it. One way of determining the answer is to examine the various alternatives against these same four measurement criteria. Practicality, as noted in the previous chapter, is usually evaluated in terms of user preference or acceptance.

Sources of performance appraisals include the team's leader, the employees themselves, peers, subordinates, and people outside the work group, such as customers, or some combination of the above. To satisfy the four criteria, appraisers must be aware of the aims and objectives of the person's job, frequently observe the employee on the job, and be capable of determining whether the observed behavior is satisfactory. Appraisers need to be aware of the objectives of a job to know what behaviors are critical to fulfilling the job requirements. They must frequently observe the person *on the job* to ensure that their appraisals are based on a representative sampling of the person's performance.[1] They must be capable of ascertaining whether the behavior is effective in order to draw correct conclusions about the employee's value to the organization. For example, we are aware of the aims and objectives of shipyard supervisors because we have

---

1. Note that relevancy rather than frequency of contact is critical for obtaining valid ratings. Appraisers who interact with ratees in a situation relevant to the dimension being rated are more valid in their evaluations than are appraisers who interact with ratees in a nonrelevant situation (Landy & Farr, 1980).

developed BOS for them. We could have completed a quarterly evaluation of them because we practically lived in the shipyards for three months. However, neither of us would qualify as an appraiser because neither of us has the ability to ascertain whether the items on the BOS are being performed properly.

During the past decade the primary focus of research on the ideal source of performance appraisals has been on peers and self (Latham et al., 1993), despite the fact that Bretz and Milkovich (1989), in their survey of Fortune 100 companies, found that only two organizations reported using self-appraisals, and less than 3 percent of the appraisals were conducted by peers. No subordinate appraisal systems were reported. This trend may be changing, as has been reported in *Fortune,* June 19, 1989, p. 201. Before addressing these and other nontraditional sources of appraisals, we will briefly discuss appraisals by one's supervisor, as they are usually the yardstick against which the nontraditional sources of appraisal are compared.

The Superior's Appraisal

In 1977, 95 percent of U.S. companies surveyed by the Conference Board used appraisals from the employee's superior, be it a team's leader, supervisor, or manager; none used peer or subordinate appraisals (Lazer & Wikstrom, 1977). This emphasis on appraisals by one's boss can be justified in terms of both practicality and theory.

The management hierarchy of most organizations reinforces the right of the supervisor to make both evaluative and developmental decisions concerning subordinates. Second, the supervisor generally controls the magnitude and scheduling of the rewards and punishments that can be administered to subordinates. Since performance is enhanced when rewards are based on performance, it is logical that the appraisal be conducted by the person who normally administers the rewards. If this were not the case, the employee would likely view the appraisal process as having little or no importance. Third, it is commonly felt that of all the sources of evaluation, the immediate supervisor is in the best position to judge the relevance of that behavior to job objectives and organizational goals.

The stratified systems theory (SST) developed by Elliott Jaques (1980) supports this position. SST states that natural hierarchies assert themselves wherever there is a group of human beings. This structuring occurs regardless of whether the group is in a factory in Calcutta or in a mine in the Namibian desert. The key to increasing productivity, according to SST, is to establish clearly demarcated levels of authority and account-ability and to make sure that people at each level of the organization are mentally equipped to do their jobs.

Despite this logic, performance appraisals conducted by the person to whom the employee reports have a drawback. They are usually heavily contaminated by bias and hence have low reliability and validity. For example, in a study of middle managers and merchandising executives, Barrett (1966) con-cluded that an employee's evaluation depends heavily on how each supervisor *thinks* the work should be performed rather than how well it is *actually* performed by the employee. Longnecker, Sims, and Gioia (1987) found that conducting appraisals is often a highly emotional process for supervisors, thus reducing any hope for objectivity and accuracy. Supervisors admitted that ratings for an employee take into account the "fallout" from the appraisal. These findings simply confirm what many employees suspect, namely, that managerial evaluations are frequently loaded with subjectivity and bias. They are nei-ther as reliable nor as valid as peer ratings. Alternative sources to supervisory appraisals are especially needed because in many instances the managers seldom see the employee on the job. Moreover, they typically spend less than 1 percent of their time observing their subordinates (Komacki & Desselles, in press). With the flattening of hierarchies that has occurred in most organizations, and with the growing emphasis on the use of teams, it is not unusual for the team members to be more knowl-edgeable and skilled technically in many aspects of the job than is the team leader.

Peer Appraisals

Peer appraisals are those conducted by one's coworkers—mem-bers of one's team or unit or people within the organization who are not in one's unit but are at the same organizational level and frequently interact with the ratee. This latter group is sometimes referred to as internal customers of the person who is being appraised. The reliability and validity coefficients are typically higher for peer assessments than for other sources, such as supervisory ratings or even psychological tests (Fox, Ben-Nahum & Yinon, 1989; Kremer, 1990; McEvoy & Buller, 1987). Hollander (1957) and Kubany (1957) reported test-retest reliability coefficients of 0.60 to 0.70 for periods ranging up to one year and interobserver reliability coefficients of 0.80 to 0.90. Moreover, appraisals made by peers after a short period of acquaintance have been shown to be as good as those made after longer periods of time (Hollander, 1965). Peer evaluations are reliable even when the person is transferred from one group to another within the same organization (Gordon & Medland, 1965).

Siegel (1982) made a paired-comparison evaluation of managerial effectiveness in a savings and loan association. Interobserver reliability was high between supervisory and peer groups.

In addition to being reliable, peer appraisals are valid predictors of job performance. In fact, they have higher predictive validities than do supervisory appraisals (Wherry & Fryer, 1949; Williams & Leavitt, 1947). Korman (1968), after reviewing the literature, concluded that peer ratings are among the best predictors of performance in subsequent jobs. These are significant findings, particularly when the appraisal is used as a basis for making promotions.

The validity of peer ratings as predictors of both objective and subjective performance criteria has been investigated extensively in military settings (Amir, Kovarsky & Sharan, 1970; Hollander, 1954a, 1954b, 1965; Wherry & Fryer, 1949; Williams & Leavitt, 1947). Peer ratings have also been shown to be valid for predicting success as a manager (Roadman, 1964), insurance agent (Weitz, 1958; Mayfield, 1970), salesperson (Waters & Waters, 1970; Mayfield, 1972), medical student (Kubany, 1957), and police officer (Landy et al., 1976). The time elapsed in these studies between the initial rating and measurement of job performance varied from several months (Wherry & Fryer, 1949) to two years (Hollander, 1965). The validity coefficients are typically around 0.40.

Brief (1980) argued against using peer appraisals, stating that the case for peer assessments has been unduly emphasized because the contextual conditions under which they are effective have not been systematically studied. Specifically, he questioned their use for allocating rewards, such as promotions. In response, Kane and Lawler (1980) cited evidence that peer assessments are effective regardless of whether peers are aware that the data will be used for this purpose.

A meta-analysis (a method of systematically cumulating the results of existing studies) by Harris and Schaubroek (1988) revealed moderate agreement between self-peer and self-supervisor and relatively high peer-supervisor agreement. Moreover, job type did not affect the peer-supervisory correlation. Peer appraisal may be an especially useful process for withstanding legal scrutiny, as it is in alignment with the North American judicial system, namely, a judgment by one's peers.

With regard to bias, DeNisi and Mitchell (1978) argued that friendship may affect peer evaluations. However, the empirical research (Hollander, 1954a; Waters & Waters, 1970; Wherry & Fryer, 1949) shows that this bias does not exist. Love (1981) compared peer nominations, rankings, and ratings and found that each method yielded reliable and valid results. None was biased by friendship.

Related to the issue of friendship is the extent to which racial differences affect validity. Cox and Krumholtz (1958) and DeJung and Kaplan (1962) found that peers gave significantly higher ratings to ratees of their own race. However, Schmidt and Johnson (1973) found that when approximately equal numbers of blacks and whites are in peer groups, no racial effects on peer evaluations are present.

Imada (1982) found that British managers rated one another accurately. He concluded that behaviorally based appraisal instruments enabled the rater to recognize the multidimensionality of performance criteria and thus minimize halo error.

The relatively high reliability and validity of peer appraisals is a function of at least three factors. First, reliability is affected positively by the daily interactions among peers. Peers see how an employee interacts not only with them but also with subordinates and the boss. In short, peers usually have a comprehensive view of an employee's job performance and thus have more job-relevant information than do other sources.

Second, the use of peers as raters makes it possible to get a number of independent judgments. The average of several ratings is often more reliable than a single rating (Bayroff, Haggerty & Rundquist, 1954). Such ratings usually provide a stable measure relatively free of the bias and idiosyncrasies of a single rater. Therefore training for minimizing rating errors may not be as critical if peer ratings are used for performance appraisal purposes rather than the supervisor's rating. The use of multiple raters can counterbalance observational errors.

Third, peer appraisals, to be reliable and valid, must be anonymous. Anonymity is important because it permits candor without fear of harming one's relationship with the person who is being appraised. A supervisor or team leader's appraisals are often too lenient because of the desire to avoid conflict with the person being appraised.

A theoretical reason for the effectiveness of peer appraisals can be found in social comparison theory (Festinger, 1954), which states that North Americans believe that rewards are based on the differential possession of abilities and competencies. Since most jobs lack objective measures of these competencies, people observe and compare themselves on the task relevant abilities of their peers. It is for this reason, Mumford (1983) argued, that peer assessments are minimally influenced by friendship, race, or sex. Attention is focused on performance.

In this vein a field study of an Israeli military training program showed that peer assessments predicted other group members' likelihood of success in the program (Fox, Ben-Nahum & Yinon, 1989). Raters who perceived peers as similar to them were more accurate than raters who perceived their peers as dissimilar; raters were better able to recall information about similar rather than dissimilar characteristics. They knew more about similar others because they spent more time with them than they did with dissimilar others. Hence they compared themselves to similar others after having ample opportunity to observe them.

Several studies have been conducted on user reactions to peer appraisals. For example, in the field study by Love (1981), user reaction was negative to all four methods of peer assessment because this use of peers redistributed power. Many people felt that only management has the right to appraise others. This finding supports Jaques' (1980) SST. However, studies by McEvoy and Buller (1987) and Farh, Cannella, and Bedeian (1991) found that employees see peer appraisals as useful if the appraisals are used for developmental rather than administrative purposes. Moreover, when the purpose was developmental, satisfaction with the appraisal process did not correlate with one's actual rating. In short, the employees valued an honest evaluation from their peers (McEvoy, Buller & Roghaar, 1988).

A manager can take advantage of the reliability and validity of peer reviews while retaining accountability for the performance appraisal. For example, in implementing peer ratings, a president and general manager encountered strong resistance from employees, who viewed peer appraisals as a way for the organization to encourage them to spy on one another.

The president overcame the problem by first stressing the concept of fairness: "Jim [the manager] and I see you only some of the time that you are on the job. Your peers see you all the time. This means your appraisals are presently based on the very limited observations of two people, Jim and me. Peer ratings minimize biases because they are averaged together. If one or two people are unfairly critical, the rating will be offset by those people who are evaluating you objectively."

Second, the president asked for their cooperation: "I need your help in order to make sure that I am rewarding people fairly. You people are aware of the aims and objectives of each other's job. You see each other working almost every day. Most importantly, you are far more skilled than I am in recognizing effective as well as ineffective behavior."

Third, he addressed the issue of spying by pointing out that the appraisals were to be completed *anonymously* and that the results were to be used primarily for counseling and development purposes: "Every week each of you voices a complaint to Jim or me regarding work that has not been accomplished by a colleague. It has been difficult for us to take action without letting that person know that you discussed the problem with us. Through peer ratings that are anonymous, I can sit down with each of you three or more times a year and express my appreciation for areas that you are doing well. Where there are areas on which you have been rated poorly, I can take steps to immediately provide you with training, remove obstacles that are getting in the way of you doing your job, or discuss with you ways of minimizing the 'erroneous' perceptions of peers who gave you a poor rating."

Finally, the president stressed to the employees that BOS completed by peers were as valuable to them as to him. "You will have a copy of each evaluation for your personal files. This document ensures that you will always be treated fairly by management. If Jim and I should play favorites regarding salary increases, promotions, or terminations that adversely affect you, you will have a document of your performance that will stand up before a labor relations board or a court of law."

Peer appraisals are now completed willingly three times a year by the employees. The president reported a sharp sustained increase in productive employee behavior within the first three months of using this technique.

A drawback of peer evaluations is that in order for them to be valid, group members must have close contact with one another (Hollander, 1954a, 1954b). Some organizations may have difficulty finding peers who have first-hand knowledge of one another's behavior. Furthermore, the interaction among peers must be relevant to the performance dimensions being evaluated. For example, it is not enough for salesmanagers who work in different geographical areas to meet once a quarter for a staff meeting; they must frequently observe one another on the job if the assessments are to be reliable and valid. If possible, our recommendation is for peers to complete the appraisal document anonymously and for the managers to use these ratings in a counseling and developmental manner with their subordinates (see Chapter 8). This procedure shifts the manager from the role of judge into the role of helper.

Another problem with peer appraisals is the time required in large departments for one person to complete the appraisal document on all employees. This problem can be minimized by the team leader and team member agreeing on the names of five or six people who frequently observe the employee to be asked to complete the appraisal instrument.

In doing peer appraisals, one can choose among three basic procedures: peer nomination, peer rating, and peer ranking. The three methods differ primarily in their ability to discriminate among members of a work group on job effectiveness (Kane & Lawler, 1978). The three procedures are described in increasing order of discriminability.

Peer nomination consists of having each employee in a work group designate a specified number of coworkers as being the highest or best in the group on some particular dimension of job performance (e.g., credit management, community relations, or inventory control). Often, each employee is asked also to nominate others in the group who are lowest or worst on each performance dimension. Employees are usually told to exclude themselves from the nominations given.

Peer rating entails having each employee rate all others in the work group on a given set of performance dimensions. This method lends itself easily to the use of BOS.

Peer ranking consists of having each employee rank order all others in the work group from best to worst on one or more performance dimensions. This method is the most discriminating of all the peer appraisal methods, since the average rank received by each employee will likely differ from that received by others.

What can be said about the relative strengths and weaknesses of these methods? According to Kane and Lawler (1978), the peer nominations are best used for identifying employees whose performance is extremely good or bad. This approach would be especially important as a basis for making decisions about promotions, layoffs, separations, and transfers. The major limitation of this method is that it is virtually useless in providing appraisal feedback to employees, because it furnishes no explanatory behavioral information about each employee's score, and it provides no meaningful information to those employees who received no nominations.

Peer rating is the most useful of the three for appraisal feedback and subsequent goal setting when the employee is evaluated in terms of specific behaviors describing the actual way each individual performed. The information that is fed back to a person is behaviorally based, not merely a comparison of the person to some extreme or nonextreme subgroup.

Peer ranking by itself is useless for feedback and goal setting unless the person is made aware of the behaviors that must be demonstrated to improve one's ranking. We would advise using peer ratings followed by peer rankings for promotion decisions and the use of peer ratings alone for coaching purposes.

Subordinate Appraisals

There are few, if any, studies on the reliability and validity of subordinate appraisals, perhaps because few organizations use them. There are at least two reasons why they are rarely used (Bernardin & Beatty, 1987). First, a top-down approach is compatible with the management styles employed in most North

American firms that continue to emphasize the separation of management and nonmanagement functions. Second, there is a fear that subordinate appraisals will undermine managerial power.

Bernardin and Beatty (1987) cited three reasons for conducting subordinate appraisals. First, subordinates are in a position to observe managerial performance from a different vantage point than most superiors. Second, like peer appraisals, subordinate assessments help eliminate one-rater-only biases. Third, a subordinate appraisal system is compatible with the employee "commitment" and "involvement" models that managers and academics alike are advocating as a way of increasing employee productivity (Lawler & Mohrman, 1989). The keys to successful subordinate appraisals include a participative management style, rater anonymity, and making the items to be rated behaviorally specific.

Levinson (1987) advocated the use of an outside consultant so as to avoid the risk of subordinates "ganging up" on the boss. People are less likely to be angry and more likely to be specific in interviews with a consultant than when confronting the boss alone or with a group of colleagues. Subordinate appraisals, when conducted in this fashion, can be a practical developmental tool for providing specific feedback to managers and thus giving them a basis for setting goals on ways to improve their performance.

That the time is ripe for implementing subordinate appraisals is evident from a survey administered to determine the likelihood of user acceptance of subordinate appraisals within eight organizations not currently using them (McEvoy, 1988). Two-thirds of the managers said that they would approve or strongly approve of subordinate appraisals. Only 17 percent said that they would disapprove or strongly disapprove of this process. The managers' receptivity toward subordinate appraisals was not influenced by their age, gender, years with employer, salary, education level, self-rated performance, or satisfaction with their last performance appraisal.

To the question "If your subordinates were to evaluate your performance, how valuable would you find such feedback for your personal development?" three-quarters of the managers responded definitely or extremely valuable. Only 6 percent said that it would be of limited or no value to them. Seventy-one percent of the managers did not approve of subordinate appraisals counting as heavily as their superiors' appraisals for determining pay and promotions; they fear retaliation from their subordinates for taking unpopular action (e.g., reprimanding an employee), and they also believe that their subordinates do not have full knowledge of their job requirements. To be accepted by managers, subordinate appraisals should be restricted to "people-oriented" as opposed to "task-oriented" dimensions (e.g., organizing, budgeting, etc.) unless the subordinates are in a position to observe them. Even then, these appraisals should supplement but not replace the superior's appraisal.

Exxon was among the first organizations to use subordinate appraisals (Maloney & Hinrichs, 1959). The "Rate Your Supervisor" program provided each supervisor with a computer printout showing the average of anonymous subordinate ratings and how the manager was rated relative to other supervisors. As a result of this program: (1) 25 percent of the subordinates said they had seen lasting changes in their supervisors, (2) 88 percent of the supervisors said they had tried to change their behavior after receiving the report, and (3) 60 percent of the supervisors and the subordinates agreed that productivity had increased as a result of the program.

A division of the Weyerhaeuser Company took this program a step further. The supervisors and their superintendents received a computer printout showing how they had been rated by both a superior and subordinates on each overall performance dimension or criterion that had been identified through a job analysis (Latham, Fay & Saari, 1979) as critical to effective performance. The printout showed the superior's ratings and the average of the subordinate ratings on each behavioral item of each BOS, as well as the person's standing relative to peers. Peer appraisals were not used, because the superintendents seldom saw one another on the job. Similarly, the supervisors seldom interacted with other supervisors.

The appraisal score was the composite of the superior's rating *and* employee ratings across four BOS. This procedure was implemented primarily to assure employees not only that their voices were being heard by management but also that their supervisor was taking action based on their input as well as that of the superintendent. Interestingly, the analysis indicated that there were some items that subordinates were more capable of observing than were supervisors.

If there is a large discrepancy between superior and subordinate ratings, management can investigate the reasons. Frequently, the cause is a personality conflict between the individual and the supervisor, which is why individuals in this organization value subordinate appraisals; the use of these multiple appraisals reduces the effects of an unfair appraisal from one person, namely, the boss.

Supervisors are allowed to keep the results of the subordinate ratings confidential for three months before showing them to their superior. In this way they have ample time to correct or improve the situation. The supervisors are trained to conduct team-building sessions with their subordinates, and they are allowed to use a consultant for the team-building process to assist them in resolving concerns that were highlighted by the subordinate appraisals. The words *team building* refer to subordinates and their supervisor discussing and resolving problems of mutual concern and thus building a productive work team. Typically, the supervisor categorizes areas in which the subordinate ratings were low in three areas: (a) areas that I won't change; here is the rationale; (b) areas that I can change immediately; and (c) areas that through discussion and help from you (subordinates) we can change together.

Through this process subordinates begin to view problems through the eyes of their supervisor, and equally important, the supervisor begins to see concerns from the perspective of subordinates. The results can be an increase in group productivity and job satisfaction within two or three months. The supervisor can then take the subordinate ratings to his or her superior and explain what has been done to maintain or improve the ratings. An additional value of subordinate ratings is that they can aid management in identifying supervisors who are promotable because of their skill in managing people.

There are, however, potential problems with subordinate appraisals. Some subordinates may perceive the process as threatening because they feel that their supervisor will reprimand them for an honest, unfavorable appraisal. Therefore anonymity is critical for increasing the likelihood of accurate ratings. As a rule of thumb, we recommend avoiding subordinate ratings if there are fewer than four subordinates. In this way subordinates can feel "safety in numbers."

Self-Appraisal

Underlying the use of self-appraisal is Bem's (1972) theory of self-perception. This theory states that just as we often infer other people's attitudes by observing their actions, we determine our own attitudes by observing our own actions.

Downs, Farr, and Colbeck (1978) hypothesized that in making inferences about one's beliefs, an individual uses the same cues that would be available to an *external observer of one's behavior.* Specifically, they argued that the theory could be usefully extended to cover self-influence concerning one's own ability to engage in specific job behaviors. The results supported the hypothesis. Employees in a training course, who were unaware of their test scores or trainer ratings of them, evaluated their own performance the same way as the employing organization that used the test scores and trainer ratings. On the basis of Bem's theory and this study, it would appear that employees can arrive at a reasonably realistic self-appraisal when it "is confined to essentially behavioral-type tests which take place within the visual field of the testee ... i.e., the testee is visually able to observe her own performance" (Downs, Farr & Colbeck, 1978, p. 276).

From a practical standpoint, the concept of self-assessment is especially intriguing, since it lies at the core of self-management, which in turn is of special importance to the productivity of the individual and to cost-reduction efforts. If people can self-regulate, the need for supervision from a monitoring standpoint decreases.

Self-management as a substitute for leadership has been examined by Manz and Sims (1980). The role of the supervisor is reduced (enhanced) to assisting "the individual in maintaining task boundaries through a consultative style of management. The essential task of management is to provide the individual with clear task boundaries within which discretion and knowledge can be exercised" (Slocum & Sims, 1980, p. 201). Self-management also fits nicely with peer assessment in that peer consultation is likely to occur where managers are not available to provide technical expertise (Mills, 1983).

Another theoretical basis for advocating the use of self-appraisals is Bandura's (1986) social cognitive theory. The application of this theory involves self-set goals, self-monitoring against one's goals, and self-administered rewards and punishers.

With regard to validity and reliability, a meta-analysis by Mabe and West (1982) showed that "taken as a whole, the data suggest that gross generalizations concerning people's tendency to overestimate their abilities is unwarranted ..." (p. 287). With regard to reliability, the test-retest reliability of the ratings was in the range of 0.76–0.90 for short time periods and 0.47–0.74 for longer periods (e.g., six months), which may reflect, in part, actual changes in employee behavior. With regard to individual differences, people high in intelligence, achievement, and internal locus of control make the most accurate ratings.

The underlying construct that explains the accuracy of self-appraisal, however, may be self-awareness. Again, the authors explained the effectiveness of self-appraisals in terms of Festinger's (1954) social comparison theory. Self-evaluation measures that require relative judgments as opposed to absolute judgments of ability yielded better approximations of criterion measures of ability. Validity also increases to the extent that the reference group with which the person is making a self-assessment is defined. Finally, there is evidence that self-evaluation is a skill that improves with practice, especially practice that includes feedback on accuracy.

Restriction of range can also be a problem with using self-appraisals in that people may rate themselves high regardless of how well they are truly performing their job. Hoffman, Nathan, and Holden (1991) found less variation in self-appraisals by maintenance employees than in the appraisals from the supervisors. Thus only the supervisory appraisals predicted the field service productivity of these employees.

Martin and Klimoski (1990), in study of university employees, also found that self-ratings had higher positive leniency than did appraisals from other sources. Relative to supervisory evaluations, the authors concluded that different information-processing dynamics occur in self-appraisals. For example, when people appraised their own performance, poor results were attributed to external causes more so than when they appraised the performance of their subordinates.

In contrast, two recent studies reported a high correlation between self-appraisals and supervisory assessments. Lane and Herriot (1990) conducted a field study of forty British unit managers to compare the predictive validity of self- versus supervisory appraisals. Subsequent performance, as measured by gross profit and the number of customers served, was predicted equally well by the two sources of appraisal.

In a field study of faculty members and their chairpersons Farh, Werbel, and Bedeian (1988) investigated the effectiveness of a performance appraisal system that incorporated self-assessments with supervisory evaluations of faculty activity reports. The results revealed a high correlation between self- and chairperson's ratings as well as criterion-related validity. Moreover, user acceptance was high, as indicated by ratings from both faculty and their chairpersons.

In explaining the differences that can occur between self- and supervisory appraisals, Campbell and Lee (1988) noted that there are informational constraints; many employees do not understand what is expected of the performance appraisal, poorly conducted previous performance appraisals contribute to this ambiguity, and the excessive time length between appraisals reduces the potential for rating accuracy. Role clarification exercises, improved job descriptions, and thorough review sessions based on behavioral criteria increase the validity of self-appraisals.

Ashford (1989) found that a person's early success experiences anchor one with specific beliefs about self. These beliefs filter subsequent information so that self-appraisal accuracy is reduced. However, she also found that self-assessments predict criterion measures of behavior when people are high in self-awareness. Self-awareness is a function of one's ability to self-observe one's own behavior. Self-aware people compare their behavior against a goal or against information relevant to their goals. Those who are self-aware are able to incorporate information from those comparisons into their self-evaluations and ultimately into their behavior. Self-awareness also results in the incorporation of the assessments of others into one's self-evaluation. As a result, self-aware people are more cognizant of how they are viewed by others, which in turn results in relatively accurate self-assessments.

Several studies have identified variables that will increase the objectivity of self-appraisals. Farh and Werbel (1986) found that telling people that their self-appraisals will be verified against other performance measures decreases positive leniency, that is, rating oneself higher than the facts warrant. Similarly, Fox and Dinur (1988) found that informing people that their evaluations would be checked against other indicators increased validity. Thus the knowledge that comparative performance information exists can reduce bias, specifically positive leniency, in self-appraisals.

Farh and Dobbins (1989) found that the correlations between self-ratings and objective measures of performance increase when the self-raters are presented with comparative performance information regarding their peers. Thus one reason for the lack of agreement between self- and supervisory ratings is that self-raters lack the comparative performance information that is available to their supervisors.

Eder and Fedor (1989) conducted a field experiment that showed that positive leniency in self-reports is reduced when employees are asked to provide documentation for their appraisals. In another field study, Somers and Birnbaum (1991) found no significant differences between staff nurse and supervisor performance ratings. These nurses had had at least two years' experience conducting self-appraisals.

In summary, the argument often given for not using self-appraisals is their lack of agreement with other sources of appraisal, especially supervisors (Harris & Schaubroeck, 1988). This can be problematic with jobs that are ambiguous in nature and hence poorly defined. The solutions to the effective use of self-appraisals include conducting a job analysis to remove this ambiguity (Campbell & Lee, 1988), making appraisals against objective criteria (Lane & Herriot, 1990), making clear to the employee that the appraisal will be verified against other performance measures (Farh & Werbel, 1986; Fox & Dinur, 1988), providing the employee with comparative information (Farh & Dobbins, 1989), requiring documentation in support of the appraisal (Eder & Fedor, 1989), and making certain that the employee has had experience conducting self-appraisals before these appraisals are compared with other sources of information (Somers & Birnbaum, 1991).

A second problem with self-appraisals is their accuracy when it comes to administrative issues, such as salary increases and promotions. This issue should not be viewed as a stumbling block. Administrative issues are only one reason for conducting a performance appraisal. The primary function of appraisals is the counseling and developing of the employee. To the extent that these two functions are done well, decisions are made regarding promotion, demotion, transfers, layoffs, salary increases, and so on. To the extent that a person can self-regulate on the basis of goal setting, self-monitoring, and self-rewarding, the administrative decisions can be left to the team's leader. No research findings suggest that only one source of appraisal (e.g., only supervisor or only self) should be used as a basis for all the appraisal-related purposes listed in Chapter 1.

The advantages of a self-review have been enumerated by Meyer (1991). First, it can enhance the subordinate's dignity and self-respect. Second, it places the manager in the role of a counselor rather than a judge. Third, it increases the employee's understanding of the need for developmental plans as well as the goals that should be formulated regarding the implementation of these plans.

Other advantages of self-appraisals include their potential for enhancing self-motivation (Baron, 1988; Lane & Herriot, 1990), and their tendency to reduce ratee defensiveness (Farh, Werbel & Bedeian, 1988; Lawrie, 1989). Self-appraisals are especially appropriate when the employee is working in relative isolation (e.g., night watchperson) or possesses a rare skill (e.g., diamond cutter). In such instances the employee usually has more information about his or her behavior than does anyone else.

With regard to user preference, a survey of eighteen hundred Minnesota Department of Transportation employees indicated that people want self-evaluations as part of their formal performance appraisal (Laumeyer & Beebe, 1988). However, employees who have experienced few supervisory appraisals (e.g., new employees) or are low in their need for independence express greater satisfaction with the traditional supervisory appraisal than they do with a self-rating procedure (Bassett & Meyer, 1968; Hillery & Wexley, 1974). Thus individual differences must be taken into account when deciding whether to use self-appraisals.

Teel (1978) recommended combining self-appraisals and managerial appraisals. In this procedure the employee and the manager independently complete the performance appraisal form one or two weeks before the performance appraisal is to take place. At the appraisal interview, the manager and the subordinate compare their evaluations. Differences of one point in the ratings are recorded on the official appraisal form at the higher rating, regardless of who assigned it. For differences of two or more points, the manager and the employee have an in-depth discussion to identify and clarify the reasons for the differences. The advantage of this procedure over traditional supervisory-based appraisals is that employees ask more questions and volunteer more comments and suggestions during the appraisal interview.

Appraisals by Outsiders

Some organizations use persons outside the immediate work environment to conduct performance appraisals. These sources include assessors in an assessment center, field reviews conducted by people in the human resources department, and evaluations from trainers.

The term *assessment center* refers to a standardized off-the-job method for assessing managerial effectiveness. Although no two programs in industry are identical, they all place heavy emphasis on the use of multiple methods of assessment, as well as the observation of behavior in simulated situations (Moses & Byham, 1977). The exercises generally include in-basket tests, business problems, and the leaderless group discussion.

In-basket tests are exercises consisting of letters and memoranda. The employees being appraised are asked to pretend that these materials have accumulated in their in-baskets and are instructed to do as much as they can to solve the problems that the materials present. This technique is an excellent measure of an individual's administrative skills regarding organization planning and decision making.

Business problems are games in which groups of employees are given capital with which to establish themselves in business. Their task as a group is to organize their business, manufacture a product, or perform a service so as to make as much profit as possible in the time allotted. During this game, each employee's skills in such areas as human relations, resistance to stress, and energy are assessed.

A leaderless group discussion (LGD) is a conference among several persons in which no formal leader has been assigned. The discussion is often of a competitive nature; each individual takes a position and tries to win its adoption by the group. Sometimes the LGD is of a cooperative nature; each person is assigned a role and told to help the group arrive at an important decision. Employees are assessed in terms of such qualities as oral communication, personal impact, and behavioral flexibility.

The assessors are typically line managers two or more organization levels above the people who are being assessed. The assessors administer the individual exercises and observe the employees. The ratio of assessors to employees is usually about 1:2 or 1:3. The employees are assessed on behavioral characteristics identified through a job analysis as relevant to success in management.

The advantage of performance appraisals conducted in an assessment center is that assessors can see five to seven employees doing the same thing at the same time under standardized conditions. Some psychologists (e.g., Wallace, 1965; McCall & DeVries, 1976) have argued that the best way to ensure objective evaluations is to establish simulated exercises in which an employee's performance can be compared to known standards under controlled, standardized conditions.

A drawback to using assessment centers for performance appraisal is that the performance being evaluated is based on simulated exercises rather than on-the-job performance. Thus employees may resent its use for appraising their present performance. However, the reliability of this procedure is high, and its validity for predicting success in higher-level jobs is impressive. When the purpose of the performance appraisal is to assess promotion potential, the assessment center is highly effective.

The *field review* derives its name from the fact that a human resources (HR) person interviews managers and supervisors about the performance of each subordinate. The HR manager then writes an evaluation, which is sent to the person to whom the employee reports, who modifies it if need be and then signs it to indicate approval. The strengths of this method are that it provides line managers with professional assistance in making appraisals, reduces the amount of time they normally have to spend in writing appraisals, and increases the standardization of the evaluation process throughout the total organization.

On the other hand, nothing is known about the reliability or validity of this technique. Also, in some organizations in which appraisals do not have the support of high-level management, it is used as an excuse by supervisors and managers to avoid their responsibility for seriously evaluating their subordinates (Wexley & Yukl, 1977).

Another type of outside evaluation is that given by the training staff. When individuals receive training, the training staff can give ratings based on what they have seen the employee do during the training program. In several studies on military personnel (Gordon & Medland, 1965; Williams & Leavitt, 1947) trainer evaluations were found to agree substantially, indicating acceptable interobserver reliability. However, it was also found that training staff appraisals were less reliable and had lower predictive validity than peer evaluations by fellow trainees; the reason is that peers usually have more information on which to make an appraisal than do the trainers.

Saari & Latham (1980) examined the validity of assessments made by two trainers immediately after training sixty-four supervisors who had attended nine two-hour leadership training sessions. The pooled judgments of the trainers correlated significantly with appraisals from the trainees' supervisors and their subordinates one year after training.

One potential advantage of using outside experts is that it may reduce the randomness in evaluations due to appraisers using different standards in evaluating performance. As mentioned previously, Barrett (1966) found that supervisory appraisals depend heavily on how the supervisor thinks the work should be done, and supervisors often differ widely on their requirements. He concluded that evaluations done by subject-matter experts outside the organization can be based on a common frame of reference and are thus more likely than evaluations by supervisors to be consistent across the organization. Smither, Barry, and Reilly (1989) found that with enhanced viewing opportunities, expert raters can provide accurate ratings, based on their detailed knowledge of the job, as well as their intelligence (Smither & Reilly, 1987).

Using outside appraisals has several disadvantages, however. As Cummings and Schwab (1973) pointed out, it is not known whether meaningful conversations take place between a manager and a subordinate about performance when the appraisal is based on input from someone outside the work unit. Furthermore, outside appraisals may sometimes be inefficient in that they can require significantly more time and personnel than do other types of appraisals. Finally, the appraisals are not often based on direct observations by the appraiser of the employee on the job. When the appraisals are based on direct observations and no other sources (e.g., peers, manager) are available, they can, of course, be valuable. This was the case in the series of studies on loggers discussed in Chapter 4. The logging supervisors were independent businesspeople who seldom, if ever, interacted with other supervisors on job sites. Many of their subordinates were illiterate and could not complete the BOS. They were reluctant to be interviewed on the performance of their boss. Consequently, the appraisal information was collected from the dealers to whom the logging supervisors sold their wood and the company foresters on whose land they were cutting timber. These outsiders are aware of the aims and objectives of the logging supervisor's job, frequently see the loggers on the job, and can discern competent behavior.

Appraising the Executive

A pervasive myth surrounding performance appraisals is that executives neither need nor want formal appraisals. A study involving eighty-four executives in eleven major organizations revealed that senior managers would value a formal appraisal of their performance with regard to both process and outcomes (Longnecker & Gioia, 1992).

Compelling arguments for appraising senior level managers, including and especially the CEO, were made by Kaplan, Drath, and Kofodimos (1987) after interviewing twenty-two executives. They found that most executives avoid acknowledging their limitations. Moreover, subordinates usually shy away from attempts to correct this situation. Worse, some subordinates act as "cheerleaders" either out of self-interest or because they have become blind to the CEO's faults.

Executive appraisal for developmental purposes is important because no executive can escape having areas in need of improvement. These areas may include difficulty in thinking strategically; a proclivity for viewing all problems through the eyes of one's specialty; a susceptibility to letting power, position, and celebrity go to one's head; or a single-minded commitment to a demanding career to the point where marriage, children, or health suffers and subsequently undermines the executive's effectiveness.

Kaplan and his colleagues identified at least three factors inhibiting the executive's development. First, the executive's power decreases the likelihood of receiving constructive feedback from others. Subordinates in particular tend to avoid critiquing the behavior of a powerful person. Second, the executive's ability to accept criticism is reduced by the need to be, and appear to be, highly competent. Third, a history of success makes the necessity for change difficult for executives to recognize in themselves. All of this is exacerbated by the tendency of most organizations to protect their executives from the indignities and problems of everyday life. Thus they lose touch with the majority of the people in the organization.

The solutions can be found in the use of peer, subordinate, self-, and outside-expert appraisals. With regard to peer appraisals, Kaplan and his colleagues found that maintaining good relations with their peers can help executives overcome the temptation to reject criticism. Because of an atmosphere of mutual respect, trusted colleagues were found to be invaluable in helping executives accept negative information.

Scott Paper Company's senior management group in Mobile, Alabama, uses peer appraisals as a team-building exercise to ensure consistency in their leadership across the plant site and to continuously develop the capability for job growth in themselves and in their people. For example, the vice-president and his immediate staff appraise one another's performance anonymously to ensure candor. Again, the process involves feedback and the setting of specific, difficult, attainable goals in relation to this feedback. In brief, each person is interviewed as to what he or she has observed each colleague do well and what he or she would like to see the person start doing or stop doing that is consistent with the organization's strategic plans. Feedback is given in a group setting. Each person is designated the role of coach, with the responsibility of helping the others grow in their respective jobs.

Two ground rules enhance the effectiveness of peer appraisals at Scott Paper. One is to focus primarily on the future rather than the past. The other is to maintain anonymity regarding the source of a particular comment that was made during the initial interviews. The rationale for the first ground rule is that the past cannot be changed, whereas control can be exerted over the future. Moreover, conflict is likely to occur as people recall the past from different vantage points. Conflict is less likely when the emphasis is on what one would like to see occur in the future. The rationale for the second ground rule is not only to ensure candor in the interviews but also to prevent anyone claiming ownership of other group members' thoughts or observations.

In the feedback session, emphasis is given to discussing and emphasizing the positive behaviors that have been observed. Here discussion of the past is welcome, so that appropriate behavior is reinforced. High-level managers are arguably less likely to receive praise than people in other employee groups, because their subordinates wish to avoid perceptions of patronization, the superior seldom sees them outside of staff meetings, and their peers are in strong competition with one another for promotion (Kaplan , Drath & Kofodimus, 1987). Hence, a strong focus on team playing, whereby a structure is provided for these managers to consciously focus on one another's development, can be critical to the organization's effectiveness.

Feedback that is negative is stated in terms of what the group would like to see occur in the future. To preserve the anonymity of the author or authors of the comment and to enhance coaching skills, each person is asked to discuss how he or she would change the behavior under discussion. Thus a third ground rule that enhances the effectiveness of peer appraisals and minimizes the likelihood of conflict is to focus on the behavior rather than the person.

After receiving feedback, each person presents and commits to three to five specific goals. These goals may be modified if the group does not believe that they are based on the feedback that was given. Once there is consensus on the appropriateness of the goals, the process concludes with a discussion of how the group can assist each individual in achieving them. In this way goal setting by each individual manager becomes a team effort. The probability that the goals will be attained is high. This final step includes agreement on the date for a follow-up meeting to reward one another for goal attainment, to provide any needed help for goal attainment, and to agree on the setting of new goals.

With regard to subordinate appraisals, Kaplan found that an effective method to ensure growth was for the executive at the beginning of each year to share his or her goals for personal change with immediate subordinates. By making their goals public, the executives committed themselves to making significant shifts in their behavior.

At Scott Paper's Mobile Division, this step is taken even further. The senior managers meet with their respective staffs to combine subordinate appraisal of a senior manager with a peer appraisal among the manager's subordinates. The group then discusses ways to help the executive and one another achieve their respective goals.

This method is especially helpful for bringing about behavior shifts in executives who are all but superstitious about altering their management style. Rather than correcting their deficiencies, many executives are inclined to build only on their strengths. Thus their success ironically becomes an inhibitor of change. Subordinate feedback and the setting of goals based on it helps executives to confront their shortcomings (Kaplan, Drath & Kofodimus, 1987).

Self-appraisal through introspection can be another invaluable source of feedback for executives. But Kaplan found that most executives do not see a connection between introspection and performance, and hence are unwilling to expend the required time and effort. Moreover, when only self-appraisals are used, many executives are reluctant to admit a weakness to themselves, let alone to others.

The best use of self-analysis and self-redirection is in response to a specific need, such as a setback at work, repeated difficulties in one's job, a career impasse, a transition to radically different responsibilities, a crisis at home, or a buildup of health-threatening stress. Such events can provoke executives to question themselves, their priorities, and the processes they are using to attain them. Hence such events set the stage for learning.

Zaleznik (1989) found that how people manage disappointment is key to growth in their careers. If they deny it, growth is retarded because the unresolved conflicts remain. Executives who react to being plateaued, demoted, or terminated by immediately finding another job and scrupulously avoiding self-scrutiny lay the groundwork for continuation of the problem in the subsequent job. To recognize a problem of one's own making, an executive must neither deny nor fight it. McCall and Lombardo (1983) found that one of the things that differentiates between success and failure at the top is a strong desire for ongoing learning. Both the executives who remained successful after reaching the top and those who were subsequently derailed had flaws. What differed was whether people dealt directly with their faults.

The use of outside experts can help CEOs learn from their mistakes. Kaplan described how the member of a board of directors in one organization heads a team of three to conduct an appraisal of the executive. This team interviews subordinates for their observations of the CEO and the CEO's staff. The information is then fed back to the CEO as a basis for making change. Other corporations use an outside consultant, who knows the organization well and who has the respect of the people in it, to collect data from key stakeholders and then feed back the information to the CEO.

As Kaplan and his colleagues noted, ironically it is the executive's experience, skill, success, and access to resources that set him or her apart from other people. These factors enable the executive to influence and accomplish great feats but these factors are also the very ones that prevent the fullest development of the executive's capabilities. Feedback and goal setting for personal development are as important, and arguably more important, for the executive as for anyone else in the organization.

Closing Remarks

The usual practice in most organizations is for an employee to be evaluated by an immediate superior. Progressive organizations have come to realize that sources other than an employee's boss can provide appraisals. These sources include the employee and his or her peers, subordinates reporting to the employee, and appraisers outside the employee's work unit.

What can be said about the use of appraisals from sources other than the individual's manager or team leader? We believe that the use of multiple sources increases the probability of obtaining a comprehensive picture of an employee's total contribution to the organization. Quite often, the performance ratings of an individual from appraisers at different organizational levels do not agree highly with one another, as the appraisers see different aspects of an employee's behavior. Therefore we recommend the systematic collection of input from supervisors, peers, subordinates, and the individuals themselves when making a performance appraisal.

The underlying issue of this chapter is the necessity for maximizing direct (first-hand) observations of an employee's performance through the use of all relevant sources of information. Only in this way can appraisals have what Locke (1976) calls logical validity. That is, an appraisal must be integrated in a noncontradictory fashion with all pertinent information relevant to the phenomenon being measured. Logical validity requires, in the case of BOS, that the contradictions among different appraiser responses to the scale be resolved. This is done by pointing out contradictions to the appraisers and by discussing with them explanations for the contradictions. Such differences result from appraisers using different frames of reference or interpreting one or more items idiosyncratically. Note that this procedure validates the appraisers, not the appraisal instrument.

6

Increasing the Accuracy of the Appraiser

Introduction

Increasing the number of appraisers with differing views of the employee's performance can increase the accuracy of the appraisal. However, no combination of appraisers will result in accurate decisions if the appraisals are affected by employee characteristics that are irrelevant to the job. Thus regardless of whether evaluations are obtained from multiple appraisers or from only the employee's immediate superior, all appraisers should be trained to reduce errors of judgment that occur when one person evaluates another. This training is necessary because to the degree to which a performance appraisal is biased, distorted, or inaccurate, the probability of increasing the productivity of the employee is greatly decreased. Moreover, wrong decisions could be made regarding whom to promote, retain, or replace, which in turn will penalize the organization's bottom line. In addition, when a performance appraisal is affected by rating errors, the employee may be justified in filing a discrimination charge. Without admitting guilt, AT&T agreed in court to compensate women and minority employees with payments that were estimated to run between $12 and $15 million. The payments were intended as retroactive compensation to possible past victims of discrimination in promotions, transfers, and salary administration (Miner, 1974).

Today few organizations incorporate training that will reduce rating errors in their performance appraisal system. They assume, incorrectly, that the careful construction of the appraisal instrument will obviate the need for training raters. Despite attempts to develop appraisal instruments that both lend themselves to counseling and developing the employee and are resistant to rating errors, evaluators continue to make errors when observing and evaluating employees.

This chapter describes common rating errors and the cognitive processes that help to explain why appraisers are often inaccurate. The extent to which the employee's sex, race, and age contribute to rater bias is examined. Most importantly, the chapter reviews training programs that help people minimize rating errors and thus increase their objectivity in making performance appraisals.

Rating Errors

Rating errors are errors in judgment that occur in a systematic manner when an individual observes and evaluates another. Rating errors may be defined technically as a difference between the output of a human judgment process and that of an objective, accurate assessment uncolored by bias, prejudice, or other subjective, extraneous influences (Blum & Naylor, 1968; Feldman, 1979). In the context of the workplace these rating errors are defined as the influence of factors other than the employee's job performance that systematically change the appraisal of that employee.

What makes these errors so difficult to correct is that the appraisers are usually unaware that they are making them. When they are aware of errors, they are frequently unable to correct them themselves (Wexley, Sanders & Yukl, 1973). The unfortunate result can be an employee who is inappropriately retained, promoted, demoted, transferred, or terminated. The most common rating errors include contrast effects, first impressions, halo, similar-to-me judgments, central-tendency errors, and positive and negative leniency.

The *contrast-effects* error is the tendency for a rater to evaluate a person relative to other individuals rather than on the requirements of the job (Wexley et al., 1972). Contrast effects are most likely to occur in personnel selection. For example, a person may interview one or more highly qualified candidates for a job opening and then interview someone who is only average; conversely, a person may interview one or more very underqualified candidates followed by an interview with an average candidate. In the first case the average applicant may be rejected only for looking bad relative to the two strong candidates; the average candidate may very well have met the requirements of the job. If the company had several job openings, the rejection was the organization's loss and possibly a competitor's gain. In the second instance of contrast effects, the average candidate may get a higher rating than would be deserved simply due to the favorable comparison to much weaker candidates.

Contrast effects are particularly troublesome in performance appraisals because of the deeply imbedded assumption by many human resources people that the distribution of ratings should resemble a normal, or bell-shaped, curve. To automatically rate on a curve is not only in violation of the 1978 Civil Service Reform Act but is also absurd. For example, work units that have experienced layoffs may have only excellent employees remaining; thus the distribution of employee ratings should pile up at the high end. It would be unethical for someone in the human resources department to insist that at least some of the employees be given low ratings on the performance appraisal form. People should be evaluated on the degree to which they fulfill the requirements of their jobs, not on how well they do relative to other people. This point is especially true if the other employees are doing different jobs. To do otherwise not only invites a possible lawsuit but also can create havoc within the organization.

Consider the following incident. One individual in a department appeared to be outstanding in contrast with the others. Consequently, that individual was promoted to a higher-paying job in another work unit but is a failure in the new job. Why? Because no one asked whether that person could fulfill the requirements of the new job, let alone how well the requirements of the original job were being performed. Instead, everyone was impressed with how well the person was doing *relative* to the poor performers in that original department.

Another example of contrast effects occurred when a company was experiencing an economic recession. An average manager working in an exceptionally good department was laid off; an equally average manager doing the same job in a poor department was given additional responsibility and subsequently promoted. Thus even though these two individuals had comparable job performance, one benefited from the mediocrity of peers, whereas the other one suffered because the peers were exceptional.

First-impression error occurs when a manager makes an initial favorable or unfavorable judgment about an employee and then ignores (or perceptually distorts) subsequent information so as to support the initial impression. For example, one individual did outstanding work the first month on the job and for the next five months did average work. The manager committed first-impression error by continuing to give the individual high ratings. Conversely, another individual initially experienced difficulties on the job for a variety of non-job-related reasons but after three months was doing extremely well. The manager, however, continued to assign mediocre ratings; the unfortunate result was that the manager still gave the challenging assignments to the first individual, who was no longer performing the job well.

The *halo error* refers to inappropriate generalizations from one aspect of a person's performance on the job to all aspects of a person's job performance.[1] For example, a person who is outstanding on only one area of the job (e.g., inventory control) may be rated inaccurately as outstanding on all areas of the job (credit management, customer relations, community relations). Conversely, if someone is rated as deficient in one area of the job, that person may be rated incorrectly as doing poorly on all aspects of the job. The point here is that people have both strengths and weaknesses, and each needs to be evaluated independently.

Now consider a different rater error. Suppose that you could find the perfect person for the job in terms of background, aptitude, knowledge, and experience. Would you rate the person lower if that individual had twelve brothers and sisters, if the father drove a bus, and if the mother was a maid? Most people would give an emphatic "no" to this question. If we persisted by asking whether such variables would influence their ratings in any way, they might wonder if we had lost our senses.

---

1. The halo effect, by contrast, refers to a person who truly is doing outstanding work on all aspects of the job.

Managers who had several years of experience in conducting performance appraisals were given a detailed job description for a position in their unit. They then observed a videotape of a person who met all the requirements of the job. However, one group of predominantly middle-class managers heard the applicant say that he had two brothers, a father with a Ph.D. in physics, and a mother with a master's degree in social work. A second group of middle-class managers received the same job description and a videotape spliced so that the applicant was heard to say he had twelve brothers and sisters, his father was a bus driver, and his mother was a maid. The first group rated the person outstanding; the second group gave this same person a much lower rating.

These managers made the *similar-to-me* error (Rand & Wexley, 1975; Wexley & Nemeroff, 1974)—raters' tendency to judge more favorably those people whom they perceive as similar to themselves. That is, the more closely an employee resembles the rater in values, attitudes, personality, or biographical background, the more likely the rater is to judge that individual favorably. By contrast, the *dissimilar-to-me* error refers to the stronger tendency to give the employee unlike the rater a low rating. Why does the similar-dissimilar error occur? We all tend to like and to think more highly of others whom we perceive as like us. This effect may sometimes be acceptable in social situations, but it is an error when making appraisals on the job because it can lead to inaccurate evaluations of people, reduce creativity if everyone sees issues in the same way, and lead to charges of employee discrimination.

Central-tendency error is committed by the appraiser who wants to play it safe and therefore consistently rates an employee on or close to the midpoint of an appraisal scale when the employee's performance clearly warrants a substantially higher or lower rating. If the manager rates the individual as average and the individual subsequently does extremely well, the manager can say, "See, I told you the employee wasn't bad." On the other hand, if the employee does poorly, the manager can justify the previous rating by saying, "What did you expect? I told you that individual wasn't all that good." In either case this rating error does disservice to both the employee and the organization.

Negative and positive leniency errors are committed by the manager who is either too hard or too easy in rating employees. In the performance appraisal process positive leniency may raise unwarranted expectations of the employee for raises, promotions, or challenging job assignments. With negative leniency the employee may get tired of banging his or her head against the wall, because no matter how hard the individual tries, the boss cannot be satisfied. In both instances the result can be the same: The employee stops working hard. It is interesting to note from anecdotal evidence that workers generally do not *like* supervisors who are tough unfairly and do not *respect* supervisors who are too lenient in their ratings. In the latter case it is demotivating to see someone who is lazy receive the same high rating as someone who is a hard worker. The importance of fairness in the appraisal process to employees is discussed in detail in Chapter 9.

Cognitive Information Processes

In his amusing and highly instructive book, Tice (1989) illustrated how we human beings seldom discover all there is to be discovered or perceive all there is to be perceived in our appraisals of others. What is obviously true to us may be restricted to only what we are able to see or what we have allowed ourselves to see. Thus we are often incorrect in assuming that we know the truth when we see it.

Consider Fig. 6.1, a picture of two women. One woman is toothless, and has a big chin and a hawk nose. Her pointy chin is in the center of her black coat. She is wearing a black hat with a feather sticking out. The young woman, who is looking back over her left shoulder, is wearing a black choker around her neck. She has the same hair, black coat, and feathered hat as the old woman. Tice used the phrase "lock on/lock out" to explain our inability to "see" the two women in the picture at the same time. By locking on to the older woman, we lock out the younger one, and vice versa. What we have locked on to is now our belief; it is the truth as we see it.

In his discussion of the blind spots in our appraisals, Tice borrowed the Greek word "scotoma," meaning blindness. A scotoma is a useful construct for explaining why we see what we

Figure 6.1
Old Woman / Young Woman

expect to see and hear what we expect to hear. Conversely, it explains why we do not see or hear what we do not expect to see or hear on the part of others. A scotoma blocks out alternative truths and thus makes us selective information gatherers. When you "see" the old woman in Fig. 6.1, you literally block out— blind yourself to—the young one. By locking on to certain aspects of an employee, an appraiser also "locks out."

High-performance people see beyond the traditional or conventional ways of solving difficult problems. They constantly look for different options to getting things done. They lock out the problem and instead lock on to finding a myriad of solutions; they lock on to the belief that "it can be done" rather than "it can't be done." Rather than locking on to their usual way of doing things, they are open minded and flexible to new ways of approaching the issues. Ironically, many executives use the locking-on principle to help them tenaciously pursue the organization's goals, but this very ability to concentrate single mindedly on an objective can become a weakness. Because they are so persistent in what they are doing, they may become blind to other options. Along with locking out distractions, they may lock out effective and efficient alternatives to achieving their goals. Tice argued that what sets high-performance people apart is that they focus intensively on their goals while remaining skeptical and analytical regarding the paths that are being followed to attain them. They recognize that they do not see the whole truth; consequently, they take creative risks in order to find more of the truth.

The application of these concepts to appraisals by one's subordinates is related humorously by Tice.

Scotomas and the Football Coach

Let me just relate something funny and dumb that happened to me years ago when I was a teacher and football coach at Kennedy High School. I had my players for four years, so I thought I knew them better than most people know anybody. See my locked-on opinion? Watch how you use this in your life and you don't even know it. By the end of the third year, I had locked on that my quarterback—a kid named David—couldn't pass the ball ten yards. To me, that's how weak his arm was; that was "the truth." How did I know? Well, I'd seen him play for three years, hadn't I? I was his coach; I ought to know.

See the detrimental attitude? But that was all right because I had also locked on that my ends couldn't catch. I knew "the truth" about them, too. I mean, they'd been dropping them all along, hadn't they? Keep in mind that once I "knew" they couldn't catch the ball, I built a scotoma to every catch they made. That whole year, I never saw my ends make a catch.

I'd also locked on that we had no speed. Being the great coach that I was, I figured the only possible way we would move the ball was if I took this big, 225-pound kid by the name of Don out of the line and made him a fullback. So we slammed the kid into the line over here for three yards, and then we slammed him over there for three yards. And to fool you, we'd come back over here with him because you thought we'd go over there. We would win 7–6, or lose 6–7. Imagine watching games like that. They were so boring, even the kids' mothers fell asleep in the stands.

I remember this one game so vividly—it must've been twenty years ago. We were ahead of Stadium High School out of Tacoma 7–0 in the second quarter. Third down, eight yards to go on Stadium's twenty-yard line. That was a long-yardage situation for us because we averaged three yards a carry with our "belly" plays—fullback into the line. So David called time out and came over to me and said, "Coach, what're we gonna call?" That made me madder than the dickens. We only had two plays, and he'd wasted a time out like that? "Hell," I thought. "Now I'm gonna have to give these kids some inspiration."

Ever get people around you who try to inspire you because they can't tell you what to do? That was me. I said, "Run 'Belly at Six' and tell those darned kids to block harder." And David said, "But Coach, couldn't we pass the ball to Marty?" Now, Marty was an end that we split way out there for a decoy. Everybody knew we wouldn't throw to him. When David said, "Couldn't we pass the ball to Marty?" that was insubordination! A bad-mouther! A kid telling you how to run your company! I said, "Don't you bad-mouth me. I got another guy that can play." I didn't, but you always say that. And they see right through it.

In exasperation, this sixteen-year-old quarterback got up enough courage to look me in the eye and say, "Well, Marty's not only been open the whole game, he's been open the whole year!" Oooh, that made me mad. So we ran my play again, naturally, where we crunched into the line for three more yards. But David sent Marty downfield anyway—and here went this kid right down the middle of our opponent's field without anybody near him. But that wasn't so bad. Every step of the way, he was making faces at me! And then he stood wide open right under the goal post. I looked at him and thought, "I'll be darned! Look at that!" Just like when you saw the old lady and then, click, you saw the young. You couldn't see it, then you could. "I'll be darned! Look at that!"

On the very next play, we sent Marty downfield again, and David faked a handoff to the fullback and threw a wobbly ol' touchdown pass to Marty. "Wobbly," of course, was my perception because, after all, I knew the kid couldn't throw. Well, we scored three touchdowns in the game on the same play. I got to thinking, "Not all year. It couldn't have been that easy. Not as hard as we've been working."

You're going to have the same feeling about your life from now on. Because it isn't just me being dumb and blind, and locked on and locked out. You'll see that you and many of the people around you are the same way. And when you see a new option for the first time, you'll be very embarrassed. You'll say to yourself, "Why didn't I see that before?"

Hold on. There's more to the story. The next day, Sunday, I went down in my basement and looked at our game films. I found out it wasn't just Marty in the clear; we had other kids in the clear all over the place. But we never called their plays. I sat there watching the film, thinking, "I'll be darned. Look at that. Look at that. Look at that." I could see now.

On Monday, I went to my office in the locker room and called in this cocky, egotistical, know-it-all junior by the name of Tommy—a halfback who was always trying to tell me how to run my team. You got any of those in your company? I said, "Tell me, Tommy. How can we score?" He said, "You know that play where you got me knocking the end down, and everybody else goes the other way? Well, once I knock him down, everybody leaves me. Even he gets up and leaves. If you wanna score, just throw me the ball." That sounded too easy. Why didn't I see that?

In the next game, so help me, that "know-it-all" kid scored six touchdowns. Not points—touchdowns. The game after that, he scored six more. That's twelve touchdowns in two games—and, before that, we had trouble scoring just one a game. Why hadn't I seen? I knew why: because I was so opinionated.

The next week I asked another kid, a halfback by the name of Joe, "Hey Joe, what's your favorite play?" And I'll be darned, I became a good coach. How come? Wasn't I working at it before? Wasn't I trying hard? Wasn't I studying? Of course, I was. But I was too locked on to my own vision of the way things is, was, and always will be, forever and ever, Amen. I was so locked on to what I thought was "the truth" about everybody else, that I couldn't see the old lady, or I couldn't see the young.[2]

Tice's conclusions are well documented in the scientific literature. For example, Feldman (1981) showed that the categorization of information affects performance evaluations by limiting information about an employee when memory-based judgments are made about an employee. Appraisals are a function of information search, information recategorization, integration and judgment processes, cognitive integration, and evaluative integration. Among Feldman's conclusions were the following:

1. No appraisal scale in and of itself can eliminate rater biases.

2. Behavioral taxonomies need to be developed. BARS and BOS provide both description and scaling in a single instrument.

3. Training programs need to capture the prototypes and category systems of experienced employees. "The development of BARS and behavioral observation scales may be seen as an attempt to define a more valid prototype of the successful and unsuccessful

---

2. Reprinted with permission of Prentice Hall from L. Tice (1989), *A Better World A Better You.*

employee. Likewise, training in the use of such scales can be seen as an attempt to teach common prototypes to a set of raters" (p. 144).

4. The use of trait ratings needs to be discouraged.

Nathan and Lord (1983) argued that human information processes are responsible for both accuracy and rating errors. Using Feldman's (1981) model, the authors hypothesized that halo error is the result of a simplifying process in which performance information is automatically stored in the appraiser's memory as part of a prototype-based category. Halo in performance appraisals occurs because distinct but similar behavior patterns are treated as being equivalent, that is, as fitting the prototype. Their categorization model shows that regardless of the observation and rating conditions, ratings of different aspects of the job result from the recall of a prototype of a general category into which the ratee has been categorized. Nathan and Alexander (1985) showed that only to the degree that a rater's implicit beliefs about performance represent an employee's actual performance will the ratings be accurate.

In support of the categorization schema hypothesis, Mount and Thompson (1987) found that rating accuracy was higher when subordinates perceived the managers to be performing in a way that was consistent with their expectations. Duarte, Goodson, and Klich (1991) found that "in-group" employees in a telephone company were rated high on a trait scale regardless of their actual performance (e.g., time taken to complete a call), whereas employees who were in the "out-group" were rated relatively accurately. Raters have a well-developed categorization schema in terms of strong expectations about the performance of their in-group members and as a result tend to give them high ratings consistent with their categorization of these people. In contrast, the performance of out-group members is highly salient to supervisors, and thus the evaluations of the employees tend to be accurate.

Employees can learn to use the appraiser's use of categorization schema to their advantage. For example, employees can influence their performance appraisal by creating a positive or negative impression on their supervisor. Wayne and Ferris (1990) found that impression management by a subordinate is particularly important initially when the appraiser is forming an impression of and categorizing the subordinate; appraisers encode an employee's behaviors in terms of general trait concepts. Partially on the basis of these trait concepts, individuals form a general evaluation concept of the person as likable or unlikable; this evaluative concept becomes the basis of the impression. Once this evaluative concept is formed, the employee's subsequent behaviors are interpreted in terms of this concept. When appraisers are asked to judge an employee, they search their memory for a general trait or an evaluative concept that specifically pertains to the judgment.

Cooper (1981) found that rating errors can be minimized by developing clear, specific, nonoverlapping performance criteria. He showed that if each criterion is internally homogeneous and descriptively rich, raters are less likely to rely on an overall impression or a few salient episodes. Unlike trait scales, these criteria help raters recall specific episodes of an employee's performance.

Cooper concluded that customized behavioral scales should be designed for each job or job family; tailor-made scales enable raters to discriminate among the performance criteria. However, if any more than nine criteria are used, the raters may be unable to discriminate among them (Kafry, Jacobs & Zedeck, 1979).

Larson, Lingle, and Scerbo (1984) found that behaviorally based scales are excellent when they are used with a time-sampling technique for determining the behavior to be observed. Such a strategy effectively minimizes the influence of selective attention and encoding by forcing the appraiser to attend to and record the ratee's ongoing behavior at predetermined moments.

Employee Characteristics

To what extent does an employee's sex, race, or age affect the appraisals he or she receives? Nieva and Gutek (1980) reviewed the literature on the extent to which an employee's gender affects a performance evaluation. Most of the studies showed a pro-male evaluation bias. They found three ways, however, to minimize this problem.

First, comprehensive task-related information must be made available to the appraiser. Their recommendation is for women to make their work highly visible to the evaluator.

Second, the performance criteria must be clear to the appraiser. Their recommendation here is threefold: (1) clarify objectives and task responsibilities; (2) use behaviorally based appraisal scales that minimize the opportunity for inference or extrapolation from available information to some other context; and (3) train appraisers to overcome rating errors.

The recommendation on training was based on the finding that level of performance affects bias regarding women. Females are evaluated less favorably than males when they perform well but more favorably than males when both perform poorly.

The third recommendation was for women to obtain incongruent sex-role jobs (e.g., engineer, airline pilot, mechanic). Positive leniency tends to occur when women who obtain such jobs are seen performing well in this "unexpected context."

Mobley (1982) conducted a field study on the performance appraisals of management employees and found that the effects of both sex and race accounted for less than 5 percent of the criterion variance. It is noteworthy that the supervisors had been trained in the use of a behaviorally based appraisal scale.

In another field study Wexley and Pulakos (1982) found no evidence to support the belief that women are tougher in their evaluations of other women than they are of men. However, female managers gave more variable ratings for male than for female subordinates and the same was true of female subordinates, in their evaluations of managers. In general, male subordinates and managers did not rate female subordinates and managers any differently than they did males, regardless of rank. The study employed behaviorally based scales that reduce the opportunity for inference or extrapolation based on nonperformance issues.

In their second field study Pulakos and Wexley (1983) investigated the similar-to-me effect and found that perceptual similarity affects managers' evaluations of their subordinates positively, whereas dissimilarity affects them negatively. Interestingly, where a similar-to-me perception existed, managers rated females slightly higher than males; where dissimilarity was perceived, males and females were rated the same, namely, low.

Likewise, Adams, Rice, and Instone (1984) found no evidence of sex-biased ratings. Male and female military academy cadets were judged the same by both their subordinates and their supervisors in field settings. The authors offered two reasons for this finding. First, sex-role stereotyping wanes over time if people observe directly the long-term performance of women. Second, training workshops had been conducted on ways to eliminate sexism.

These studies support Landy and Farr's (1980) literature review showing that rater sex does not have a consistent effect on appraisals, especially if the rater is trained and behaviorally based appraisal scales are used. Peters et al., (1984) obtained a main effect for sex of ratee, but it accounted for less than 1 percent of the variance in the ratings. Females were rated slightly, albeit significantly, higher than males. As those authors noted: "One is hard pressed to argue for the unfair treatment of women on managerial performance evaluation" (p. 352). Six subsequent field studies have shown that the effect of gender on performance appraisal is either nonexistent (Griffeth & Bedeian, 1989; McFarlane Shore & Thornton, 1986; Simpson, McCarrey & Edwards, 1987), or of very small magnitude (Greenhaus, Parasuraman & Wormley, 1990; Pulakos et al., 1989; Sackett, DuBois & Wiggins Noe, 1991).

Rather than focus on the relatively vague variable of sex typing, Trempe, Rigny, and Haccoun (1985) reasoned that gender may be a proxy variable that masks a number of other important variables. In a field study involving French Canadians, they showed that subordinates were less concerned with the gender of the supervisor and more with the influence the supervisor can exert over higher-level managers. One implication of this study is to train women how to exercise such influence.

In a study involving a police department, Wendelken and Inn (1981) found significant effects for ratee race, past performance, rater race, and a ratee-rater interaction. But all of these sources combined accounted for no more than 4 percent of the total variance in performance ratings. Fowler (1985) showed that findings of this low magnitude should be considered trivial because psychological variables, in general, share on the average about 4 to 5 percent common variance.

With regard to race, Kraiger and Ford (1985) performed a meta-analysis that showed that both white and black raters give significantly higher ratings to members of their own race than to other races. But again, the variance accounted for was statistically significant but practically minuscule. With regard to these trivial differences, the authors concluded that "no firm conclusions can be reached regarding the extent to which the results found are due to rater bias or ratee performance" (p. 62).

Subsequent research showed that the effect of race accounted for less than 1 percent of the variance in performance rating in one study (Pulakos et al., 1989), 3 percent of the variance in performance ratings in a second study (Waldman & Avolio, 1991) and 4 percent of the variance in job performance evaluations in a third study (Greenhaus, Parasuraman & Wormley, 1990). Waldman and Avolio (1991) found that when the effect of ability, education, and job experience were controlled, race of ratee did not contribute to the prediction of performance ratings. In a meta-analysis of two large data sets, Sackett and Dubois (1991) failed to find support for Kraiger and Ford's conclusion that black raters tend to rate blacks higher than they rate whites.

As for the influence of age, Cleveland and Landy (1981) studied the effect of rater and ratee age on the appraisals of exempt managers; they then replicated their findings with a second sample. No influence of rater and ratee age was found regarding six of eight performance criteria. Where the influence of age was found, it accounted for only 1 to 4 percent of the variance in the appraisal ratings.

In summary, it would appear that when employees make their work visible to appraisers, when appraisers and appraisees together clarify objectives and task responsibilities, and when the appraiser uses behaviorally based appraisal scales, ratee characteristics, such as age, race, and sex, have a negligible effect on the resulting performance appraisal.

Training Approaches to Increase Accurate Appraisals

For years, psychologists have stressed the importance of providing training to improve objectivity and accuracy in evaluating an employee's performance. But only recently have training programs for reducing rater errors appeared. Training is necessary for minimizing scotomas or cognitive schemata that interfere with an appraiser's ability to make an accurate or valid appraisal.

Levine and Butler (1952) made one of the first known attempts to improve supervisors' rating practices. They worked with twenty-nine supervisors in a large manufacturing plant in which the supervisors overrated those working in the higher job grades and underrated those in the lower grades. These evaluations were unfair because the supervisors were obviously not rating the individual's performance as much as they were the job that the individual held. Consequently, those supervisors in the control condition were given no training or information. Supervisors in a second group were given a detailed lecture on the theory and technique of performance ratings. The lecturer explained to the supervisors the problem caused by their previous ratings and what each supervisor needed to do to correct the problem. In the discussion group the supervisors met to discuss the nature of the problem and how it could be solved. The discussion leader merely acted as a moderator, avoiding interjection of his own opinions. After generating a number of ideas, the group arrived at one solution acceptable to all, namely, to focus solely on the extent to which the person is fulfilling the requirements of the job.

The results showed that the lecture method had practically no influence on changing the supervisor's method of rating. The same was true for the control group, which had received no training. Only the group discussion method, in which the members participated in arriving at solutions to the problem, was successful in overcoming the rating errors.

Two limitations of this study were that it dealt with only one rating error, and the effects of the training were not assessed over time. Nevertheless, a major conclusion of this research was that *knowledge alone* (i.e., lecturing) *is not sufficient to change rating behavior.*

Similarly, in a university setting Wexley, Sanders, and Yukl (1973) found that warning individuals to recognize and avoid contrast effects did not reduce this error. Only an intensive workshop resulted in a behavior change. The workshop was based on psychological principles of learning—active participation, knowledge of results or feedback, and practice. Specifically, the workshop gave trainees a chance to practice observing and rating videotaped individuals. In addition, the trainees were given immediate feedback regarding the accuracy of their ratings.

A review of the literature by Spool (1978) indicated that the majority of the approaches to reducing rating errors suffer from one or more methodological problems. For example, many training programs do *not* give trainees an opportunity to practice the skills learned; nor do they provide them with feedback on how well they are performing (Bernardin, 1978; Bernardin & Walter, 1977). Other studies failed to include a control group (Borman, 1975), and some did not evaluate the effects of training at all (Burnaska, 1976).

Worse, many training programs have taught trainees inappropriate behaviors. For example, in the training programs developed by Bernardin (1978), trainees are shown rating distributions such as those shown in Table 6.1. He told the trainees that the ratings provided by Rater 1 probably contain halo error, whereas those provided by Rater 2 probably do not. Explicit in this training was that certain rating distributions were desirable. As another example, skewed distributions were said to be an indication of leniency error, and raters were encouraged to conform more closely to a normal distribution across ratees. This training was inappropriate because it taught raters to use the entire range of the scale when such advice may be unwarranted and to give low rather than high ratings (Bernardin & Pence, 1980). This training focuses the appraiser's attention on the distribution of ratings rather than on how well the employee performed the job. It is therefore not surprising that rater reliability and accuracy (validity) do not improve as a result of this approach to training.

Table 6.1
Rating Distributions on Performance Criteria

Rater/	Technical Ability	Human Relations	Organizational Commitment	Safety	Overall
1	5	6	5	5	5
2	5	3	6	3	4

Bernardin and his colleagues (Bernardin & Buckley, 1981; Bernardin & Pence, 1980) therefore concluded correctly that rater training programs, if they are to be effective, should concentrate on enhancing the accuracy of ratings through discussion of the multidimensionality of work performance, the importance of recording objectively what is seen, and the development of specific examples of effective and ineffective employees. This is an advantage of using BOS, an approach that specifies standards of what is meant by effective/ineffective performance for the observer. Finally, Bernardin & Buckley (1981) concluded that only training programs similar to that used by Wexley, Sanders, and Yukl (1973) are likely to be effective in improving rating accuracy.

On the basis of Wexley's earlier work in laboratory settings, Latham, Wexley, and Pursell (1975) developed a performance training program to help people minimize rating errors when observing and evaluating others. In addition, they developed a group discussion method similar to that used by Levine and Butler. Both methods were selected because each one had previously been effective in reducing at least one type of rating error. They have subsequently turned out to be the only two programs that have been shown to systematically reduce rating errors and increase rating accuracy in organizational settings. In fact, they have been described as "the most advanced rater training programs related to rating job performance" (Borman, 1979, p. 412).

In a study to evaluate the effectiveness of this training program, sixty personnel people and line managers were randomly assigned to one of three conditions: a workshop, a group discussion, or a control group that was not to receive training until it was certain that at least one of the two training methods could attain the objectives for which it was designed, namely, to reduce rating errors. The training required six to eight hours of instruction, depending on the amount of discussion generated among the trainees. Note the marked contrast with previous training programs, which lasted from five minutes to an hour (e.g., Bernardin, 1978; Bernardin & Walter, 1977) and did not bring about a lasting behavioral change.

The workshop consisted of exercises showing videotapes of job candidates being evaluated. The trainees gave a rating on a 9-point scale according to how they thought the manager in the videotape rated the candidate; they also rated the candidate. Group discussions concerning the reasons for each trainee's rating of the job candidate followed. In this way the trainees had an opportunity to *observe* other managers making errors, to *actively participate* in discovering the degree to which they were or were not prone to making the error, to receive *knowledge of results* regarding their own rating behavior, and to *practice* job-related tasks to reduce the errors that they were making. The relationship between the training content and the actual job was similar in principle so as to facilitate *transfer of learning* back to the job.

The first exercise focused on the similar-to-me error. The trainees were given a job description and a list of the job requirements for a loan officer's position. They were then shown a videotape of an interview with a below-average individual. The content of the interview revealed a strong attitudinal and biographical similarity between the manager and the applicant. Relatively little job-related information from this below-average applicant was elicited by the manager. When the tape ended, the trainees were asked to give two ratings in response to two questions: (1) How would you rate the applicant? (2) How do you think the manager rated the applicant? Their ratings were then discussed in relation to the similar-to-me effect. The trainees discussed possible ways of minimizing this error in performance appraisal situations. Typical of the many solutions brainstormed by the trainees for minimizing this error in performance appraisals are the following:

1. Establish the standards of performance expected on all jobs before rating employees.
2. Make certain that all criteria on which employees are evaluated are clearly job related.
3. Rate employees solely in relation to the job responsibilities, not in terms of how similar they are to oneself.
4. Have employees evaluated by multiple raters with different backgrounds and attitudes from one another.

The second exercise focused on the halo error. The trainees were again shown a videotaped situation and then rated how they and the manager on the tape would rate an individual who was outstanding in only one area of the job.

The trainees were again asked to brainstorm solutions to halo error in performance evaluation settings. The solutions suggested most frequently by the workshop participants are as follows:

1. Do not listen to comments about a person until you have made your own evaluation.

2. When an individual is to be evaluated by multiple raters, be certain that the raters assign their ratings independently; group discussion about the employee should come after everyone has had an opportunity to observe and evaluate the individual.

3. Rate the individual solely on the behavioral items that define a given criterion (e.g., safety). Recognize that different performance measures are not always related. A person can do well on one criterion and perform poorly on another (e.g., a professor may be a good researcher and a poor teacher).

The third exercise dealt with contrast errors. The trainees were given a job description and a list of the job requirements for an accountant's job. Trainees were then given a resume of a highly qualified applicant and asked to make a rating. The procedure was repeated with a second highly qualified applicant and then with an average applicant. The fact that evaluations of job applicants can be affected by the suitability of immediately preceding applicants and that subordinates are often evaluated in comparison to other subordinates rather than on established standards was discussed. The necessity of basing ratings on predetermined job standards was then emphasized.

Solutions to the contrast error are:

1. Appraise a large number of people at the same time; the error is more frequent when only a few individuals are interviewed or appraised.

2. Base your performance evaluations on specific *predetermined* job requirements or standards.

3. Do not rate people in any particular order (i.e., don't rate the best or the worst people first).

4. Rate people on the extent to which they fulfill the requirements of the job; compare people after, not

before, an evaluation. For example, Kim received an A in Algebra while Pat received a B. Kim's score was compared with Pat's after each test was graded in accordance with predefined standards, namely, the answer key. The two students were not rated on a curve relative to each other.

5. Avoid appraisal scales with vague benchmarks, such as "excellent," "above average," "average," and so on. Use scales on which one merely records the frequency with which a behavior has been observed or on which the benchmarks themselves are defined behaviorally.

The final exercise was a demonstration of the effects of *first impression.* The trainees were given a job description and a listing of the specific job requirements for an insurance rater and were then shown a videotape of an interview, which began with the applicant presenting a poor impression by her answers, actions, and appearance. The remainder of the interview showed that the applicant was acceptable for the job; however, the interviewer continued to act according to the initial impressions. Again, the trainees gave two types of ratings—their ratings of the applicant and ratings they thought the interviewer made. The trainees discussed their individual ratings, as well as ways to reduce the rating error in the performance appraisal. Among the solutions mentioned by the trainees were:

1. Reserve all judgments about an employee until the end of the time period for which the appraisal is scheduled.

2. Be a note taker rather than an evaluator during the interval between performance appraisals. Ideally, supervisors should record daily a subordinate's behaviors that they observed lead to adequate or inadequate performance on job assignments. The incidents should be reviewed later by the manager when it is time to assign ratings. Read the incidents in an order other than the recorded sequence. For example, first read the incidents that occurred during the middle of the appraisal period, then read those that occurred toward the beginning of the appraisal period. The recording of incidents should be done regardless of whether BOS or BES are used. The advantage of using BOS is that

when the incidents have not been recorded daily, the items on the BOS can facilitate recall of incidents.

The final exercise dealt with positive and negative leniency. Again, raters were trained to record exactly what they saw and to compare what they recorded with critical job behaviors/standards required in a job description or contained in the appraisal instrument.

In the group-discussion method, each error was defined by the trainer. An example of each error was given in the context of a performance appraisal, a selection interview, and an off-the-job situation. This procedure was followed to ensure that the trainees thoroughly understood the error. The trainees were then divided into groups to discuss their personal experiences in these three situations. Then the trainees generated solutions to the problem. These solutions were similar to those given in the workshop.

The advantage of the group-discussion procedure over the workshop method was that it was less formal. Thus the trainees could be more relaxed. In addition, the expense of preparing the videotapes and renting equipment was not necessary.

The disadvantage of the group-discussion method was that the trainees did not have an opportunity to experience the errors or to practice solutions to the errors. Thus they were able to obtain knowledge from the trainer and from one another about their understanding of the problem but not about their own specific behavior with regard to the problem. Note that in neither the workshop nor the group discussion were examples given of good/bad rating distributions or intercorrelations among ratings. Instead, training focused solely on the necessity for recording exactly what was said or done by the person on the videotape so as to be able to justify a given rating in terms of the job description/responsibilities the trainees received prior to viewing the videotape.

Training Results and Implications

A critical limitation of most training programs is that no attempts are made to assess their long-term effectiveness. That is, managers may know that the training program was or was not effective in modifying an individual's behavior immediately after training; however, they have no measure of its effectiveness once the person has returned to the job. There is a danger that many concepts and principles taught in training are forgotten or discarded soon after the trainee returns to the daily pressures of the job. For this reason the long-term effects of training programs must be evaluated to see if they bring about a relatively permanent change in trainee behavior.

The results regarding a change in rating behavior immediately after training were disappointing. In general, the trainees in the two training conditions continued to make rating errors, as did the trainees in the control group. Rating errors, as previously noted, are well-established habits that are highly resistant to change.

The results of the two training programs were evaluated again six months after training on the basis of two criteria: reaction measures and behavioral samples. The reaction measures consisted of the trainees' opinion on a 9-point rating scale of the extent to which they believed that they benefited from the program after they returned to their jobs. The mean ratings given to the workshop and the group-discussion methods were 8.8 and 6.3, respectively.

These results were surprising in that the researchers had predicted that the greater freedom in the group-discussion method to participate in informal evaluations of their own and their peers' understanding of each rating error would result in trainees being more satisfied with the training than those in a highly structured workshop. Furthermore, it was felt that the workshop trainees might become embarrassed and defensive after committing rating errors in the presence of fellow trainees.

The actual results, however, are congruent with studies done in other settings that show that participation in itself is not always desirable. For example, Hillery and Wexley (1974) compared trainee satisfaction in a program that permitted trainees a great deal of participation in evaluating their own performance versus one in which they were allowed comparatively little participation. Results of the study indicate that in a training setting, people generally want to be told how they are doing; employee participation in this situation is not highly valued.

The second group of measures for assessing the effectiveness of the two training programs were behavioral samples. Trainees, as well as the people in the control group, were given the requirements for a specific job and then shown videotapes, which none of them had previously seen, of a job candidate being interviewed for that job. The trainees were instructed to rate each applicant as to suitability for the job. Ratings were to be made solely on the basis of what each individual actually said or did.

The results showed that the control group committed the similar-to-me, halo, and contrast-effects errors; the group-discussion trainees committed only one error—a sizable recency, or last-impression, error. The trainees in the workshop did not commit any rating errors. It would appear that managers need an opportunity (e.g., six months) to practice on the job the skills that are taught in these training programs before the beneficial effects of the training become evident.

That the workshop appears to be more effective than the group-discussion method in eliminating rating errors could be a result of one or more factors. First, the trainees in the group discussion were able to obtain *knowledge of results* from the trainer and from one another about their personal understanding of the errors and their solutions, but unlike the trainees in the workshop, they did not receive feedback about their own specific behavior in committing an error.

Second, the trainees in the workshop recorded that the highly structured format of their program made them feel that the time taken away from their jobs was being used wisely, which was not always the case with the trainees in the group discussion. Although this latter group was given greater freedom to participate in the structuring of the training content, the participants wanted more feedback from the trainer than from one another. Consequently, some of them expressed a lack of interest in the program.

The primary disadvantage of the workshop approach is that it is costly and time consuming to develop. On the other hand, once the materials are developed, the training of the trainers is relatively easy compared to the training required for the group-discussion leaders, because a major part of the workshop program includes the use of the videotapes. In light of the rating errors eliminated and trainees' reaction to the program, a workshop procedure would appear to be the more effective training approach. When the cost and time for developing a structured training program are prohibitive, the group-discussion method appears to be a beneficial alternative technique for minimizing these errors.

Replication of Training Effectiveness

The results of the workshop approach were repeated by Bernardin and Buckley (1981) in what they called frame-of-reference training (FOR). This training is effective because it creates a common frame of reference, or cognitive schemata, of effective and ineffective performance for those who rate on the basis of idiosyncratic standards (Bernardin & Beatty, 1984). The training program culminates with the trainee developing behaviorally based scales as a means of overcoming rating errors. A field test of FOR showed an increase in interobserver agreement (Bernardin, 1980).

Further Studies on Rater Training

Psychologists have spent years attempting to develop the ideal rating scale that would be resistant to rating errors. Suggestions have ranged from using a 2-point scale to a 22-point scale, using BOS and BES, or a ranking system versus a forced-choice format in which the rater has to select from equally favorable and unfavorable alternative statements in describing an individual. But comparatively little has been accomplished toward solving the problem of rating errors. Why? Because, as we have pointed out, people must be *trained* to minimize these errors. Rating errors are well-entrenched habits that are difficult to break.

A study by Fay and Latham (1982) found that rating errors are made regardless of whether BOS, BES, or trait scales are used. Once raters are properly trained, however, the rating format or scale is important for reducing rating errors.

For example, there was no difference between BOS and BES with regard to rating errors after the raters had received the workshop training described earlier in this chapter. Both BOS and BES were superior in this regard to trait scales. This finding contradicts the conclusions of Borman (1979) and Warmke and Billings (1979) regarding the effectiveness of the training procedures described in this system.

As another example, using the same structured videotaped program as Latham, Wexley, and Pursell (1975), Borman (1979) found that training had little effect on rating errors. Warmke and Billings reached the same conclusion after using the group-discussion approach to training. Although different trainers and different rating formats were used in those three studies, the most parsimonious explanation for the differences in conclusions is based on the motivation level of the subjects and the time devoted to training. Where training has been shown to be effective, the trainees were managers (Latham, Wexley & Pursell, 1975), foremen (Pursell, Dossett & Latham, 1980), or business students (Fay & Latham, 1982). They had the knowledge or experience prior to receiving training to appreciate the relevance of the program to them personally. The subjects in Borman's study, drawn primarily from a liberal arts college, may not have seen the necessity of acquiring the knowledge and principles taught during training. Moreover, these liberal arts students, unlike the managers, supervisors, and business students in the previous studies, did not appear to understand some of the performance dimensions on which they were to rate people (Borman, 1979).

A second factor that may explain the differences in conclusions is training time. It took Wexley, Sanders, and Yukl (1973) two hours to eliminate only one rating error. Latham, Wexley, and Pursell (1975) exposed the trainees to six to eight hours of training to minimize four rating errors. In the Fay and Latham (1982) study the trainees received four hours of training to reduce three rating errors.

In the two studies in which training was not found to be effective, the trainees received only two to three hours of training (Warmke & Billings, 1979; Borman, 1979, respectively) to reduce three to four rating errors (Borman, 1979; Warmke & Billings, 1979, respectively). The additional hours of training that trainees received in studies in which training proved to be effective may have been critical for allowing the trainees to practice those skills necessary to minimize these different rating errors.

A third explanation for the discrepancy in findings on the value of this type of training may be that Borman did not spend sufficient time teaching the trainees to focus on behavioral observation skills. Similarly, Warmke and Billings reported difficulty in keeping the discussion of their trainees on the subject matter. In the studies in which the training has proved effective, the one question that is asked over and over again is: "What did the individual *do* to deserve the rating that you made?" The trainer stresses again and again the necessity of focusing on observable job behavior and ignoring all non-job-related factors so as to maximize productivity and minimize legal challenges to these decisions. This emphasis on productivity and legal challenges is well accepted by business students, foremen, and managers; it has been greeted with derision by people in our introductory psychology classes, perhaps because they are similar in attitude to the people trained by Borman.

A final explanation was reported by Bernardin and Pence (1980). These two authors suggest that both Borman and Warmke and Billings made the mistake of including in their training program the teaching of inappropriate response sets discussed earlier (e.g., "never give one person the same rating on different criteria; use the entire scale in evaluating a person").

A limitation of the Latham, Wexley, and Pursell (1975), Borman (1979), and Fay and Latham (1980) studies is that all three were conducted in a laboratory setting or involved managers using simulated criterion measures. A fourth study of the effectiveness of the structured videotape-based training was conducted in the field (Pursell, Dossett & Latham, 1980). The purpose of that study was to validate a selection system for hiring electricians.

For years, psychologists have worked on the development of reliable and valid selection systems (e.g., reference checks, interviews, weighted application blanks, aptitude tests, personality inventories). In many instances the results have proved to be reliable but not valid. Were the selection tests not good? Not necessarily. The tests may have been quite good; rather, the criterion against which they were evaluated may have been quite poor. In general, psychologists have ignored the criterion problem (Ronan & Prien, 1971).[3]

Pursell, Dossett, and Latham (1980) correlated the results of a selection battery with performance appraisals of journeyman electricians. The relationship was essentially zero. Rather than concluding that the tests were poor and going through the costly and time-consuming procedure of choosing or developing new tests plus retesting the applicants, the researchers concluded, on the basis of their job analysis, that both the selection and

---

3. The criterion problem refers to the failure to take into account the reliability of performance measures, reliability in the observation of performance, the multidimensionality of performance, and situational factors affecting performance. Traditionally, psychologists have focused primarily on the predictor side of the predictor-criterion equation. In this particular study the problem had to do with the observation/recording of performance.

the performance appraisal instruments were satisfactory. The problem, they believed, was with the supervisors who used the appraisal instrument. The researchers felt that the performance ratings were contaminated by rating errors.

Consequently, the supervisors, who were unaware of the employee test scores or that the validation study was a failure, received the training workshop described by Latham, Wexley, and Pursell (1975). They were then asked to reevaluate the employees' performance. This time four of the five test scores correlated with the performance measures. The result was a validated selection process that predicted employee performance. Thus it would appear that the training described in this chapter not only reduces rater bias but also improves rater accuracy or validity.

In a different approach to rater training, Hedge and Kavanagh (1988) applied decision-making principles based on cognitive information processing to develop a workshop training program that incorporated the learning principles contained in the Latham, Wexley, and Pursell (1975) approach. In addition to a control group, two other training programs were used. The first was a lecture-discussion format aimed at reducing the rating effects of halo, leniency, range restriction, and similar-to-me errors. The final training program, aimed at improving observational skills of trainees, was based on procedures from both the FOR and workshop approaches. The results showed the traditional lecture reduced classic rating errors but had a detrimental effect on rating accuracy, whereas both observer and decision-making training increased rating accuracy. The authors concluded that this was due to the inclusion of elements from the workshop training developed by Latham, Wexley, and Pursell (1975).

Closing Remarks

A major problem that must be overcome in developing measures of a person's job performance is the elimination of bias in the observation and appraisal of behavior (Ronan & Prien, 1966, 1971). Observer bias in performance appraisals can be attributed largely to well-known rating errors, such as first impressions, halo, similar-to-me, and contrast effects. Rating errors are faulty judgments that occur in a systematic manner when an individual observes and evaluates another. They lie at the core of decisions that adversely affect women and minorities. In order to minimize the occurrence of rating errors and costly litigation battles, the observer must be trained. For this reason, organizations, regardless of the appraisal instrument that they use, are well advised to expose people who evaluate employees to a training program to minimize rating errors.

The probability that a training program will bring about a relatively permanent change in behavior can be estimated prior to training by looking at three factors: (1) the extent to which the trainees *actively* participate in applying the principles during the training; (2) the degree to which they receive knowledge of results about the extent to which they are performing the skills correctly; and (3) the opportunity they are given to practice the new skills.

Training programs designed to reduce rating errors must refrain from telling trainees: "Don't give too many high ratings; don't rate a person high or low on all factors." Trainees must be taught the necessity of defining effective/ineffective employee behavior on the basis of a job analysis. They must record the frequency with which they see an employee engage in these behaviors. This is the advantage of using BOS; such scales define explicitly what the observer is to look for on the part of an employee. The observer's task is reduced to that of a recorder.

Training alone, however, is not sufficient for bringing about reliable and valid appraisals. It is highly unlikely that the extinction of the behaviors acquired during training is due to memory decay or faulty cognitive categorization procedures. The study of appraiser affect in addition to cognition is needed if training is to bring about a relatively permanent increase in rating accuracy. A study on affect and perceived or anticipated outcomes in terms of their effect on such cognitive variables as self-efficacy (the conviction that I can indeed make accurate appraisals) and outcome expectations (my beliefs regarding what will occur as a result of my making accurate appraisals) is likely to provide a parsimonious explanation for why the positive effects from training raters may sometimes be short-lived. Raters may want to avoid the ramifications of a deserved but harsh appraisal of a subordinate. As Longenecker, Sims, and Gioia (1987) noted, accuracy is not the primary concern of an executive in appraising subordinates. Their results showed that the primary concern of executives is how best to use the appraisal process to motivate and reward subordinates. Managers in that study made it clear that they would not allow appraisal accuracy to cause problems for themselves and that they used the appraisal process to their own advantage. The authors concluded that the formal appraisal process is in fact a political one and that few appraisals are made without some political consideration. Thus "counseling in the legal ramifications of appraisal should become part of executive training" (p. 191). The legal ramifications of performance appraisal were discussed in Chapter 2. Ways of motivating and rewarding employees through performance appraisal is the subject of the next chapter.

7

Goal Setting in Leadership and Motivation

Introduction

Motivating employees through performance appraisal involves five basic steps. First, a manager, supervisor, or team leader must determine what the employee is required to do on the job—the critical aspects of effective job performance. That is why BOS developed from a systematic job analysis are so useful; they identify the behaviors that employees must follow to fulfill the requirements of the job.

Second, an appraiser must be able to recognize effective performance when it is demonstrated. Inaccurate appraisals can lead employees to discouragement and apathy. So care must be taken to select observers who are aware of the aims and objectives of an employee's job, who frequently observe the employee on the job, and who are capable of discerning competent performance. Further, training must be given to ensure that the observations are recorded accurately.

Third, the appraisal process must focus on the setting of specific performance goals. Specific goals that are difficult but attainable have been shown to consistently lead to effective performance.

Fourth, steps must be taken to ensure that the perceived consequences of goal attainment are positive; otherwise, the goals will not be accepted. If the outcome expectancies regarding goal attainment are positive, the probability is high that the person will be truly committed to attaining the goal.

Finally, employees must be allowed to participate in solving problems preventing goal attainment that are of concern to both them and their supervisors. In this way effective work teams are formed; groups that people find rewarding because they approve of the group goals tend to be cohesive (Levine & Moreland, 1990).

Successful performance appraisal consists of both a *system* of rules, regulations, procedures, and training necessary for conducting effective appraisals and a *process* designed to instill the desire for continuously improving one's performance. The purpose of this chapter is to discuss applicable principles of leadership and motivation underlying the performance appraisal process.

Goal-Setting Theory

Goal setting has received a great deal of attention in the scientific literature within the past twenty-five years because it underlies motivation theories (Locke & Latham, 1990). Nevertheless, many people in industry have downplayed its importance because they believe that almost everyone sets goals. This assumption is incorrect in that the concepts underlying goal setting are not systematically applied throughout most organizations. Whenever one group of employees is required to have specific goals, group members invariably increase their productivity substantially over that of groups who do not set goals. This is true regardless of whether the employees are engineers and scientists (Latham, Mitchell & Dossett, 1978), typists (Dossett, Latham & Mitchell, 1979), or loggers (Latham & Yukl, 1975).

In a series of laboratory experiments (Locke, 1968) individuals were assigned different types of goals on a variety of simple tasks (e.g., addition, brainstorming ideas, assembling toys). It was found repeatedly that individuals who were assigned *difficult* goals performed better than individuals who were assigned moderate or easy goals. Furthermore, individuals who had *specific* goals that were challenging outperformed individuals who were merely told to try to do their best. Finally, it was found that incentives, such as praise, feedback, participation, and money, led to an improvement in performance only if they caused individuals to set and commit to attain specific difficult goals.

There are three related reasons why goal setting affects performance. Primarily, the setting of goals has a directive effect on what people think and do. Goals focus activity. Simultaneously, goals regulate energy expenditure, since people typically put forth effort in proportion to the difficulty of the goal, given that the goal is accepted. Finally, difficult goals lead to more persistence (which can be viewed as directed effort over time) than do easy goals. These three reasons—direction (choice), effort, and persistence are the three central aspects of the goal-setting process.

Application of Goal Setting

Superordinate Goals

The performance appraisal process will be valued up and down the organizational hierarchy to the extent that it is aligned directly with the organization's superordinate goal—its vision. The development of a vision that inspires people is a key variable that differentiates effective from ineffective leaders (Locke et al., 1991).

Although the development of a vision is more an art than a science, there do appear to be common underlying factors that differentiate effective from ineffective visions. For example, an effective vision galvanizes people, giving them a cause to rally around. It conveys clearly and forcefully that what they are doing is worthwhile, meaningful, and contributing to a common good.

Some political leaders who were adept at developing visions that inspired people were Winston Churchill, John F. Kennedy, and Martin Luther King. As bombs dropped on London during World War II, Churchill intoned that in 1000 years people will read with pride that this was indeed England's finest hour. He exclaimed that never had so few done so much for so many. He promised that England would fight the enemy on the land, England would fight them on the beaches.... Kennedy's inaugural address implored Americans to ask not what their country could do for them but rather what they could do for their country. Martin Luther King eloquently expressed a dream that one day little black children and little white children would walk hand in hand to school together.

For decades we in the Western hemisphere have wondered why third-world countries embraced communism. One reason is the power of a cogent vision: "Redistribute wealth to the needy." To the extent that people were unable to provide shelter for their families and were suffering from malnourishment, this vision might provide them with a cause that would rally them to support it wholeheartedly. In industry Lee Iaccoca has been effective in rallying North American employees around nationalistic themes to get consumers to buy North American products, especially automobiles, and to beat the Japanese in terms of the quality of goods and services produced.

It would be wrong, however, to conclude that an effective vision or superordinate goal is formulated only by the titans of countries, movements, or companies. Effective visions are often generated "bottom up." They can be derived from asking employees two questions: What is our reason for existing? Who would miss us if we were gone? The answers are usually expressed in words that are loaded with meaning to the employee. These expressions contrast sharply with the trite remarks that afflict many top-down vision statements.

In the early 1980s, for example, Scott Paper Company's corporate headquarters in Philadelphia decided to sell its Timberlands division in the northwestern United States. Ron Stoppler, a middle-level manager of Timberlands, called his people together to announce that the rumors they had been hearing about a possible sale were true.

Did productivity and morale soar or plummet as a result of this announcement? The answer is that both increased dramatically as measured by profits and attitude surveys. Stoppler had included a vision, or superordinate goal, in his announcement of the sale. "We will send Philadelphia a message—we will make them choke." But before discussing the ramifications of this vision, a note of caution about superordinate goals needs to be given.

Visions are often no more than rhetoric. Worse, they raise employee expectations only to have them dashed. Instead of energizing people, they demoralize them because people feel betrayed. Cynicism is often the result of frustrated idealism. Thus in order for a superordinate goal to motivate employees, it must be accompanied by specific challenging goals.

Specific Challenging Goals

The purpose of goal setting is to make the superordinate goal concrete. Goals move the vision from a dream to the action steps that must be taken to move toward it. Thus the setting of specific goals makes clear what people will have to start doing, continue doing, or stop doing in order to move reality closer to the vision. Consequently, Churchill set specific goals for involving the United States in World War II; JFK established the Peace Corps; King and his supporters worked actively for the passage of Title VII of the 1964 Civil Rights Act; Iaccoca set goals about the quality of cars to be built by Chrysler Corporation.

Stoppler asked the unionized loggers to express his vision in a palatable fashion. It was the union that subsequently had its members' shirts emblazoned with the superordinate goal, "Excellence our standard; perfection our goal." Together, Stoppler and the union then set specific challenging goals for production, quality, and costs in order to become so efficient and effective that either Philadelphia would rescind the decision to sell Timberlands or the employees would become so valuable that the new buyer would hire them to manage the land.

Difficult but attainable goals are motivating because they provide people with a sense of challenge, recognition, and accomplishment through working toward their attainment. Thus loggers who were given tallymeters to keep count of the number of trees cut down in relation to the goals that were set (Latham & Kinne, 1974) and truck drivers who kept count of the number of trips to the mill from the woods, experienced the same feelings of accomplishment (Latham & Baldes, 1975) as those who keep count of the number of strokes in a game of golf. Tracking one's performance in relation to a goal can turn an otherwise meaningless activity into a challenging game.

The power of goals that are specific and challenging is that they focus effort and instill persistence. Therefore, the goals should be approximately three to seven in number. If too many goals are set, the lengthy list is likely to disappear into one's desk drawer. In short, there will be no goal commitment.

Several investigators have examined the benefit of involving the employees in setting specific performance goals. A study at General Electric examined the results of allowing middle-level managers to participate in setting specific performance goals during their performance appraisal (Meyer, Kay & French,

1965). Meyer found that goals were attained more often when the employee had a say in them than when they were assigned by a supervisor. However, this was true only for employees with a supervisor whose managerial style throughout the year encouraged employee participation in decision making. Employees with a supervisor who did not normally encourage participation performed better when the goals were assigned to them. Meyer concluded that the way a goal is set is not as important as it is to set a specific challenging goal.

The Weyerhaeuser Company examined the benefits of involving engineers and scientists in the setting of goals during the performance appraisal (Latham, Mitchell & Dossett, 1978). Using BOS, the company found that participation in goal setting resulted in higher goals being set than when the goals were assigned unilaterally by a supervisor. Interestingly, employee perceptions of goal difficulty were the same regardless of whether the goal was assigned or set participatively, even though they were truly more difficult in the latter condition. Consistent with goal-setting theory, individuals with challenging, participatively set goals performed significantly better than did individuals who were urged to do their best. Finally, as the theory states, giving employees specific feedback without setting specific goals on the basis of the feedback had no effect on their subsequent performance.

In a second study conducted at Weyerhaeuser, female clerical personnel were randomly assigned to participative, assigned, or do-your-best goal conditions on a clerical test (Dossett, Latham & Mitchell, 1979). With goal difficulty held constant, goal attainment in terms of test scores was higher in the assigned than the participative condition. The performance appraisal results of these same people on BOS showed that assigned goals resulted in higher performance and greater goal acceptance than did participatively set goals.

In reviewing these results, Likert (personal communication, August 1977) commented that when assigned goals have been effective, the supervisor has always behaved in a highly supportive manner. Three key aspects of modern organizational theory (Likert, 1967) are supportive relationships with employees, participative decision making, and goal setting.

Latham and Saari (1979b) tested this assumption in a laboratory setting; students were given a brainstorming task, and goal difficulty was held constant between the participative and assigned-goal-setting groups. The experimenter behaved in either a supportive or a hostile manner. Supportiveness led to higher goals being set than occurred when the experimenter was nonsupportive. The setting of specific goals led to higher performance than did urging people to do their best. Finally, participation increased performance by increasing the individual's understanding of how to attain the goals.

In summary, goal setting is effective because it clarifies exactly what is expected of an individual. Employees at Weyerhaeuser commented that by receiving a specific goal from the supervisor, they were able to determine what was expected of them. Moreover, the process of working for an explicit goal injects interest into the task; it provides challenge and meaning to a job. Through goal attainment, feelings of accomplishment and recognition (from self and/or supervisor) occur.

Goal Setting and MBO

The principles of effective goal setting are basic to most MBO programs. The primary difference between the thesis of this book and that of MBO advocates is that the latter emphasize the use of cost-related measures (e.g., number of sales) for performance appraisal purposes, whereas we argue for the use of behavioral measures for counseling and developing an employee. We have no objection to the use of MBO as a vehicle for planning the focus and effort of an organization, department, or individual for one to three years. Nor do we object to the inclusion of such objectives on the performance appraisal instrument. Cost-related objectives can clarify the context or situation in which the employee's behavior will be appraised. Rather, the BOS we advocate clarify how the employee is to behave when attempting to attain those objectives. We therefore agree with Kearney (1979) that the missing link in MBO is behavior.[1]

---

1. Campbell (1977) has made a similar argument about the use of cost-related measures of performance in the field of leadership. In fact, he cited the use of these measures as a major factor impeding the development of useful information in this area: "We should not be using 'objective' organizational measures of subordinate performance, such as the amount of productivity, total sales, etc. We should not be using summary indices of work group performance (e.g., total absenteeism). All of these measures that are determined by many factors besides the influence of a leader and, even in the best of all possible worlds, the leadership factor may account for only a small portion of the total variability in these criteria" (p. 233).

In general, there will be close agreement between the employee's performance and performance outcomes (e.g., costs, profits). As we have repeatedly stated, good cost-related outcomes generally come about because someone did something correctly. The purpose of BOS is to specify what it is the person did correctly. Where there is disagreement between the BOS scores and performance outcome measures, there are four possible explanations.

First, the BOS may not be comprehensive; hence the importance of a systematic job analysis. Second, BOS may be contaminated by rater errors, which is why the careful selection and training of raters are so important.

Third, the cost-related measures may be contaminated by judgmental errors. A problem inherent in MBO programs is that the employee is likely to get systematically more credit (or blame) than is deserved, because people are seen as more "causal" than they, in fact, are for performance outcomes (Feldman, 1979). Thus the appraiser is likely to overstate the contribution of the employee for any positive or negative outcomes.

This problem is especially troublesome when the employee belongs to a group not prevalent in the organization (e.g., women or minorities). To the extent that the supervisor is pleased or displeased with the cost-related outcomes, the probability increases that attributions of causality will be assigned incorrectly to the person rather than to the situation (Feldman, 1979). If the employee is well liked or highly disliked by the appraiser, biases in the causal attribution of behavior will benefit the liked employee and harm the disliked person. No one can dispute the number of products produced or sold. But one person will receive undeserved credit for good outcomes; the other person will receive undeserved blame for poor outcomes. The use of comprehensive BOS are helpful here because they alert the manager to look elsewhere for situational factors that may account for the good/bad outcomes when the BOS scores are incongruent with the outcome measures.

Finally, sometimes the BOS scores are low and the cost-related measures high because the employee is engaging in unethical behavior or in behavior that has at best a short-term positive effect on performance outcomes. For example, Likert (1967) has shown that highly autocratic managers who behave in a nonsupportive manner may achieve performance outcomes superior to those of managers who do not behave in this manner. The superiority is short lived as peers, subordinates, or clients respond adversely over time to such conduct.

Setting goals is not synonymous with setting standards. If people are measured on goal attainment, they may create ingenious ways to make easy goals look difficult so that their attainment is ensured, as are any concomitant rewards.

As an example, a manager was encouraged to set stretch goals regarding costs in the building of a new plant. After contractors over whom he had marginal control exceeded their budget, the manager did not receive his Christmas bonus and was penalized again in February at his annual performance review. Vowing never to make this mistake again, he has subsequently attained his easier goals year after year and has been promoted to Senior VP of Operations—but at what cost for the company or its stockholders? A focus on goal attainment can be a recipe for bringing about mediocrity.

A standard is a benchmark for assessing performance. An example of standards in educational settings is the grading system: 90 for an A, 80 for a B, 70 for a C). Treating a goal and a standard as synonymous can have the dysfunctional consequence of rewarding and penalizing the wrong people. For example, two students may have as goals getting an A and a C, respectively. The first student may receive an 85 and get a B+; the second student may get a 72 and get a C. If goal attainment were rewarded, only the second individual would be eligible. But if performance were rewarded, both individuals might be eligible.

Goal Commitment

A problem with setting specific challenging goals is finding ways to get employee commitment to them. Understanding a person's perceived consequences of an action, providing feedback systems, linking pay to performance, modeling desired behavior, being accessible, building a team, clarifying roles, measuring performance, and encouraging self-management are ways that leaders can encourage employee commitment to goals.

Perceived Consequences

Consequences affect behavior largely through their informative and incentive values (Bandura, 1986). That is, consequences affect behavior antecedently by creating expectations in the employee of similar outcomes on future occasions. Thus the likelihood of an employee's engaging in particular actions is increased by anticipated reward and reduced by anticipated punishment.

The principle of reinforcement refers to the consequences of behavior (Skinner, 1987). It can be broken down into four basic subprinciples when applied to performance appraisal. First, the reinforcer must be made contingent on the desired or appropriate behavior. If the presentation of a reward is not perceived to be a consequence of a given behavior, the behavior will not increase in frequency.

Second, in performance appraisal the employee must clearly perceive the relationship between the desired behavior and the reinforcer. This is critical if money is administered with the expectation that it will reinforce high performance. A few behavioral scientists (e.g., Herzberg, 1968) have reported that money does not motivate employees to increase their productivity. The reason is that the money was not made contingent on the employee's performance. Rather, money is often given as a function of the employee's hours on the job, tenure with the company, or negotiations on behalf of a union.

Third, the reinforcer must be administered soon after the desired behavior has occurred. Skinner (1987) contended that a reinforcer must be administered immediately after a desired behavior occurs if it is to increase the probability that the behavior will be repeated. But research involving human beings rather than rats and pigeons does not support this view. People are able to process and synthesize feedback information from sequences of events over periods of time regarding the conditions necessary for reinforcement, as well as the pattern and rate with which actions produce outcomes (Bandura, 1986). Nevertheless, it is true that to the extent that a reinforcer is delayed, its effectiveness is sometimes decreased. This occurs because an employee may not clearly see the connection between the reinforcer and the behavior. Even worse, delayed reinforcers may inadvertently reinforce inappropriate behaviors. For example, a new vice-president's performance in a start-up operation may initially be at a high level, which the senior-management group may attempt to reward with a salary increase. Unfortunately, the salary increase may not be approved until months later, by which time the vice-president's high level of performance may have diminished. When the salary increase finally occurs, the vice-president is, in effect, being reinforced for mediocre performance.

Fourth, the reinforcer must be a valued outcome for the employee. Thus if recognition for fasting for a cause is valued by an individual, food will not be a reinforcer, but attention from others may be effective in maintaining abstinence. Similarly, it has been found that employees sometimes set self-imposed limits on the amount of work they do, and anyone who tries to exceed the limit becomes a rate-buster in the eyes of coworkers. Here social factors may be far more important (reinforcing) to the employee than money. However, in organizations in which workers have initiated self-imposed limits, it is interesting to note that the money is almost always given after a considerable lapse of time since the occurrence of the desired behavior.

A straightforward approach that leaders can use to understand why an employee accepts or rejects a goal is depicted in Table 7.1. All the positive consequences that an employee receives as a result of engaging in a desired behavior (e.g., a mechanic working ten rather than six hours) can be listed in cell 1; all the aversive consequences or punishers for engaging in this desirable behavior (e.g., fatigue, arriving home late for dinner), in cell 2. These steps can be repeated for the perceived consequences of engaging in undesirable behavior. These steps can be discussed with the employees. This approach can provide a rational way for understanding why people behave the way they do. More importantly, it provides a basis for motivating them to do what you want them to do by indicating the consequences that need to be changed in order to change their behavior. The approach is straightforward and costs little; however, the cost of

Table 7.1
Goal Commitment

	Consequences	
	+	−
Desired Behavior	1	2
Undesirable Behavior	3	4

changing the consequences sometimes exceeds the benefits of changing the behavior. The advantage of this approach is that people can estimate the costs, knowing, with a high degree of certainty, that if the consequences are changed, the behavior will change.

This approach was used successfully by Emery Air Freight. Emery found that efficiency was reduced by 45 percent because people on airport loading docks shipped items in the wrong containers, at an annual cost to the company of more than $1,000,000. Rather than implementing a training program, Emery examined the positive consequences to the employee of loading containers properly. This analysis revealed that there were few, if any, consequences of any kind; moreover, most employees believed that they were performing efficiently.

Emery instituted a goal-setting program that required each employee to fill out a behavioral checklist similar to BOS. All employee improvements in performance were reinforced with praise by a supervisor, regardless of whether the goals were attained. Failure to attain a goal was reinforced by praise for honesty in reporting that failure. In this way behavior was shaped toward desired objectives through praise. Criticism and blame can lead to defensiveness, discouragement, and dishonest behavior on the part of employees. Dishonest behavior occurs when the honest behavior of reporting failure is punished; the dishonest behavior of exaggerating success is inadvertently praised.

Providing feedback about the consequences of behavior gives employees a feeling of task accomplishment because it lets them know how they are doing on the job. It increases acceptance of present goals and encourages the probability of setting more difficult goals. Feedback on performance is important because many employees only know how well they are getting along with their supervisor.

Feedback Systems

The keys to the design of effective feedback systems are three-fold (Locke & Latham, 1990). First, feedback must be based on behaviors over which the employee has control. Second, feedback must be provided on a frequent basis. Immediate feedback, as previously stated, is more effective than either delayed or infrequent feedback. Third, *specific goals* must be set in relation to the feedback.

The goal-setting program at Emery increased productivity from 45 percent to 90 percent *within one day*. The cost of the program was $5000—travel costs of $4900 for one person to travel from Emery's various facilities and $100 for developing BOS for providing feedback to the employee.

Pay Linked to Performance Appraisal

A recurring issue in the performance appraisal literature is whether money should be tied to performance. Is this an effective way of securing goal commitment? The arguments for linking money with performance include the following issues outlined by Lawler (1971) and Mobley (1974):

1. Linking money to a performance appraisal is a relatively objective and logical way to allocate financial rewards.

2. It establishes a performance-reward contingency for the employee. To the extent that pay is a valued reward, linking it, along with other desirable rewards (e.g., praise), to performance enhances goal commitment.

3. It helps ensure that compensation and appraisal decisions do not work at cross-purposes. Separating pay from performance can only raise questions among employees as to the importance of an appraisal and the equity of pay decisions.

4. Although praise from others is a powerful source of feedback, money tells employees how much they are truly valued by their organization.

5. Most managers want their pay to be based on performance (Andrews & Henry, 1963; Lawler, 1971).

There are, however, several arguments *against* linking pay to performance appraisals. Among the leading advocates of this position are Meyer (1975) and Deci (1972). These arguments are as follows:

1. Tying pay to performance appraisal may encourage people to avoid difficult goals, which is a problem with many MBO programs. As discussed earlier, this prob-

lem can be overcome by always evaluating performance rather than goal attainment.

2. It may fail to reflect total performance by emphasizing the measurable to the exclusion of more subjective, yet nonetheless important, aspects of the job. This argument poses a problem for MBO programs that emphasize cost-related measures, but the argument is not an issue with BOS that are content valid.

3. It may place undue emphasis on individual as opposed to team performance. But this problem is almost always overcome with content valid BOS that specify team-playing behaviors that are required of each employee (see the Appendix).

4. Installing an incentive plan for workers rather than managers is difficult because considerable effort is required to build a trusting relationship between management and workers. Many employees do not trust an organization to administer incentive schemes properly. But the issue of trust needs to be resolved regardless of whether pay is tied to performance. Team building is an excellent way of increasing trust and in fact has led to the development of effective incentive plans (Hinrichs, 1978), which in turn increases trust among supervisors and employees.

5. Tying pay to performance introduces conflict into the appraisal by making the appraiser both a judge and a counselor. However, this conflict role always exists in relationships between managers and employees. It is a naive employee who believes that management is not evaluating performance on an ongoing basis. It is even more naive for an employee to believe that during the appraisal the manager will suddenly stop being an evaluator and become a counselor only.

6. It is difficult to measure performance. But the advantage of BOS is that they are based on observable behavior and hence are measurable. Employee input is used as the raw data for developing BOS so that everyone understands and agrees on the performance measures. The appraiser is trained to minimize rating

"Barkley, I perceive my role in this institution not as a judge but merely as an observer and recorder. I have observed you to be a prize boob and have so recorded it."

errors so that objectivity is increased and observer bias is decreased. This helps to increase trust and reduce conflict between the supervisor and employee.

7. Large amounts of money must be given to the good performers if employees are to place a high value on good performance and the raises to which it leads. This is true; but performance should and must be rewarded if productivity is to improve significantly.

8. Money can diminish interest in a task. It detracts from the feeling of doing a job well for its own sake. This

argument has little empirical support for it. As Bandura (1986) noted, monetary incentives can increase performance, decrease performance, or have no effect whatsoever, depending on the way in which the rewards are used and the activities involved.

For example, decreases in performance may reflect employee reactions to how the incentives are presented rather than to the incentives themselves. Incentives can be used in a coercive manner: "Sam, you will not receive the bonus unless you do . . . do you hear me!" Coercive contingencies may evoke oppositional behavior. Incentives can also be presented in a supportive, appreciative manner: "Sam, this is what we think your performance is worth." As Bandura noted, "It is unlikely that concert pianists lose interest in the keyboard because they are offered high performance fees. Indeed, they would feel devalued and insulted by low fees" (Bandura, 1977, p. 111).

In summary, tying money to performance can bring about large increases in performance (Yukl & Latham, 1975; Latham & Dossett, 1978). However, the process is admittedly more complicated than may at first appear.

1. Money must be valued, or desired, by the employee. But for some employees money beyond a set amount has little or no effect. Thus systematic interviews or questionnaires must be given to ascertain the extent to which employees perceive money as reinforcing.

2. The money must be tied to all important facets of the job. For example, quantity is often achieved at the expense of quality in many incentive programs because the incentive is tied to a piece-rate system only. BOS developed from a job analysis, however, take into account both the quality and the quantity involved in performing the work.

3. The employees must perceive that money is tied to performance. In other words, the incentive program must be easy to understand. This is a crucial requirement. Programs that employees do not understand seldom motivate them.

4. The amount of money must be seen by employees as worthy of their efforts. Again, systematic interviews or questionnaires are critical to determining what constitutes a perceived equitable bonus.

5. The money must be given soon after the desired behavior or outcome has taken place. As anyone who has been to Las Vegas or Atlantic City knows, in this way money has its greatest impact on behavior.

6. The employees must trust management to dispense the rewards equitably.

In closing this discussion, it is appropriate to summarize the results of a survey administered to all exempt managerial and professional employees of a large manufacturing organization (Landy, Barnes & Murphy, 1978). Performance appraisals are considered fair and accurate by employees when supervisors evaluate performance frequently, are familiar with the employee's performance levels, are in agreement with the subordinate on what constitutes the important job duties, and set specific plans or goals with the employee for eliminating performance weaknesses. The process of goal setting in a performance appraisal has positive effects on the credibility and acceptability of the entire performance appraisal system. Thus it would appear that frequent feedback and the setting of specific challenging goals are two primary ways of increasing the performance of employees. The researchers found that discussing salary during the evaluation *does not* negatively affect perceptions of the appraisal, as some earlier researchers (Meyer, Kay & French, 1965) thought.

Modeling

Leaders can foster goal commitment by modeling what needs to be done to achieve the goals that will move the vision toward reality. This is sometimes referred to as "integrity" in that effective leaders, in the words of their employees, "practice what they preach" by "walking the talk."

Modeling is an effective way of building an employee's self-efficacy (Bandura, 1986). When people see someone they admire do something successfully, they imitate that action. To the extent that one perceives that engaging in the action is doable, high self-efficacy occurs. Training is sometimes given to ensure that the person has the requisite knowledge and ability to do this (Wexley & Latham, 1991). High self-efficacy, the belief that one can successfully engage in a course of action, is as important, if not more so, than outcome expectancies in bringing about goal commitment (Bandura, 1986; Locke & Latham, 1990). Through modeling, leaders convey to their people what is important; they signal what truly needs to be done.

The disadvantage of being a model is that one is constantly under a microscope, especially by one's employees. Thus leaders who are effective are sensitive to sending inadvertent signals. Weyerhaeuser Company, for example, had long been an advocate of corporate wellness as a means of reducing costs (e.g., employee benefits). George Weyerhaeuser himself is an active athlete, and the question arose as to the optimal time for him to use the company gymnasium. If he used it before 8:00 A.M. because he is an early riser, at noon because he often forgoes lunch, or after 5:00 P.M. because he is no longer expecting telephone calls, he would have unintentionally signaled that corporate wellness is secondary to one's primary job responsibilities. The intended signal was that one's physical wellness is a primary job responsibility. Thus he decided that he would use the gym on an ongoing basis during regular business hours. But at what hour? Cognizant of the power of modeling, George knew that if he used the gym at a set time, the gym would be overused then and underused by employees at all other times of the day. Therefore, he uses it on an intermittent schedule. The result is that Weyerhaeuser employees use the physical facilities and the jogging trails outside corporate headquarters at all hours of the workday. Corporate wellness is a goal that is being attained at Weyerhaeuser Company.

Accessibility

Another way effective leaders can foster goal commitment is one that is also effective in building the self-efficacy of subordinates and ensuring that outcome expectancies are in alignment with the organization's vision—accessibility. The importance of leaders being accessible to their employees was argued forcefully by Peters and Waterman (1982), who coined the acronym MBWA—management by wandering around.

The underlying importance of accessibility is twofold. First, leaders need to let people know that they both notice and appreciate what employees are doing in relation to the goals. Recognition is a powerful antidote to job burnout if the recognition is tied to specific goal-related behavior. If the recognition is expressed in a general way (e.g., "Pat, you are outstanding"), the employee might interpret the praise as endorsing behavior that the leader wished, in fact, the person would do differently. Thus an anomaly can occur whereby performance gets worse rather than better as a result of praise.

The power in making the praise specific is that it increases the probability that the behavior will be repeated as the person learns exactly what is valued. It reduces feelings of favoritism among others if they see (outcome expectancies) what is valued, model the same or similar behavior, and subsequently receive praise.

A second reason for being accessible to one's subordinates is to encourage them to express concerns, doubts, and any skepticism they may have regarding goals. Overcoming resistance to change is exceedingly difficult when one does not know the basis for the resistance. Leaders who are effective encourage the expression of concerns and then focus on clearing the pathways of obstacles, real or imagined, to the goals so that outcome expectancies are positive (Evans, 1970, 1972).

A potential problem with accessibility is that the authority and responsibility of one's direct reports may be unintentionally usurped by a leader who becomes directly involved in clarifying the path-goal relationship rather than ensuring that the clarification is done by the appropriate party or parties. To the extent that leaders try to fix everything themselves, the people who were not involved, but should have been involved, feel devalued. Therefore, in being accessible to subordinates, leaders must be sensitive to empowering them by helping them to ask the right questions and pointing to paths that they can explore to solve their own problems. This process is sometimes referred to as team building.

Team Building

The assumption underlying team building is that when people work together to solve problems, they form an effective work group, or team (French, Bell & Zawacki, 1989). Allowing employees to participate in solving problems is a useful device for increasing the group's knowledge and thereby improving decision quality. It can lead to better decisions through input from subordinates and allows employees to begin seeing things from a supervisor's perspective, and vice versa.

Team building is especially applicable to performance appraisal when the appraisals are completed anonymously by an employee's peers or subordinates. The employee can categorize such feedback into the following three areas:

1. Things I can change immediately

2. Things I can't change (e.g., organizational policies) even if my life depended on it, and here's why

3. Things I think we as a group can change with your help

The group then sets priorities for the specific issues it wants to resolve over a given time period (typically three months). The meetings generally are held twice a month for up to three hours. The key question answered at the end of each meeting is: "Who is going to do what by when?" This question is the crucial goal-setting step.

A similar approach was used effectively to reduce turnover (Krackhardt et al., 1978). Managers in twenty-five branches of a West Coast bank were trained to discuss with the tellers as a team possible solutions for reducing turnover. They then met with each of their tellers individually. Together they set specific goals about ways to resolve issues of employee concern. For those branches at which goals were implemented, turnover was reduced significantly.

When team building is conducted with hourly employees, the supervisor generally works with five employees who have been nominated by the group to represent their viewpoint. The advantage of using five employees is that it increases the probability that everyone's voice will be heard (Slater, 1958). When there are fewer than five people present, group members are frequently too tense, tactful, and constrained. The fear of alienating one another seems to prevent them from expressing their ideas freely. When there are more than five people present, team members are often seen as too competitive and inconsiderate of one another.

It is explicitly understood prior to team building that the function of the team is to make proposals; management makes the final decisions. However, when a proposal is rejected, management must explain why in words that the employees can understand.

Although team building is a straightforward process, the approach has been received unfavorably by managers who believe that it will raise employee expectations to levels that management cannot meet. This fear is seldom warranted. It is justified only when the team building is allowed to drift to issues peripheral to productivity. The approach has proved effective in the aerospace industry, where product quality increased appreciably; at General Motors, where absenteeism and grievances decreased significantly; and at the Valspar Corporation (a paint manufacturing plant), where there was a significant improvement in product quality and reduction in employee turnover (Hinrichs, 1978).

Role Clarity

The purpose of role clarity is to define role expectations and obligations of group members to improve effectiveness. Often people do not have a clear idea of the behaviors expected of them by others and of what they can expect from others to help them fulfill their own roles. The process of reaching agreement on role requirements is as follows:

1. Individuals write down their views of the rationale for the existence of their jobs, specific duties, and job contribution to the goals of the unit, division, or organization.

2. The specific duties and behaviors are listed on a chalkboard for discussion by the entire team.

3. Behaviors are added and deleted until the group is satisfied that they have defined the role completely.

4. Individuals list their expectations of the other roles in the group that most affect their own role performance.

5. The group discusses these expectations and agrees on any modifications or additions.

6. The group members decide what they want from and expect from the person in a given role.

7. The person in each job writes a summary of the role as it has been defined by the group. This role profile,

derived from the steps above, provides a comprehensive understanding of what is expected of each individual.

8. The written profile, or job design, is reviewed again at a following meeting before another role is analyzed.

This intervention can be a nonthreatening activity with a high payoff for productivity. Often the mutual demands, expectations, and obligations of interdependent team members have never been publicly examined. Individuals wonder why the other employees are "not doing what they are supposed to do" while in reality they are performing as they think the job requires. Collaborative problem solving by the team members not only clarifies who is to do what but also ensures commitment to the role once it has been clarified, which in turn ensures the likelihood of positive performance appraisals for individuals and the group.

BOS can play an integral role in team building/role clarity so as to bring about a lasting behavior change among the team members. The following approach has been used successfully by the authors in a wide variety of organizational settings.

1. The division vice-president and the staff defined broad five-year objectives.

2. BOS were developed (see the Appendix). They made explicit what was required of each manager to influence the attainment of these objectives.

3. The vice-president and the managers completed the BOS on one another anonymously every quarter to give each person periodic feedback as to the appropriateness of behaviors in influencing the broad division targets.

4. The mean rating for each item on the BOS was calculated.

5. The group met together for an entire day. Participants identified items on which they felt they had been rated too low.

6. The peers were asked what a given participant must *do* in the subsequent appraisal period to receive a higher score. Discussion was always on the future; specific examples of past behavior were not allowed. Peers had to provide specific examples of acceptable behavior

for each individual and ways they could facilitate goal attainment.

7. The specific action steps for each individual were recorded. Specific goals for each individual were set in relation to the feedback from peers. A copy of each person' goals was subsequently distributed to each person in the group.

Immediate changes in behavior occurred. The employees knew what was expected of them. The BOS served as a communication tool for facilitating explicit feedback about how the employee was perceived by peers in doing what was expected. The employee could either reject the feedback and risk peer condemnation or accept the feedback and win peer approval that is contingent upon engaging in specific job behaviors critical to attaining organizational objectives.

Measurement

Effective leaders bring about goal commitment by focusing on measurement; hence the importance of performance appraisal. The late Mason Haire at the University of California, Berkeley, is credited with the maxim "That which gets measured gets done." Measurement conveys clearly and forcefully what is in fact valued by the organization. Thus measurement can highlight hypocrisy. For example, leaders who preach quality but focus on costs should not be surprised when the former is ignored in favor of the latter. To minimize hypocrisy, effective leaders ensure that the measurement is in alignment with the vision as well as the specific goals that were set to attain it.

Measurement not only fosters the setting of specific goals but also increases the likelihood of goal commitment for those who want to be valued by the organization. In the absence of the explicit feedback that measurement provides, employees cannot gauge their progress toward the goal. Thus they are likely to be satisfied with performance that falls far short of the goal. A useful way to understand the relation of measurement to vision and goal is as follows: Measurement tells people what is; goals tell them what is desirable. Measurement involves information; goals involve evaluation. Goals inform individuals as to what type or level of performance is to be attained so that they can direct and evaluate their actions and efforts accordingly.

Measurement allows them to track their performance in relation to their goals so that adjustments in effort, direction, and strategy can be made as needed (Locke & Latham, 1990).

Self-Management

Training in self-management (Kanfer, 1980) involves teaching people to assess their problems, to set specific difficult goals in relation to those problems, to monitor ways in which the environment facilitates or hinders goal attainment, and to identify and administer reinforcers and punishers for working toward or failing to work toward, respectively, the attainment of a self-set goal. In essence this training teaches people skills in self-observation, to compare their behavior with goals they set, and to administer reinforcers and punishers to bring about and sustain goal commitment (Karoly & Kanfer, 1982). The procedure is sufficiently powerful that it enabled unionized employees to overcome problems with absenteeism (Frayne & Latham, 1987; Latham & Frayne, 1989), as follows.

An orientation session was conducted to explain the principles of self-management; the next week the reasons given by the trainees for using sick leave were listed and classified into nine categories: legitimate illness, medical appointments, job stress, job boredom, difficulties with coworkers, alcohol and drug-related issues, family problems, transportation difficulties, and employee rights (i.e., "sick leave belongs to me"). Of these nine, family problems, incompatibility with supervisor or coworkers, and transportation problems were listed most frequently. Sick leave was the focus of discussion in this session because it accounted for 49.8 percent of the recorded absenteeism in the organization.

The trainees were taught to develop a description of the problem behaviors (e.g., difficulty with supervisor), to identify conditions that elicited and maintained the problem behaviors, and to identify specific coping strategies. This constituted the session on self-assessment. In this session, as in all sessions, the employees were assured that their comments would not be shared with anyone outside the training group.

The third week focused on goal setting. The primary goal was to increase one's attendance within a specific time frame (e.g., one month/three months), along with identification of specific behaviors that the respective individual had to engage in to attain the goal.

The fourth week focused on the importance of self-monitoring one's behavior. Specifically, the trainees were taught to record their own attendance, the reason for missing a day of work, and the steps followed to deal with the constraint(s) to subsequently get to work. This was done through the use of charts and diaries, with emphasis on the importance of daily feedback for motivational purposes as well as accuracy in recording.

In the fifth week the trainees identified reinforcers and punishers to self-administer. The training emphasized that the reinforcer must be powerful and easily self-administered (e.g., self-praise, purchasing a gift). The punisher was to be a disliked activity, easily self-administered (e.g., cleaning the garage). Each individual developed specific response-reward contingencies.

The sixth week was essentially a review of the previous five sessions, accomplished by asking the trainees to write a behavioral contract with themselves. Thus each trainee specified in writing the goal(s) to be achieved, the time frame for goal achievement, the consequences for attaining or failing to attain the goal(s), and the behaviors necessary for goal attainment.

The seventh week emphasized maintenance. Discussion focused on issues that might result in a relapse in absenteeism, planning for such situations should they occur, and developing coping strategies for dealing with these situations. During the last week of training, the trainer reviewed each technique presented in the program, answered questions from the trainees regarding these skills, and clarified expectations.

The result was a significant increase in job attendance relative to the people who had been randomly assigned to a control group. When the control group too was trained, their job attendance increased to the level of the originally trained group.

Closing Remarks

Frank (1983) described an event that occurred in 1944 when Allied aircraft began bold air strikes into Europe. After a factory was hit by bombs, the Germans ordered prisoners to one end of the building remains, commanding them to shovel the debris into carts and drag it to the other end of the compound. The next day the prisoners were ordered to move the high pile of debris back to the other end of the compound. Day after day the prisoners hauled the same mountain of rubble back and forth from one end of the camp to the other. After several weeks of this meaningless drudgery, one man began sobbing uncontrollably and was led away by the guards. Another screamed until his captors beat him into silence. Then another man, who had survived three years in prison, darted away from the group and raced toward an electrified fence.

This activity continued until dozens of prisoners went mad and ran from their work, only to be shot by the guards or electrocuted by the fence. Why did the Germans require this activity? The commandant of the camp later explained that this was an experiment in mental health to see what would happen when people were given meaningless work.

In *The House of the Dead* the Russian novelist Fyodor Dostoyevsky (1911) wrote that if one wants to utterly crush a human being, just give the person completely senseless, irrational work. In describing his own ten years in Russian prisons, Dostoyevsky reported that if a convict had to move a heap of earth from one place to another and back again, he would hang himself, preferring death to such humiliation. Deprived of meaningful work related goals, men and women lose their reason for existence.

Goals provide people with a sense of purpose. They minimize feelings of meaninglessness, and provide a basis for people to take pride in what they accomplish.

If corporate goals are not defined clearly in terms that employees understand, accept, and are held accountable for, the employees often see their tasks as meaningless. In the absence of clearly stated goals, employees do not know whether they have performed their jobs well.

A key aspect of effective leadership is addressing the question with employees as to why the organization exists and what its goals are. In developing these goals people create a shared vision, which drives employees to take their company to the top. Once people commit to a goal, they immediately ask: "How do I do it?" "How can I get it?" And they start planning a strategy.

But it's the goal that comes first. Once the goal is set, there is a sense of purpose in searching for and being alert to the information, the finances, and the resources needed to attain it.

It is from goals that we derive a sense of accountability. As Tice (1989) has noted, the goal comes first; then you see.

It is absolutely vital that we have goals in order for us to change and grow. Goals provide targets for us to aim toward, to look forward to in the future. Most importantly, goals give feedback its significance. Once we target a goal, we become alert to where we are in relation to it. This feedback allows us to make adjustments so that we can grow and develop in ways to attain the goals, which in turn gives us the confidence to set even higher goals.

Feedback alone isn't enough to change behavior. To change behavior, the feedback must be given in relation to the goal. But even here, the feedback must be accepted if people are to have the desire to continuously improve their performance. In Chapter 8 we discuss ways of minimizing employee defensiveness to constructive feedback.

Effective goal setting in performance appraisal should take into account the following points:

1. Setting specific goals leads to higher performance than does adopting an attitude of "do your best." That is, a specific score on BOS should be specified, along with the key behaviors that the employee needs to work on to improve or maintain the score.

2. Participation in goal setting is important to the extent that it leads to the setting of higher goals than those that are assigned unilaterally by superiors. Participation does not necessarily lead to greater goal acceptance than when goals are assigned by a supportive manager (Latham, Erez & Locke, 1988). However, employee understanding of how to attain them may be increased as a result of participating in the goal-setting process (Latham, Winters & Locke, in press).

3. Given the employee's goal commitment and ability, the higher the goal, the higher the performance. However, the goal should be reasonable. If the goals are unreasonable, employees will neither accept them nor derive a sense of accomplishment from pursuing unattainable goals. People with low self-confidence or ability should initially be given more easily attainable goals than are given to people with high self-confidence and ability.

4. Performance feedback is critical for showing employees how they are doing relative to the goals, maintaining the employees' interest in the goals, revising goals, and prolonging effort to attain the goals.

5. If employees are evaluated on overall level of performance rather than goal attainment, they will continue to set high goals regardless of whether the goals are attained. High goals lead to higher performance levels than do easy goals. If employees are evaluated on goal attainment regardless of the difficulty of the goal, they are likely to set low goals or reject difficult goals imposed by supervisors.

6. There must be some latitude for the individual to influence performance. If performance is rigidly controlled by technology or work flow (such as the typical assembly line), goal setting may have little effect on performance.

7. Employees must not feel threatened that they will lose their jobs if they increase their performance under the goal-setting procedure. Most people have enough sense not to put themselves out of work by being too productive.

8. Goal setting is most effective when the supervisor behaves in a supportive manner when interacting with subordinates.

8

Effective Coaching: The Interplay Between Formal and Informal Appraisals

Introduction

Despite the importance of performance appraisals for both maximizing employee productivity and minimizing the probability of litigation suits, many supervisors avoid giving the results to employees. Giving feedback is avoided because in many instances the appraisal is tantamount to a "bad joke" for both the appraiser and the appraisee. It is a bad joke because the appraisal is often based on the wrong instrument (e.g., trait scales). Thus the employee argues that the appraisal does not provide a thorough assessment of what is required in the job, thus attacking the content validity of the appraisal instrument. The result is that the employee discredits the measuring instrument and the person who used it (Meyer, 1977, 1991).

But even if a content-valid instrument is used, the performance appraisal is frequently ineffective because the wrong person(s) make the appraisal. The appraisers are frequently unaware of the aims and objectives of the person's job, seldom see the person performing on the job, and are incapable of discerning competent behavior. Therefore the use of multiple appraisers, particularly peers, was stressed in Chapter 5.

The performance appraisal often fosters feelings of inequity among employees, due to different appraisers using different standards. Two employees who do exactly the same things are often rated differently by two different supervisors. Uniformity and objectivity are necessary to ensure feelings of equity among employees, especially when monetary rewards are tied to performance. This is why training to increase observer accuracy is so important for ensuring effective appraisals.

Even when such training takes place, people often avoid conducting formal appraisals because their outcome expectancies are so low. In two field studies involving a newsprint facility and a bank, Napier and Latham (1986) found that this was true even when self-efficacy was high. That is, supervisors felt that they could indeed appraise their people accurately but nevertheless avoided conducting appraisals because they perceived that the outcome of evaluating subordinates was the same regardless of how well or how poorly the employees were performing the job. In short, the supervisors could see no relationship between how a person was appraised and how that person was subsequently rewarded or penalized. It is noteworthy that in neither organization did the appraisal instrument reflect the organization's strategic plan. As noted in Chapter 7, the appraisal must reflect the steps that must be taken to move the superordinate goal from a vision to reality if appraisals are to be taken seriously in an organization. The appraisal instrument must reflect the steps necessary for implementing the organization's strategic plan.

Another reason why performance appraisals are disliked by both supervisors and employees is that the employee's performance can sometimes drop to a level below where it was prior to conducting the appraisal (Meyer, Kay & French, 1965). This drop occurs because the motivational principles described in Chapter 7 are not followed. If the appraisal is to bring about a behavior change or to sustain a high level of output, it must be conducted on an ongoing basis, explicit feedback must be provided, specific goals must be set on the basis of this feedback, and criticism that is perceived as destructive must be minimized. For example, telling employees once a year to "keep up the good work" or "try harder" is going to have little or no effect on their behavior.

The underlying theme of this chapter is that what an employee needs to start doing, stop doing, or continue doing must be specified in terms of explicit goals and subsequently discussed on an ongoing basis. In this chapter we will focus on the characteristics of effective formal appraisals conducted by supervisors, discuss three ways of conducting formal appraisals, and conclude with ways of conducting informal day-to-day appraisals. The emphasis in this chapter is on supervisors or team leaders—the people who conduct most appraisals.

Characteristics of Effective Appraisals

In a seminal article Burke, Weitzel, and Weir (1978) summarized six major characteristics of effective performance appraisals based on their review of the literature. Their findings are still applicable today.

1. High levels of subordinate participation in the performance appraisal result in employees being satisfied with both the appraisal process and the supervisor who conducted it (Nemeroff & Wexley, 1977; Wexley, Singh & Yukl, 1973). The importance of this statement is that subordinates' participation in the appraisal interview appears to increase their acceptance of the supervisor's observations.

   Subsequent research (Leung & Li, 1990) has shown that merely increasing participation in the decision-making process, however, does not necessarily enhance employee perceptions of fairness. It is especially necessary to show those people who will be affected by a negative appraisal that their views were taken into account before the final appraisal was made.

2. Employee acceptance of the appraisal and satisfaction with the supervisor increase to the extent that the supervisor is supportive of the employee (Latham & Saari, 1979a; Nemeroff & Wexley, 1977). In addition, perceptions of rating fairness are increased to the extent that the appraiser demonstrates sensitivity to the employee's self-image. Interestingly, perceptions of fairness are not a function of the rating that the employee receives (Greenberg, 1988). (This fascinating phenomenon is explored in detail in Chapter 9.)

3. The setting of specific goals to be achieved by the subordinate results in up to twice as much improvement in performance as a discussion of general goals (Bassett & Meyer, 1968; Meyer, Kay & French, 1965;

Latham & Yukl, 1975). The positive effect that goal setting has on performance is among the most replicated findings in psychology (Locke & Latham, 1990).

4. Discussing problems that may be hampering the subordinate's job performance and working toward solutions has an immediate effect on productivity (Maier, 1958; Meyer & Kay, 1964). In a longitudinal study of ten business units, Nathan, Mohrman, and Milliman (1991) found that appraisals that focus on issues in terms of behavioral criteria and also include a discussion of the person's career correlated with subsequent improvement in performance. These two variables, plus allowing the employee to participate in the appraisal process, also correlated significantly with subsequent job satisfaction.

The same study revealed that with regard to organizational satisfaction, a well-conducted appraisal compensated for a poor interpersonal relationship between the employee and the appraiser. Conversely, a good interpersonal relationship between a superior and subordinate compensated for a poor appraisal interview.

5. The number of criticisms in an appraisal interview correlates positively with the number of defensive reactions shown by the employee. Those areas of job performance that are most criticized are least likely to show an improvement. There appears to be a chain reaction between criticisms made by the supervisor and defensive reactions shown by the subordinate, with little or no change in the subordinate's behavior (Kay, Meyer & French, 1965; Nemeroff & Wexley, 1977). However, subsequent research has shown that when an appraisal is negative, employees are receptive to the feedback when they are allowed to participate in the feedback session, the feedback is based on factors clearly relevant to their work, and subsequent goals are set in relation to this feedback (Dipboye & Pontbriand, 1981).

In a field study of nurses in Scotland, Anderson and Barnett (1987) found that when the emphasis in the formal appraisal was placed on the employee's performance rather than personality, she left the appraisal session feeling encouraged to improve her performance. Equally important, the appraisal was perceived as fair. This is important for employee morale; it is also important in a litigious society.

6. The more that subordinates are allowed to voice their opinions during the appraisal, the more satisfied they will feel with the appraisal (Greller, 1975; Nemeroff & Wexley, 1977; Wexley, Singh & Yukl, 1973). In a survey of middle managers Greenberg (1986) found that the solicitation and use of employee input prior to the final appraisal, the use of a two-way conversation during the appraisal process, and the opportunity to challenge or rebut the appraisal are among the primary determinants of employee perceptions of fair performance evaluations.

Burke and his colleagues' (1978) conclusions regarding the six characteristics of effective formal appraisals were based on their research in a large hospital in the Midwest. Employee responses to both the participation items and the job-related items on a questionnaire (i.e., solving job problems, setting specific goals) correlated with the employee's satisfaction with the appraisal process. However, only the job-related items correlated with an improvement in the employee's performance. Setting specific goals clarifies the behavioral paths or strategies that the subordinate can take to fulfill job requirements. Resolving job problems removes present or potential obstacles in the paths of these requirements.

In addition, Burke and his colleagues found that the amount of thought and preparation subordinates spent analyzing their job responsibilities, problems encountered in the job, and the quality of their work correlated positively with improved performance. The employees who took this time were those who perceived that organizational rewards are contingent on the results of one's performance. "These data suggest that managers in organizations would get better mileage from their appraisal system if they made the appraisal of performance a priority managerial activity and overtly utilized appraisal results for distributing discretionary 'rewards'" (Burke, Weitzel & Weir, 1978, p. 917).

Three Approaches to Conducting Formal Appraisal

Maier (1958) suggested three approaches for conducting a formal appraisal: tell and sell, tell and listen, and problem solving.

Tell and Sell

The purpose of the tell-and-sell approach is to let employees know (tell) how well they are doing and to assign them specific goals for improvement (sell). Thus the approach maximizes points (3) and (5) above. The approach is effective for increasing the performance of trainees (Hillery & Wexley, 1974), as well as experienced employees who have been socialized to accept a directive leadership style (Dossett, Latham & Mitchell, 1979). In addition, this approach is efficient in that it takes less time to conduct than allowing employees to participate in the appraisal process (Latham & Saari, 1979a).

The problem with the tell-and-sell approach is that it can do more harm than good with many employees. When subordinates think that their interests and the supervisor's are no longer compatible, performance can and often does deteriorate (Maier, 1958). The day-to-day relationship between the supervisor and the subordinate may become strained, and job satisfaction often decreases for both of them. Finally, the approach can encourage subservience in that the underlying philosophy of the approach is that the boss knows best. The boss sets the goals and dispenses the rewards and punishments. Thus when the method works, it is likely to develop dependent, docile behavior; when it fails, the result can be a rebellious employee.

Tell and Listen

The purpose of the tell-and-listen method is to communicate the supervisor's perception of the employee's strengths and weaknesses and to let the employee respond to these statements. The approach maximizes employee satisfaction with the process. The supervisor actively listens to the employee's attitudes and feelings, makes effective use of pauses to encourage the subordinate to speak, paraphrases the employee's statements to ensure understanding, and summarizes the employee's feelings at the end of the interview. Thus the employee knows that he or she has been "heard." Unfortunately, no specific goals are set;

thus there is little subsequent change in the employee's performance.

Problem Solving

The problem-solving approach maximizes the principles of allowing employee participation in the appraisal, discussing and solving employee problems, and setting specific goals. As such, the approach combines the steps outlined in the tell-and-listen method. The steps to conducting an effective appraisal are as follows:

1. Explain the purpose of the meeting, namely, that it is to provide recognition for areas in which the employee is doing well and to discuss any problems that the employee may be experiencing on the job. The employee should be given sufficient notice of the meeting so that the discussion can be truly two sided.

2. At the beginning of the meeting, ask the employee to describe specifically what was done that deserves recognition and why it deserves recognition. Ask the employee to be specific so that it is clear to both of you what needs to be done to maintain this level of performance. "Self-observe–self-remember" is a key to self-management.

3. Ask the employee to specify what he or she should start doing, stop doing, or be doing differently. The discussion may include projects, tasks, or behaviors. As with the tell-and-sell approach, the emphasis of the discussion is on the future rather than the past and on employee learning and development rather than the assignment of blame.

4. Ask the employee if there are areas where you can provide assistance. The purpose here is to show that you truly want to help the employee.

5. After the employee has completed steps 1 through 4 and after you have probed the employee to increase mutual understanding, you give your input with regard to the employee on steps 2 through 4. If the employee has failed to mention in step 3 areas that you feel are important, discuss no more than two to

four areas for improvement. Focusing on more than two to four broad criteria (e.g., technical competence and interaction with subordinates on BOS) can overwhelm an employee and increase defensiveness. And again, focus strictly on issues from a behavioral perspective rather than personalities. Simply explain what you have seen and why it concerns you.

There is no question that an evaluative process can be threatening to some employees. This anxiety is heightened not by the clarity of an issue but by its fuzziness. When the appropriate behaviors are well known to both the employee and the supervisor and when the measurement of these behaviors is discussed openly, anxiety is reduced, and the relationship between the employee and the supervisor can be candid and comfortable. This is another reason why BOS are so important as appraisal instruments. They make clear to all parties what is required of an employee.

6. As will be emphasized later in this chapter, focus on what you want to see occur. For example, a tennis coach should continually reinforce a pupil for paying attention to keeping the wrist stiff as opposed to the converse: "Look, you are bending your wrist." People who focus on bending their wrist continue to do an excellent job of bending their wrist.

7. Ask for and listen openly to the employee's concerns regarding your observations. It may well be that your initial concerns are not justified because you did not have all the facts.

8. Come to agreement on steps to be taken by each of you. This is the crucial goal-setting step.

9. If BOS are used, mutually agree on a specific score that the employee will strive to attain on the subsequent appraisal.

10. Finally, agree on a follow-up date to determine the extent to which the employee's and your concerns have been eliminated and progress has been made on the goals that have been set. As will be discussed in

the section on informal appraisals, the follow-up date should occur long before the next formal appraisal.

The problem-solving method is particularly appropriate for peer ratings because it minimizes the role of the supervisor as a judge and increases the supervisor's role as a counselor. The supervisor simply feeds back the information provided anonymously by the employee's peers. If an employee becomes defensive because of a specific rating, the supervisor, rather than being required to defend the rating, can shift the discussion with the employee to the future. Specifically, the two-way discussion can shift to what the employee is doing or can stop doing or consider doing differently to get peers to change their "erroneous" perception. In this way team leaders or supervisors can serve in the role of coach rather than critic.

If a content-valid appraisal instrument is used, it is unlikely that peers will fail to point out an area that is of concern to a supervisor. What makes this process so effective is that by using peer ratings, a supervisor can focus attention during an appraisal interview on ways of helping the employee correct problems rather than jeopardizing the success of the interview by defending his or her own appraisal of the employee and providing criticism after criticism to justify that appraisal.

Administrative Versus Developmental Objectives: An Ongoing Controversy

The performance appraisal serves a myriad of purposes in two broad categories: administrative and developmental. The former has to do with decisions regarding promotions, transfers, demotion, layoffs, terminations, salary increases, bonuses, etc. The latter has to do with ways of enhancing employee ability and motivation. These two categories are obviously interrelated in that an employee's ability and motivation affect subsequent administrative decisions, and administrative decisions affect an employee's subsequent ability and motivation. Meyer, Kay, and French (1965) argued for the need to separate the administrative from the developmental aspects of the appraisal interview by conducting two separate interviews. They stated that to do otherwise would result in the employee selectively attending to the administrative (e.g., monetary) information at the expense of the developmental. Moreover, the appraiser would spend more time explaining and justifying administrative decisions than on generating ideas on how the employee can grow and develop in the organization. This conclusion sparked a debate that has continued for more than a quarter of a century.

In support of the argument for separating the administrative from the developmental purposes of an interview, Harackiewicz and Larson (1986) found that supervisors provided less information about an employee's competence during the appraisal interview when they were also required to administer financial rewards. An employee survey showed that 81 percent of the respondents preferred to have discussions of their salary separated from a review of their performance.

In contrast, a survey involving multiple organizations (Prince & Lawler, 1986) found that including a discussion of salary in the performance review was particularly important to employees at lower hierarchical levels. The reason is that a discussion of salary communicates loudly and clearly the specific aspects of the person's performance that are valued by the organization. Moreover, the inclusion of salary in the discussion enhanced the information content of the appraisal by forcing managers to provide specific feedback to support the evaluation. Similarly, Dorfman, Stephan, and Loveland (1986) showed that discussions of pay and advancement correlated significantly with employee satisfaction with the appraisal process.

Why hasn't this debate been resolved? Our belief is that the wrong question continues to be addressed. The important issue is not whether the administrative and developmental aspects of an appraisal should be combined into one session but whether there is value in the "one session" regardless of the content. We believe that the formal appraisal should serve as no more than a summarization of the ongoing feedback that has been given and as an occasion for goal setting and goal commitment. It should contain no surprises if the employee and the appraiser have had ongoing discussions. This is the crucial "if"— the issue that should be the focus of concern for academics and practitioners. An athletic coach, for example, would be fired if appraisals were done only at the end of the baseball, basketball, or hockey season. Coaching must be done on an ongoing basis if it is to be effective in improving behavior. Similarly, supervisors and team leaders need to provide ongoing coaching in industry, or else they too should be replaced. When coaching is ongoing, the issue of whether to mix discussions of salary with developmental discussions during a formal appraisal becomes moot. Our guess is that when researchers find that combining administrative and developmental aspects in the formal interview is inappropriate, it is because ongoing coaching has not taken place; when researchers find that it is appropriate, ongoing coaching has taken place.

At best, only a small amount of improvement in performance can be attributed to the once-a-year formal appraisal (Nathan, Mohrman & Milliman, 1991). In sports, performance often decreases rather than increases because the golfer or tennis player is trying unsuccessfully to unlearn old habits while attempting to master new ones. The key to increasing effectiveness is to take lessons on an ongoing basis. Without ongoing coaching, the formal appraisal can satisfy administrative requirements, but it will have little or no positive effect on the developmental component.

Informal Day-to-Day Coaching

The underlying theme throughout this book is that the results of performance appraisals must be given frequently to an employee if they are to bring about a change in an employee's behavior or to maintain a high standard of excellence. Employees need feedback on how well they are doing. Employees must accurately perceive the consequences of their efforts and be able to set goals on the basis of this feedback (Locke & Latham, 1990). This does not mean that formal appraisals must be conducted on a daily basis. But on an informal basis, this is exactly what managers do each and every day; they appraise people. There is no reason why a manager cannot feed back this information informally to employees.

For coaches to instill the desire within employees to continuously improve performance, at least two key variables must be addressed, namely, an employee's outcome expectancies and self-efficacy (Bandura, 1986). Addressing outcome expectancies, often the easier of the two to improve with an individual, involves clarifying for people the relationships between their behavior and its consequences, such as the acquisition of a new skill, an increase in social status, or a transfer to an exciting job.

Goal setting can be an important technique for coaches to use in this regard in that goal attainment can become an expected outcome of engaging in various courses of action.

The difficult job of coaching is finding ways to instill a high sense of self-efficacy in an employee, to instill the belief that "I can learn that; I can do that; I can be that." Success requires not only skills but also the strong belief in one's capabilities to exercise control over events to accomplish desired goals. People with the same skills may perform poorly, adequately, or extraordinarily, depending on whether their self-appraisal of their capability enhances or improves their motivation and problem-solving efforts (Bandura, 1988). Highly self-efficacious people have the deep belief that they can cause, bring about, or make something happen. High self-efficacy is, in a word, conviction. Self-efficacy is the result of a self-appraisal of one's ability.

Note that self-efficacy and self-esteem are not synonymous. Self-esteem refers to how one feels about one's self, whereas self-efficacy refers to how one appraises one's ability about a specific set of tasks. For example, I can like myself the way I am and have little desire to change me. Simultaneously, I can have low self-efficacy about anything that is mechanical in nature. Hence I can like me while believing that I have little ability to repair my car. Conversely, I may believe that there is no engine that I cannot fix and simultaneously not like me as a person very much.

Interestingly, it is self-appraisal that keeps people from improving their knowledge and skills in that their ability often exceeds their self-efficacy. Thus the key to maximizing an employee's ability is for coaches to strengthen the employee's self-efficacy. People with low self-efficacy set low goals despite high ability. It is their beliefs that keep them from trying to develop their knowledge and skills.

Sadly, employees with low self-efficacy do not dream the big dreams; they do not buy into the vision; they do not set high goals. They do not make a commitment to attain that which they believe they cannot "cause, bring about, or make happen." They do not allow themselves to want or desire what they truly believe is unattainable for them. When working to achieve a goal that they perceive is difficult, they quickly abort their efforts in the face of obstacles. By contrast, those who have a strong sense of efficacy exert greater effort to master challenges than they would if the challenge were not present (Bandura & Schunk, 1981). People with low self-efficacy make up their minds, for example, that they are incapable of learning math, mastering spelling, or acquiring a new language. It is not their lack of ability that prevents the acquisition of this knowledge or skill but rather their self-appraisal. Consequently, such people often lower the goal to match their self-appraisal, rationalizing that they are being "realistic." Even worse, these people may abandon the goal altogether as a result of searching for ways to find fault with it. This self-protective action allows them to maintain their self-esteem in that they behave in ways that are consistent with their self-appraisal.

People usually look for ways to escape or avoid activities that they believe exceed their coping capabilities (Bandura, 1982). People don't allow themselves to truly want or desire what they don't believe they can master. The issue is not low self-esteem; the issue is low self-efficacy regarding the task or goal in question. Therefore the job of coaching is to strengthen an employee's self-efficacy regarding a specific task or tasks so that there is an inextinguishable sense of commitment that is resilient to setbacks and rejections. The importance of doing so has been described by White (1982) with regard to people who achieved eminence in spite of repeated rejection.

James Joyce's *The Dubliners* was rejected by twenty-two publishers. Gertrude Stein submitted poems to editors for twenty years before one was finally accepted. The Impressionists had to arrange their own art exhibitions because their works were routinely rejected by the Paris Salon. Van Gogh sold only one painting during his lifetime. Frank Lloyd Wright's architectural works were widely criticized during much of his career. Fred Astaire was initially rejected for being only a balding, skinny actor, who could dance a little. Decca records turned down a recording contract with the Beatles because groups of guitars are "on the way out." As Bandura (1988) noted, persistence in the face of massive unintermitting rejection defies explanation in terms of reinforcement or utility theories. It is a person's self-beliefs of efficacy which determine how much effort they will exert in an endeavor, and how long they will persevere in the face of obstacles. It is their belief in their capabilities that affects how much stress and depression people experience. People who believe they can cope with difficult tasks and situations are not upset by them.

Self-efficacy can be enhanced in several ways, including persuasion, enactive mastery, modeling, and physiological arousal.

Persuasion

Persuasion can come from one's self or others. Self-talk refers to an ongoing internal dialog (Meichenbaum, 1977). When people experience failure and attribute it to internal stable factors (e.g., one's ability), the self-talk that follows serves to reinforce their belief that they cannot succeed in a given course of action. Even worse, because of the individual's ability for symbolic visualization and forethought, the person may experience the one failure again and again (Bandura, 1986). What people say to themselves influences their subsequent behavior (Bandura, 1988; Meichenbaum, 1974).

Therefore one important aspect of coaching is to teach employees self-statement modification, that is, to get them to change their self-talk so that it is constructive (Meichenbaum, 1977). For example, people can be taught the danger of self-fulfilling prophecies. What you tell yourself often ends up to be what you get: "I never make the sale"; "I can't get the job"; "I've always been a poor speaker"; "Look, I am bending my wrist when I return a serve." People predict an outcome with their self-talk and then make it happen. In short, one's intentions influence one's behavior (Latham & Saari, 1984).

Another key to changing self-talk is to help people change their explanatory style when assigning blame or failure (Burns & Seligman, 1990). A person assigns a cause for negative events in a characteristic manner. People who attribute blame to internal, stable factors regarding themselves have a pessimistic explanatory style. They believe that they are helpless in controlling outcomes.

The emphasis in this aspect of coaching is cognitive—to help the person identify self-depreciating statements and to replace them with positive ones (Burns & Seligman, 1990): "I can do that"; "I can make the sale"; "I can get high teacher ratings"; "Look, I keep my wrist stiff when I return a serve." Next, people are taught to connect their self-statements to evidence supporting those self-statements.

The job of a coach is to teach people to know when they are or are not responsible for a failure. The coach teaches people to replace inaccurate self-statements and attributions with accurate ones. Employees are taught to replay in their minds their past successes. They are taught to affirm what they want to achieve, what they intend to bring about. By contrast, people who judge themselves inefficacious in coping with environmental demands dwell on their personal deficiencies. They imagine potential difficulties as more formidable then they are in fact. Visualizing scenarios regarding failure undermines performance (Bandura, 1988). Conversely, people who have a strong source of efficacy shift their attention and effort to the demands of the situation and are spurred to find ways to overcome obstacles (Bandura, 1982). By visualizing success scenarios, they consistently see their goals within their reach.

Another source of persuasion that is effective in increasing self-efficacy is the role played by one's significant others, because most people view themselves in ways that are congruent with how they believe others whom they respect see them. Wood and Bandura (1988), for example, told one group of managers that decision making is a skill that is developed through practice. They told a second group of managers that decision making reflects a basic intellectual aptitude. Managers who regarded decision-making ability as an acquirable skill maintained a strong sense of efficacy in the face of difficulties, set challenging goals, used good problem-solving strategies, and did well in fostering employee productivity. Conversely, those who were told that decision making reflects basic intellectual capacities lost confidence in themselves as they encountered problems, lowered their goals, demonstrated poorer problem solving, and had less productive employees. In short, their belief system undermined the effective use of their capabilities because it directed their attention from how to master the tasks to a preoccupation with a depreciating self-appraisal. Interestingly, they also tended to find fault with their employees.

The effect that supervisory expectations alone can have on an employee's performance has been examined by Eden (1988) and his colleagues. For example, Eden and Shami (1982) found that trainees who were designated as having high command potential in the Israeli military performed significantly higher than a control group on an objective achievement test.

Eden and Ravid (1982) replicated these results and provided further insight into the nature of this pygmalion effect. Specifically, these authors tested the influence of the pygmalion effect when manipulated independently on the trainee as well as the trainer. Trainees in clerical courses in the Israeli Defense Force were randomly assigned to one of three conditions in which the instructors were informed that trainees had high potential for success, or regular potential for success, or insufficient information prevented prediction of trainee success. The trainees in the third condition were then randomly assigned to two groups. The trainers were not given any predictions about these trainees, who had been assigned to either a group told that it had high potential for success or a group told its members had regular potential for success. Success in training was subsequently measured by instructor performance appraisal ratings, as well as by an objective performance examination.

The results of this study demonstrated highly significant pygmalion effects for both the instructor-expectancy and trainee-expectancy conditions. Instructor expectancy accounted for 52 percent of the variance in mean performance ratings; trainee expectancy (i.e., self-efficacy) accounted for 35 percent of the variance. As for the objective performance exam, instructor-expectancy accounted for 27 percent of the variance in scores; trainee-expectancy accounted for 30 percent of the variance. Interestingly, these results persisted despite a midcourse change to instructors who were unaware of the pygmalion manipulation. Thus the effects of the initial expectancy induction "carried over" to the relief instructors, whose expectations had not been experimentally manipulated.

The results of this research demonstrate the powerful effect of supervisory beliefs on a subordinate's subsequent beliefs and behavior. Employees who believe that others, whom they think highly of, respect their capabilities develop a strong sense of self-efficacy and thus exhibit high performance. People who are assigned inferior labels, implying limited competence, perform activities at which they are skilled less well than when they do not bear a negative label (Bandura, 1982).

Still another way coaches can ensure the self-efficacy of others through persuasion is to give them recognition. In a study at the Weyerhaeuser Company, Latham and Saari (1979a) found that employees who received recognition for their work were generally the outstanding workers and the poor performers. Recognition for the poor performers often took the form of reprimands from supervisors, which in turn resulted in approval from colleagues. The outstanding employees frequently received recognition in terms of awards, promotions, and stock options.

The majority of employees were neither poor performers nor outstanding workers. They did an adequate job, and their work habits seldom warranted criticism. In short, they did what was expected of them. They came to work every day; they were seldom, if ever, late; they got along well with others; and they caused little or no problems for anyone. Typically, these people received no recognition for their work; they were viewed as "average" employees. Yet their manager's job would have increased in difficulty if they suddenly stopped doing what was expected of them and became poor performers. To prevent such an occurrence, they were given praise from a supervisor for those things that were originally taken for granted. To borrow academic phraseology, the primary objective was to keep a C student from becoming a D or an F student. In many instances the outcome of giving recognition is a B or even an A student. The emphasis in this aspect of coaching is primarily behavioral rather than cognitive. Weyerhaeuser supervisors were trained to take the following actions:

1. Clearly describe to the employee *specifically* what was done to deserve recognition. Specific praise can increase both job satisfaction and productivity. Also, making the praise specific increases the probability that the employee will perceive it as sincere. Blanket praise sometimes generates skepticism as to motives behind the comment.

   An advantage of using BOS is that they specify the behaviors that a manager should look for to praise the employee. Many managers have no problem noticing and commenting on ineffective behavior. These same managers often appear to ignore effective behavior on the part of their subordinates.

2. Express your personal appreciation to the employee. This may amount to nothing more than saying thank

you. The rationale behind giving specific praise and expressing appreciation is simply to let the employee know that you both *notice* and *appreciate* what is being done on the job. This conversation does not need to take place in an office. It can occur anywhere the two of you meet. Preferably the conversation should occur *immediately* after the desired behavior on the part of the employee takes place.

3. Ask the employee if there is anything you can do to be of assistance regarding job-related problems. Many managers are reluctant to follow this step because they are afraid of being "hit with a laundry list" of complaints. In the literally hundreds of cases in which we have trained people to follow this step, this fear has never materialized. In most cases the employee simply looks at the supervisor in awe. In other cases the employee has said thank you and later commented that it was the first time in literally years that anyone had commented in this fashion. As most motivational theorists hypothesize, and as almost all employees are painfully aware, most people are starving for recognition. Recognition that is tied to specific behaviors is a powerful motivator for increasing productivity. Through this step, you may subsequently be among the first rather than the last to know of sources of irritation among your work force. This is why management by wandering around is so important; it is a vehicle for letting people know that what they are doing is noticed and appreciated. It provides the time necessary for managers to listen to the concerns of others.

4. If necessary, plan a specific follow-up meeting to determine whether the employee's concerns have been resolved. If you cannot resolve a concern, you need to explain to the employee what you have done and why it was ineffective. In this way the employee knows that you tried.

A pitfall in steps 2, 3, and 4 is the tendency to mix criticism with praise: "Chris, if you would only do this well in accounting, you'd be outstanding." Leave criticism for a separate discussion. Criticism has a tendency to generate criticism.

Employees suddenly find it very easy to find fault with the supervisor. If praise is usually mixed with criticism, the praise that is being given is not heard because the employee is waiting for the punch line. However, just as criticism has a tendency to generate criticism, the same effect occurs with praise. Employees suddenly find reasons to compliment a supervisor. The result is a positive and contagious work climate. Eight months after this training at Weyerhaeuser, the union executive committee began encouraging the membership to look for ways to give specific praise to the supervisors. This occurred despite the fact that there had been a wildcat strike a year previously.

Enactive Mastery

In many instances the very act of providing training for an employee does more than increase a person's ability. It shows that the organization believes that the person has the ability to master the skill; it sends a message that the person is valued by the organization. Thus in addition to persuasion through self-talk, conveying positive expectations, and giving recognition, coaches can increase a person's self-efficacy through enactive mastery of progressively difficult or intimidating activities (Bandura, Reese & Adams, 1982).

Positive experiences and success with the task tend to increase self-efficacy; failure leads to a lowering of efficacy. For example, Bandura (1982) found that self-efficacy increases when one's experiences fail to validate one's fears and when the skills one acquires allow mastery over situations that the person once felt threatening. But in the process of completing a task, if an employee encounters something that is unexpected and intimidating or if the experience highlights skill limitations, self-efficacy decreases even if the person's performance was "successful." Only as people increase their ability to predict and manage perceived threats do they develop a robust self-assurance that enables them to master subsequent challenges. It would appear imperative that coaches arrange subject matter in such a way that trainees know in advance what they will be taught and that they experience success in that arena through active participation with the subject matter.

Enactive mastery is the most influential source of efficacy self-appraisals because it is based on authentic mastery experiences (Bandura, 1982). In a study on creativity, Locke et al.

(1984) demonstrated that training programs are effective only to the extent that they increase a person's self-efficacy. After their ability to think creatively was measured, trainees were taught strategies for improving evaluative thinking. The more the training increased a trainee's beliefs in his or her capability, the higher the goal that the person set, the higher the commitment to the goal, and the more productive the person became in generating creative ideas. In short, employees' beliefs about their capabilities profoundly affect the results of a training program.

Modeling

As discussed in Chapter 7, modeling the desired behavior is a highly effective way for coaches to increase the self-efficacy of others. Seeing others who are similar to oneself perform a task or tasks successfully raises efficacy expectations in observers who judge that they too possess the capability to master the observed activities. A model conveys to observers the effective strategies for dealing with challenging or threatening situations as well as information about the nature and predictability of environmental events. For modeling to be effective, the coach must use a model that people can identify as similar to themselves. For example, there is only one way either of us would enter a training program that teaches basic mechanical skills for simple home repair jobs; we would do so only if we saw someone whom we judged to be equally unmechanical as we are before he or she received the training doing well afterward.

When applied to training, complex activities, such as leadership skills, are often modeled on videotape. Effective modeling teaches general rules or strategies. Trainees use role playing to apply these rules to different people under different circumstances. This approach to training, as noted earlier, was done effectively by Weyerhaeuser Company in teaching supervisors how to interact with a unionized work force (Latham & Saari, 1979b).

To help them master a skill, people are sometimes shown videotapes of their own performance. The danger here is that watching one's own mistakes can weaken self-efficacy. The person begins to doubt his or her capabilities (Hung & Rosenthal, 1981). To bring about the desired change in behavior, coaches who use this technique must direct the trainee's attention to successes and improvements. This is evidence that they can and

will continue to improve their skills. The most beneficial modeling focuses on the right ways rather than the wrong ways of
accomplishing a task (Bandura, 1988).

After a person masters a skill in a training session, the
training must be transferred to the job. Allowing time for practice during training is essential for the mastery of most competencies (Wexley & Latham, 1991). But these new competencies
will not be demonstrated on the job for long unless they are put
into practice successfully. People must experience success using
what they have learned during training in order to believe in
themselves and in the value of applying their newly acquired
competency.

For example, at Weyerhaeuser Company (Latham &
Saari, 1979b) the supervisors, at the end of each training session, were given the learning points that described what the
model did effectively. Having practiced these points during the
session, the supervisors were asked to use these skills with one
or more employees within the following week. Problems that
were encountered were discussed and reenacted during the subsequent training session. In this way the trainees developed the
conviction that they were capable of dealing with increasingly
difficult situations.

In summary, modeling, to be truly effective as a coaching
technique, must allow for sufficient practice for employees to
achieve proficiency in the modeled skill. It must then be followed
by guided practices that allow people to experience success in
using these skills on the job.

Gist (1989) found that self-censorship stifles creativity
through self-judgments (e.g., "My idea is no good"). She argued
that cognitive modeling may be more appropriate than behavior
modeling when the performance deficiency is due to inappropriate thoughts rather than to overt behavior or skill.

Cognitive modeling is a self-instruction technique that
involves visualizing one's thoughts as one performs an activity.
The results of Gist's study of a federal research and development
agency showed that people in the cognitive-modeling condition
had significantly higher self-efficacy than did their lecture-
trained counterparts following training (Gist, 1989). In addition,
the cognitive-modeling subjects were superior to the lecture/prac-
tice group in generating divergent (i.e., creative) ideas.

Physiological State

Effective coaches realize that people rely in part on their physiological state when appraising their capabilities. They interpret their visceral arousal when they feel stressed as a signal of their vulnerability to dysfunction. Effective coaches assure people that it is natural to feel intimidated and to question one's ability. What is not okay is to lower the goal or to abandon the vision because of a low self-appraisal. Coaching involves helping people realize that initial feelings of tension do not signal incompetence. Among the ways to maximize physiological arousal so that it increases rather than decreases one's self-efficacy are the following:

1. Engage in positive self-talk. Think positively about the situation by becoming challenged. Recall similar situations or other challenges about which you felt doubt initially but successfully overcame the doubt and executed the task well.

2. When you make a mistake, use it as a source of information to make a change. Tell yourself that mistakes are natural and that you are learning from them.

3. Practice deep breathing to help you relax and lower your pulse rate while you remain focused on the task at hand.

Team-oriented Appraisals

An emerging trend in industry is to focus on the team rather than the individual when setting goals and giving feedback in relation to progress toward goal attainment. This trend has been fueled by Deming (1986), who observed that when the focus of the appraisal is on the individual, the goals that are set are often incongruent with those of the group and the overall organization. He thus concluded that the annual individual appraisal is the most powerful suppressor to quality and productivity in the Western world because it encourages dysfunctional competition, especially lack of teamwork. Consequently, people push themselves forward for their own good rather than for the good of the unit, division, or organization.

We agree with Deming's observations; we disagree with his conclusion. Abandoning the focus on the individual is akin to "throwing out the baby with the bath water." No athletic coach would ever consider embracing Deming's conclusion; no manager in any other organizational setting should embrace this conclusion.

A focus on the individual is necessary for several reasons:

1. meeting legal requirements in legal proceedings (Cleveland, Murphy & Williams, 1989)

2. validating hiring and promotion decisions (Cleveland, Murphy & Williams, 1989)

3. motivating the individual through feedback, recognition, and goal setting (Longnecker & Gioia, 1992)

4. developing the employee (Cleveland, Murphy & Williams, 1989)

5. clarifying the reasons for personnel decisions regarding such issues as promotion, termination, transfer, and salary increases

As we said earlier, Deming's observations are correct. The solutions include abandoning a sole emphasis on an annual appraisal and outcomes achieved in favor of ongoing coaching and an emphasis on the behaviors engaged in to achieve the outcomes. The team should be evaluated, as should the team members. Peers—the people on the team—are the people who are capable of doing this; they should be given the responsibility to ensure that the team's goals are aligned with those of the division and that each team member's goals are aligned with those of the team. And because organizational outcomes are affected by factors beyond the control of any one individual, the individual should be evaluated on what he or she does (behavior) to attain the organization's goals.

A paper company, for example, found that it was consistently failing to attain its projected bottom line. This is because the timberland's division looked for ways to attain its goals by delivering poor quality wood at maximum cost to the pulpmill; the pulpmill looked for ways to deliver marginally acceptable pulp to the tissue mill; the tissue mill discovered ways to give minimally acceptable paper to the finishing division; the finishing division was equally creative in coming up with ways of delivering an inferior product to distribution. In short, each manager of the five divisions was more interested in maximizing his bottom line than he was in maximizing the bottom line of the company. Consequently, the vice-president, to whom these managers reported, shifted the emphasis to job behaviors that impact outcomes rather than only on the outcomes themselves, and to a peer rather than a boss-subordinate appraisal. The behaviors on which the managers were evaluated are shown in the Appendix. The team of senior managers developed the instrument themselves and subsequently decided when each formal appraisal should take place. Feedback was *ongoing* among them to ensure favorable appraisals. To ensure candid formal appraisals, they were done anonymously in accordance with the discussion in Chapter 5. The result was a significant turnaround in the company's bottom line within eighteen months largely as a result of teamwork (e.g., actively looks for ways to hurt his/her bottom line for the overall good of the division).

Closing Remarks

The key to making formal appraisal effective is to focus on its developmental role on an ongoing basis. Administrative decisions can be made at the completion of a task cycle or the attainment of an important milestone. Leaving the developmental aspect of formal appraisals until the "end of the season" is unconscionable. To enhance the employee's ability and motivation, coaching must, on an ongoing basis, focus on the employee's outcome expectancies and self-efficacy.

Self-motivation is best summoned and sustained through the setting of specific challenging goals (Bandura, 1982, 1986; Locke & Latham, 1990). Goals raise one's expectation levels; they create inner discontent with the status quo. Once goal commitment occurs, people become attentive to the various ways of attaining the goal. They see new options and paths to the goal because they are now processing information differently.

Some people abandon the goal because their outcome expectancies are low. They too quickly seize on their inability to answer all the "hows" for goal attainment as justification for lowering it. The danger in lowering goals is that it retards employee development and growth. The danger in abandoning all goals is that work becomes meaningless.

People who tend to lower or abandon goals may have high outcome expectancies yet low self-efficacy (Frayne & Latham,

1987; Latham & Frayne, 1989). Self-efficacy is affected by information that is perceived as persuasive. Thus, for example, if people believe that intelligence tests are good predictors of performance and if people score poorly on the IQ test, they will in fact perform poorly even if the IQ score they were given was erroneous (Wood & Bandura, 1988). Similarly, people may be unduly influenced by what Tice (1989) refers to as a "Who Said of the Greatest Magnitude." That is, if someone whom they respect states that they lack the capability to do well, they generally do poorly. Conversely, if a "Who Said" tells them that the IQ test is incorrect, they act accordingly. One message for us as parents, let alone supervisors, is to focus on what we want rather than what we don't want. If we are respected by our children and we continually inform them of how sloppy they are in the home and in the school, they are likely to act accordingly. Conversely, if we tell them how neat and conscientious they are in both domains, they are likely to act in the way we described until someone else replaces us as a "Who Said."

Similarly, we must be alert to our own self-talk. We believe what we tell ourselves; we tend to do what we say (Latham & Saari, 1984). If we tell ourselves we are incapable of losing weight, we will likely lose very few pounds. If we say we are likely to slice or hook the golf ball, especially when we are on the first tee, we are likely to do so.

What we need to do is focus on what we are doing *right*. We need to visualize it; we need to rehearse it again and again until we convince ourselves that we have the will to repeat the performance successfully. Most of us have no difficulty waking up in the middle of the night to berate ourselves for failure. We need to give equal time to our successes. When we experience failure, we need to focus on what we learned from the failure, visualize it, and incorporate it into our self-talk. When people we respect make disparaging remarks about our ability, we need to forgive them with the knowledge that no one is always right, including them. In this way we can admit to ourselves that they may be correct in that we may not know the answer at this moment, but we are correct in knowing that we can determine where to go to find it. We may not be able to do "it" right now, but we know where to go to learn ways of getting it done. High self-efficacy means believing that "I can take that hill."

9

Letting People Go
with Class

Introduction

No matter how effective the coach, some people simply lack ability or motivation and should not remain on the team. Yet most managers experience considerable guilt at the very thought of terminating those individuals. They see the termination as an admission of their own failure to instill in the employee the ability and the desire to find ways to continuously grow and develop knowledge and skill in the organization. They question the humanity of turning an employee out into an environment in which it may prove exceedingly difficult to find suitable employment. They worry about how remaining employees will view the termination and the legal ramifications of their decision. Thus many managers choose to avoid the situation by allowing the person to remain in the present job or by transferring the individual and the problem to another area of the organization.

Such avoidance behavior should cause as much, if not more, guilt on the part of the manager who engages in it. The implicit signal to other employees is that inferior performance is acceptable in the organization. Employees who are performing well become demoralized when they see that they are treated no differently from a "social loafer," or someone who willingly allows other members to compensate for his or her deficiencies. If the problem is allowed to continue for years before appropriate action is taken, the employee may legitimately ask "why now?" and file a discrimination suit. Pleading to a judge that a rating of "acceptable" never truly meant "acceptable" is unlikely to lead to a ruling favorable to the employer.

Although layoffs and terminations are an ongoing phenomenon of organizational life, there is surprisingly little empirical research on what managers should do when requiring a person to leave the organization. There are, however, theories that strongly suggest effective ways to approach this issue, namely, organizational justice and impression management. The underlying emphasis is on ways of being perceived as treating employees fairly.

The importance of being perceived as fair was underscored with the demise of Eastern Airlines. Frank Lorenzo, president of Texas Air, the parent company of Eastern, developed a reputation with Eastern's machinist and pilot unions as being extremely unfair. When the unions went on strike, they made it clear that they would be willing to make significant concessions to outside parties who might be interested in purchasing the airline; they made it equally clear that they were *not* in favor of making any concessions to Lorenzo. Eastern lost more than $1 billion in one fiscal quarter and was forced into bankruptcy. Certainly, Eastern had other problems as well. But employees concentrated their hostility specifically on the president.

In this chapter we examine factors that contribute to employee perceptions of a just organization. Specifically, we examine the nature of procedural and interactional justice, the importance of "voice," and the role of impression management in contributing positively to perceptions of organizational justice. Finally, we present steps that can be taken in informing an employee of termination.

Organizational Justice

Taking a behavioral perspective, Podsakoff and his colleagues (Podsakoff, Todor & Skov, 1982; Podsakoff & Todor, 1985) found that when punishment is a direct consequence of a person's ineffective behavior, group cohesiveness and productivity, as well as the satisfaction and performance of the individual who was punished, are higher than when punishment is *not* contingent on behaviors. This vicarious effect on the surrounding members of the work group suggests that the beneficial effect of punishment is a function of how the recipient and coworkers interpret the disciplinary event.

The theory of organizational justice (Greenberg, 1987) explains how this occurs. The theory states that content and process issues affect an employee's judgment of justice. Content refers to the specific decision that was made regarding the employee; process refers to the procedural steps leading to the decision. The latter is more important than the former in bringing about and sustaining perceptions of fairness.

Procedural Justice

To enhance perceptions of fairness, seven procedural elements should be in place in an organization (Leventhal, 1976). These elements are worded as questions to enable you to determine whether your perception that the organization in which you are working is fair.

1. Do employees have input into the *selection of agents* who will make decisions about the allocation of rewards? Unions guarantee this through the election of employee representatives for bargaining sessions and grievance and disciplinary hearings. At most universities the faculty are ultrasensitive to issues of process; the university administration, not wanting a union, asks professors to make tenure, merit, and promotion decisions.

2. Are the *ground rules* for decisions established and understood before the decision-making process? Are people made aware of the behaviors that lead to rewards and punishments? University faculty members know that there is no quicker way to lose tenure than to be perceived as guilty of age, race, or sex discrimination in or outside the classroom. With regard to salary increases, the faculty know the 40–40–20 rule. That is, 40 percent of the weight in determining whether a professor will receive a salary increase is based on teaching performance, 40 percent is based on research publications, and 20 percent is based on service to the university and the community.

3. Are there *agreed on procedures* for obtaining and using information about employees? Decisions about faculty

teaching at many universities are restricted to the students' ratings. If suddenly the administration deviated from this practice by asking department chairpersons or deans to evaluate the course syllabi, without having given prior notice and without having provided a rationale, there would be an uproar of dissent from the faculty.

4. Is there a *decision structure* for the allocation process? What is the ordering of individual and group decisions? At the University of Washington, for example, the full and associate professors as a group evaluate each assistant professor; the full professors as a group evaluate each associate professor. The decision of the individual department chairperson is weighted equally with that of the faculty as a whole.

5. Are there *safeguards* for ensuring that the decision-making body does not abuse its power? Before a final salary decision is made at the University of Washington, for example, each department chairperson meets with the dean in a group setting. The dean makes a decision about each faculty member before learning the evaluation of the faculty and the respective department chairperson. The dean and each chairperson must explain their respective decisions in terms of the 40–40–20 rule. This is done as a safeguard against the possibility of favoritism. Similarly, before a faculty member can be required to leave the organization for inappropriate behavior, the reasons for the decision, at the faculty member's request, must be heard by a group of "disinterested" faculty, that is, faculty from other areas of the university. That group determines whether the decision is justified and then forwards a recommendation to the president to either support or reject the termination decision.

6. Is there an *appeal process?* The existence of an appeal process is necessary but not sufficient for ensuring perceptions of fairness. People must feel comfortable using it when they view a decision as inappropriate.

7. Are there *change mechanisms?* Can allocation decisions about rewards and punishers be altered? In

answering these questions, one can understand the popularity of unions. Unions strive hard to ensure due process rights for their members. It is almost always far simpler to terminate a salaried employee than a union member.

In examining the adequacy of these procedural elements in an organization, Leventhal, Karuza, and Fry (1980) identified six procedural issues that employees ask themselves before deciding whether a decision is fair.

1. Are the decision rules applied *consistently* across people and time? Before changes in decision rules are made, is ample notification given to all affected parties? Were their concerns listened to before the decision was made? Was the rationale for the change made known?

2. Is *bias suppressed?* Employees look for indications that the decision maker had a vested interest in the outcome. Did the termination allow the decision maker to get rid of someone who was a rival for a coveted position in the organization? Was the decision maker so influenced by prior beliefs about the person that other points of view did not receive consideration?

3. Are decisions based on *accurate information?* If someone is terminated on the basis of hearsay, the action will obviously be seen as unjust.

4. Is a poor decision *correctable?* Again, employees will look to see whether appeal procedures can be invoked. Will the discharged person be allowed to correct incorrect information or supply information that was missing when the original decision was made? For perceptions of fairness to exist, employees must believe that there is indeed a chance to change an inappropriate decision.

5. Does the decision reflect the viewpoint of a *representative sample* of the organization's members? For example, few employees tolerate stealing. But until a few years ago, few employees would tolerate an administrator's desire to ban smoking in the workplace. This ban is sanctioned today only because we have been

educated to the dangers of breathing cigarette smoke, even though some of us remain addicted to cigarettes. In short, when someone is terminated, people ask themselves whether the decision reflects the idiosyncracies of an administrator or the values of the organization at large.

6. Is the decision *ethical?* Is it aligned with prevailing societal standards? Most people understand why a person is let go for stealing thousands of dollars. Would they be equally understanding of terminating a person for stealing a pad of paper from the office?

"Voice" has been found to play an important role in influencing perceptions of a fair process. Voice is the opportunity to express one's views regarding a perceived inequity. However, for voice to have this effect, people must believe that what they said was subsequently considered by the decision maker before the decision was made (Tyler, 1989). Note that this concept goes beyond participation in decision making. If people perceive that being asked to participate in the decision making is merely a manipulative device for inducing employee loyalty and commitment, anger and frustration will occur (Cohen, 1985).

In a review of the literature, Greenberg (1982) found that it is not the outcome that determines whether a decision is perceived as fair but rather the *process* that was followed in determining the outcome. This is true regardless of the grade a person receives (Tyler & Caine, 1981) or the issuance of a traffic ticket (Tyler & Folger, 1980).

Interactional Justice

Even when an organization puts into practice policies and procedures in accordance with the principles above, employee perceptions of unfairness may persist due to interpersonal relationships in the workplace. Thus Bies and Moag (1986) argued for the inclusion of an intervening factor that influences perceptions of organizational justice, namely, interactional justice. Specifically, they argued that organizational justice is a function of the procedures in place, the interactions among members, and the resulting outcomes.

Tyler and Bies (1989) found that procedural fairness is a function of the perceived sincerity and adequacy of the explana-

tion. This finding is particularly relevant to termination decisions. An adequate explanation for a termination reduces the
time taken by the employee, as well as colleagues, to come to
terms with the situation. It helps to focus the thinking and
actions of the terminated employee toward searching for a new
job. In short, one of the most important factors affecting perceptions of procedural justice is how employees feel about the quality of the interactions they have experienced with management
(Greenberg & McCarty, 1990). This emphasis on interactional
justice may be especially important in minimizing wrongful-dis-
missal suits, which often reflect a desire to "get even" with the
person who made the decision to terminate the employee. For
example, a young, highly respected and well-liked manager in a
pharmaceutical company was fired for submitting the same
expense item on more than one expense account. This was the
only violation of ethics that the manager had knowingly made.
The manager was fired within the week that the company's
internal security people discovered the act. This was done
despite the manager's commitment to the goals of his work
team. The amount of money involved was relatively minuscule
in light of his salary and his contribution to the organization.
Nevertheless, the outcome was perceived as fair for two reasons.
First, the company's strong adherence to ethical behavior was
well known throughout the organization. Second, the person
who terminated the manager had been "like a father" to him. All
the members of the team were aware of the quality of this relationship. Everyone knew that the person who terminated the
manager was sincere in his regret that the manager had to be
told to leave the organization. In explaining the situation to others, he said:

> No one will miss Pat more than I. If a teenager picks-up a
> dollar off my living room floor and sticks it in his or her
> pocket, I would be annoyed. If one of you did likewise, I
> would be more than annoyed. My trust in you would be
> damaged. It is not the amount of money that is important
> in this situation; it is the signal that the action sends to
> all of us in the company about integrity. Similarly, if one
> of us tells an ethnic joke, it would be in bad taste. But if a
> member of the President's Cabinet tells the same joke, the
> person may be asked to resign from the position. This has

indeed happened; recently a cabinet minister of a former President of the United States was asked to resign not because of telling an ethnic joke per se, but because of the signal it would have sent to the American people regarding tolerance for others had he been allowed to continue working in his position.

Distributive Justice

This third component of organizational justice refers to outcomes, such as pay or layoffs, that are distributed throughout the workforce. A survey of government employees revealed that perceptions of the outcomes received are independent of perceptions of procedural justice. More importantly, a perception of procedural justice was the more important of the three types of justices regarding feelings of job satisfaction, evaluation of the supervisor, and trust in management (Alexander & Ruderman, 1983).

Impression Management

Impression management focuses on managers' communication of fair and equitable behavior to others (Greenberg, 1988). Because of the ambiguity inherent in most situations, it is necessary, yet not sufficient, for a manager to act fairly in order to be viewed as fair; one's actions must be interpreted as fair as well. For the latter to occur, people must understand the reasoning underlying a termination decision.

In 1987 the president of Ohio State University fired the university's football coach one week before the final game of the season. Claiming that such matters must be kept confidential, the president refused to divulge why the coach had been fired, let alone why he had been fired just before the biggest game of the year against Ohio State's arch rival, the University of Michigan. This secrecy generated tremendous ill will toward the president by the university community, the local press, and even the national press. Not surprisingly, Ohio State's football coach emerged as a sympathetic, victimized hero (Greenberg, 1990).

A long-term strategy for impression management is reputation building. Two tactics for creating a reputation for fairness are assertive and defensive actions. In a downsizing situation assertive tactics may take the form of a corporate communications campaign explaining the steps that will be taken to allow or facilitate early retirement. An open policy should be adopted whereby employees are informed of both legislatively required severance pay levels and the organization's own policy relating to such factors as relocation counseling. A participative approach that involves employees in deciding whether they should volunteer to leave the company gives people a sense of control over their destiny.

A well-publicized and hence well-understood reward system is key to minimizing the unpleasantness associated with terminating employees (Balkin, 1992). The Age Discrimination in Employment Act makes it illegal in the United States for an employer to force an employee to leave on the basis of age (only a few job categories, such as top management, are exempt from this law). But an early-retirement incentive package can make it financially attractive for senior employees to volunteer to leave the company. Such packages may accelerate the age requirement of older employees within the company for the sake of retirement benefits.

In 1991 IBM announced an early-retirement incentive program to reduce its workforce. Employees with 30 years of service qualified for full retirement benefits, and received a lump sum of one year's salary under the plan. Service credits were capped at 30 years so that people who chose to work beyond 30 years did not get further credit in the calculation of retirement benefits. The result was a significant redirection in the existing workforce which, in turn, significantly reduced fixed pay costs. Less expensive junior employees were given the opportunity to advance quickly in the organization to fill some of the gaps created by those who voluntarily left IBM.

Outplacement benefits can complement a voluntary severance plan. The advantages of doing so were experienced by Scott Paper Company's plant in Winslow, Maine, in 1991–1992 where the outcome was a significant improvement in union management relations as well as in the division's bottom line. The plant's senior management team and the executive committee of five union locals formed a steering committee. The company's financial officer taught everyone how to read a balance sheet, and how corporate headquarters interprets numbers as indicating whether a division should receive capital, be left alone, or shut down. The plant's financial books were then opened to the union. The rationale for employee downsizing in order to keep the plant viable in Scott Paper Company was clearly understood by salaried and unionized employees alike. With union officials and managers working together as equal partners, action steps were developed that included job location assistance from professional career counselors, office space for terminated employees, along with training in job-search skills, such as interviewing and resume preparation. For the first time in the history of Scott Paper, active and successful attempts were made to transfer unionized as opposed to only salaried employees to other Scott locations throughout the United States. There were no strikes due to the permanent lay-offs; there were no grievances. Perceptions of procedural justice, interactive justice, and distributive justice were exceedingly high. Further, by assisting departing workers with their transition to new jobs, Scott Paper maintained its image in the Winslow community as a good corporate citizen. In addition, the anxiety levels of the remaining employees decreased as they viewed the company as being fair, despite regrets about the departure of their friends.

Defensive actions to manage impressions can be combined with assertive tactics. Defensive actions include justification and even apologies for necessary decisions. Justification can include both situational and personal factors. Apologies indicate remorse and hence self-punishment.

Perceived Fairness in Performance Appraisal

The adequacy of performance appraisals has been traditionally judged in terms of Thorndike's (1949) criteria: validity, reliability, freedom from bias, and practicality. In a compelling essay Folger, Konovsky, and Cropanzano (1992) argued that there has been an overemphasis on the development of reliable and valid appraisal instruments and the training of raters to be accurate. Too little recognition has been given to the importance of perceived fairness in performance appraisals. Due process is important for creating the perception of fair appraisals. A principal feature of due process, they argued, is curbing the effect of self-interests through the focus on the rights of others. This is accomplished through adequate notice, a fair hearing, and judgments based on evidence.

Giving *adequate notice* should be simple in practice. It can be accomplished through the publication, distribution, and explanation of standards of performance. It can be accomplished by giving people time to prepare for the discussion in a formal appraisal. Yet in a study involving 700 manager-subordinate dyads at General Electric, Lawler, Mohrman, and Resnick (1984) found that subordinates were often surprised by formal appraisal interviews called on short notice. Two-thirds of the subordinates reported that the appraisals were not based on pre-determined objectives. Adequate notice entails a thorough discussion and understanding of standards, as well as ongoing feedback throughout the year regarding one's performance against those standards.

A *fair hearing* in performance appraisal involves the inclusion of self-appraisal with a supervisor's evaluation. As noted in Chapters 5 and 8, self-appraisal involves the employee gathering information that will be appraised, making an evaluation of the information, and participating in an evaluation of that information. This process has been shown to increase perceptions of fairness (Lissak, 1983; Kanfer et al., 1987).

With regard to the perceived accuracy of the *"evidence"* used when evaluating performance, an appraisal that has as its foundation job analysis, behavioral rating scales, and rater training enhances employees' perceptions that appraisals have a rational basis (Folger, Konovsky & Cropanzano, 1992). Greenberg (1987) found that appraisers who use diaries to record information throughout the appraisal period are viewed as more fair than those who do not use them.

Greenberg's (1987) research showed that perceptions of outcomes and procedural justice are relatively independent. Therefore appraisers should devote their efforts to making well-presented, reasonable decisions rather than placating employees with inflated ratings. In short, appraisers must discuss with employees not only the rationale for a given appraisal but the rationale underlying the decision-making process itself (Folger, Konovsky & Cropanzano, 1992).

Terminating the Employee

Adopting the viewpoints above regarding due process does not guarantee that the outcome will be favorable appraisals for the employee. When an individual performs inappropriately, fairness also requires that corrective action be taken. A supervisor who has given adequate notice, a fair hearing, and has made a judgment based on evidence should feel little guilt in terminating someone who had been given ample opportunity to succeed in the job.

A progressive disciplinary process should be followed, regardless of the employee's position in the organization or the presence of a union. In fact, many organizations that wish to remain nonunion follow a four-step process whereby a person who is behaving inappropriately receives a verbal warning, then a written warning, and then a suspension before a termination decision is made. The focus in the first three steps is on coaching the employee on ways to correct issues regarding ability or motivation to do the job effectively. A progressive disciplinary process is seen as fair in that there is little or no surprise when a person is terminated because the person was given ample opportunity to correct the situation.

Obviously, the severity of a person's actions is taken into account when administering progressive discipline. For example, someone who shoots the boss is unlikely to be given only a verbal warning. The rationale underlying progressive discipline is that the issue is correctable; hence the person is receiving adequate notice of the issue and a reasonable time period for correcting it.

Progressive organizations use a five-step process in correcting performance problems (Goldsten & Sorcher, 1974; Latham & Saari, 1979b; Wexley & Silverman, 1993). The initial step is problem solving, assuming that this is the first rather than the twenty-first time discussion of the performance issue with the employee has taken place. The steps are as follows:

1. *Focus on the problem.* Stay away from personalities. For example, you might say, "Sam, there is a production problem, and I'd appreciate your ideas on how to solve it. Production has decreased; I would appreciate your input on ways to increase it."

   Focusing on personalities is tantamount to criticism, which usually puts an employee on the defensive. The employee then feels the necessity for justifying the behavior and consequently resists changing it. And yet many supervisors feel that their role is that of a disciplinary agent similar to that of a grade school teacher or police officer. The role of the supervisor is to solve problems efficiently and effectively. Focusing on the issues rather than on personality is the effective way to solve problems.

2. Ask for the employee's help and discuss the ideas given on how to solve the problem. Employee participation in problem solving helps reduce resistance to change. Equally important is the likelihood that the ideas offered by the employee are good ones. In fact, it may be that in the final analysis the poor performance was not due to the employee after all but rather to improper work procedures. Regardless of the cause, when an employee offers ideas, there is an admission that the problem is worthy of discussion. Thus the key point in this step is to get ownership of ideas rather than a guilty plea.

3. Come to agreement on steps to be taken by each of you. This step is critical. It ensures not only the setting of specific goals but also goal clarity and understanding, as well as clarity and understanding on the part of the speakers. A key substep is to paraphrase, or repeat to the other person, what you believe has been said. An example of paraphrasing is: "Sam, if I hear you correctly, you will check with the computer people by Monday, and you will have the program debugged no later than Friday."

4. Plan a *specific* follow-up meeting. The word specific is emphasized to stress the necessity of making clear to the employee when the problem is to be corrected.

5. When the issue is resolved, praise the person for resolving it.

If the employee gives answers in step 2 that are clearly excuses that will not solve the problem, company labor relations personnel, union business agents, and research data (Latham & Saari, 1979a) stress that the same learning points should be followed. This procedure allows the employee to save face and to protect his or her self-esteem. The employee knows that you are aware of the problem and the time limit for correcting it. Most employees in these circumstances will correct the situation and will remember that you gave them the opportunity to do so without criticizing them or engaging in disciplinary action.

Discussing Poor Work Habits

Sometimes criticism cannot be avoided. If the poor performance does not improve or if it is impossible to avoid personalizing the issue (e.g., the employee has been leaving work early), the following points should be covered:

1. Explain to the employee, *without hostility,* what you have seen and why it concerns you. The discussion should *not* be an emotional one on your part. You as a manager are paid to solve problems; your role is not to act as the judge, jury, and executioner. Your tone should be no different from that of a newscaster.

2. Explain why the behavior cannot continue in words the employee can understand. For example, what happens when a report is late? Does the department really come to a standstill if the employee is absent? If you have a difficult time thinking of a rationale, possibly the behavior does not constitute a problem, and perhaps the rules should be changed.

3. Ask for and listen openly to the employee's reasons for the behavior. This step is critical for ensuring that your decisions are made on the basis of all available facts.

4. Focus on *one* specific problem. Do not allow the employee to lead you into a discussion of unrelated issues. For example, you may discuss the fact that the employee leaves work early. The employee may counter your comments with the perception that his or her work is outstanding in terms of quantity and quality, with no loss in productivity. You may respond with the observation that the quality of the person's work leaves much to be desired. In the heat of the ensuing argument, the original issue of leaving work early is forgotten.

5. Ask the employee for ideas on ways to solve the problem. Again, participation in problem solving increases commitment to change. In this case the employee's

behavior is the problem; the employee's ideas on the subject are a necessity.

6. Offer your help in solving the problem. In so doing you are communicating to the employee that you are truly interested in solving the problem rather than finding a way to take disciplinary action.

7. After agreeing on the cause or causes of the problem, come to agreement on steps to be taken by each of you. This ensures goal setting, clarity, and understanding between you and the employee about what is going to be done to solve the problem.

8. Set a specific follow-up date. This last step is the timetable for ensuring that the problem has been resolved.

Company labor relations personnel and the research data suggest that for minimizing or winning legal or union difficulties, this first discussion should be labeled a "problem-solving meeting." The meeting should be documented—the date of the meeting, the content of the discussion, the steps that were agreed on, and the timetable for implementing the steps. The employee should receive a copy of a memo summarizing this information. If a second, third, and fourth meeting are required because the issue has not been resolved, the employee should be given a formal verbal warning, a written letter, and a suspension/termination, respectively.

Salaried employees should be treated *no* differently from union employees. In too many cases, the salaried employee is simply terminated. A union guarantees that a person's security needs will be protected by clearly delineating the steps an organization must follow before the employee can be discharged. An organization can reduce feelings among salaried personnel for the necessity of instituting a union by treating them as fairly as they do their unionized work force.

Disciplinary Action
If the performance problem is not resolved and a subsequent discussion is necessary, the following points should be followed:

1. Define the problem in terms of lack of correction since the previous discussion. In other words, specify the exact issue or issues that have yet to be resolved.

2. Again explain, in words the employee can understand, why the behavior cannot continue. Do not simply cite company regulations or a union contract. What is the rationale underlying these regulations? Presenting a strong rationale depersonalizes the situation.

3. Ask for and listen openly to the employee's reasons for the continued behavior. This step should be followed even if there was a previous discussion on this subject months earlier. It is imperative that you attempt to collect all the facts before you take disciplinary action. For example, we know an employee who used his seniority to bump back from the day to the night shift. This was followed by excessive absenteeism. When he was at work, he was frequently away from his job. Almost always he could be found in the bathroom. Why?

   The company and the union had negotiated a no-fault absentee contract policy. If a person had sixteen days off during a year, no questions were to be asked. Was the employee taking advantage of this policy by adding days to his vacation time?

   After the seventeenth day away from work, the employee's manager asked for an explanation. The employee explained that he had cancer and had to go for treatment during the day to a hospital ninety miles away. The chemotherapy made him nauseous, which is why he spent so much time in the bathroom. He told no one of his illness because he did not want others to be staring at him or asking questions. No disciplinary action was discussed in this situation.

4. If disciplinary action is necessary, indicate specifically what the action will be, your reasons for taking this action, and when the action will take place. It must be stated explicitly whether the disciplinary action constitutes a verbal warning, a written warning, or a suspension. For example, if the phrase "verbal warning" is not used, an arbitrator or a court is likely to rule that none was given.

5. If the action does not require terminating the employee, stress that the employee is responsible for solving the problem, but that you are willing to help in any

way you can. The point here is to show that you are not picking on the employee. You should be truly disappointed that disciplinary action is needed, but your job is to correct problems as well as praise good performance. It is not your fault, for example, that the employee is repeatedly late for work, but it is your responsibility to work with the employee to find a solution to the problem.

6. Plan a specific follow-up meeting to praise the employee for correcting the problem.

Progressive companies usually give a suspension to salaried employees with pay. The issue is not to find ways of hurting the person's pocketbook. What is required is a change in the person's behavior. Therefore the employee is requested to return from a suspension with a three- to five-page action plan as to what he or she will start doing, stop doing, or begin doing differently to correct the situation; alternatively the person can initiate discussions regarding severance from the company.

When step 4 requires termination, the discussion can and should be brief because a problem-solving session, a verbal warning, a written warning, and a suspension have already preceded it. Once the termination has been announced, the supervisor should leave the room. To remain is to invite debate and argument. This recommendation means that the termination should occur in a room other than the supervisor's office. When the boss leaves the room, a neutral party, such as someone from Human Resources, should enter to discuss with the person concerns that may not have been answered. Typical questions from a discharged employee include:

1. Can I transfer to another location in the organization?
2. How long will my benefits continue?
3. Is there a severance package?
4. When can I clear out my office?
5. When do you want me to return company property (e.g., a computer) from my home?
6. What will my peers and my subordinates be told?
7. Will I receive a recommendation?
8. I would like an appointment to see a person in higher authority (e.g., my boss's boss) to discuss this situation.

Progressive companies allow the neutral party and the former employee ample time to discuss the situation in a private setting. A primary goal of the neutral party is to help the person understand the reasons for what has happened and to engage in constructive coping responses that will retain or restore the person's sense of control. Often the neutral party will offer to drive the person home if the anxiety level is sufficiently high that the discharged employee's driving ability might be impaired. The neutral party takes the initiative to contact the former employee several days later to answer questions that were not thought of at the time of the termination.

Closing Remarks

To reduce bias in the appraisal of employees, managers should use the best measurement technology available, including job analysis, behavioral rating scales, and systems of rater training. But as Folger, Konovsky, and Cropanzano (1992) noted, it is essential that appraisers not regard a package of measurement technologies as comprising the elements that ensure due process. Measurement technologies at best bear the imprimatur of science. No scientifically devised system provides a fool-proof check on human frailties. Thus, managers need to be as concerned with perceptions of fairness as they are with the reliability and validity of their decisions. Even if perfect accuracy were attained, employees could still feel unfairly treated if they perceived that some aspect of the decision making or implementation process violated procedural justice. As Folger, Konovsky, and Cropanzano concluded: "The due process metaphor suggests that if we cannot be sure of being correct, we can at least try to be fair . . ." (p. 171). Letting people go with class requires that due process be followed and that employees perceive that it was followed. Viewing terminations from a psychological rather than from only a legal perspective may do much to lower both the organization's and the employee's costs in this area (Latham et al., 1993).

Appendix

Behavioral Observation Scales for Managers in _____ Company's Strategic Planning Group (SPG)

Manager _____

Date _____

This checklist contains key job behaviors that managers have reported as critical for improving their contribution as SPG managers to the effectiveness/efficiency of Northwest (N.W.) operations.

Please consider the named individual's behavior on the job for the past six months. Read each statement carefully. Circle the number that indicates the extent to which you believe this person has demonstrated this behavior. For each behavior a 4 represents almost always, or 95 to 100 percent of the time. A 3 represents frequently, or 85 to 94 percent of the time. A 2 represents sometimes, or 75 to 84 percent of the time. A 1 represents seldom, or 65 to 74 percent of the time. A 0 represents almost never, or 0 to 64 percent of the time.

An example of an item is shown below. If a manager comes to meetings on time 95 to 100 percent of the time, you should circle a 4. If the manager hardly ever comes to meetings on time, you should circle 0.

Example: Comes to meetings on time.

Almost Never   0   1   2   3   4   Almost Always

Key Behaviors

I. Team Playing

1. Invites the input of SPG managers on issues that will directly affect them before making a decision

   Almost Never   0   1   2   3   4   Almost Always

2. Explains to SPG the rationale behind directives, decisions, and policies that may or will affect other divisions

   Almost Never   0   1   2   3   4   Almost Always

3. Keeps SPG informed of *major* changes in the department regarding people, policies, projects, construction, etc.

   Almost Never   0   1   2   3   4   Almost Always

4. Continually seeks input of SPG as a group on capital policy and plans rather than engaging primarily in interactions with individual managers

   Almost Never   0   1   2   3   4   Almost Always

5. Is open to criticism and questioning of decisions from SPG members at SPG meetings

   Almost Never   0   1   2   3   4   Almost Always

6. Supports SPG decisions

   Almost Never   0   1   2   3   4   Almost Always

7. Spends time learning about other SPG members' ongoing operations (e.g., their targets, timetables, interrelationships of targets within and between departments)

   Almost Never   0   1   2   3   4   Almost Always

8. Develops ways of combining departmental objectives with the overall objectives of N.W. operations

   Almost Never   0   1   2   3   4   Almost Always

9. Admits when doesn't know the answer

   Almost Never   0   1   2   3   4   Almost Always

10. Participates in SPG discussions (e.g., asks questions, brainstorms with group)

    Almost Never   0   1   2   3   4   Almost Always

11. Encourages candid comments (e.g., not offended by loss of temper by others)

    Almost Never   0   1   2   3   4   Almost Always

12. Acknowledges the expertise of fellow SPG members

    Almost Never   0   1   2   3   4   Almost Always

13. Looks for ways to support fellow SPG members (e.g., ideas, work hours)

    Almost Never   0   1   2   3   4   Almost Always

14. Keeps discussion in SPG meetings on key SPG issues

    Almost Never   0   1   2   3   4   Almost Always

15. Generates new ways of tackling new or ongoing problems

    Almost Never   0   1   2   3   4   Almost Always

16. Solicits comments from SPG members on the effectiveness of the structure of the organization

    Almost Never   0   1   2   3   4   Almost Always

    Total Score = _____

II. Planning/Forecasting

1. Operates on a crisis basis

   Almost Always   0   1   2   3   4   Almost Never

2. Sets goals that are difficult but attainable

   Almost Never   0   1   2   3   4   Almost Always

3. Establishes a realistic timetable to get the job done

   Almost Never   0   1   2   3   4   Almost Always

4. Planning/forecasting is based on investigation of facts

   Almost Never   0   1   2   3   4   Almost Always

5. Surfaces important issues for which there may be no immediate answers

   Almost Never   0   1   2   3   4   Almost Always

6. Identifies problems not previously considered by SPG that may affect N.W. operations

   Almost Never   0   1   2   3   4   Almost Always

7. Identifies opportunities to improve the value of N.W. assets

   Almost Never   0   1   2   3   4   Almost Always

8. Has broad overall strategy statements for the department that define where the department is to be five years from now

   Almost Never   0   1   2   3   4   Almost Always

9. Measures the success of the department and functional areas against the standards of SPG and/or N.W. operations and PPD

   Almost Never   0   1   2   3   4   Almost Always

10. Talks about day-to-day issues at SPG meetings only to the extent that they surface a new condition or situation that affects long-term strategies of SPG and/or N.W. operations

    Almost Never   0   1   2   3   4   Almost Always

11. Finds ways of incorporating/integrating the programs and objectives of the corporate office with those of the department/functional areas

    Almost Never   0   1   2   3   4   Almost Always

12. Identifies jobs, job requirements, as well as workforce needs and skills that are anticipated within the next three to five years in areas of own responsibility

    Almost Never   0   1   2   3   4   Almost Always

13. Establishes measures for evaluating the efficiency of the department/functional area to determine whether operating within an acceptable margin

    Almost Never   0   1   2   3   4   Almost Always

14. Establishes mechanisms for spotting trends/patterns on key departmental/functional areas

    Almost Never   0   1   2   3   4   Almost Always

    Total Score = _____

III. Interactions with Subordinates

1. Communicates objectives of SPG to the people he/she works with

   Almost Never   0   1   2   3   4   Almost Always

2. Requires managers to engage in planning and forecasting

   Almost Never   0   1   2   3   4   Almost Always

3. Encourages key managers to consider the value of team-building activity for their respective departments

   Almost Never   0   1   2   3   4   Almost Always

4. Clearly defines the role responsibilities of the key managers

   Almost Never   0   1   2   3   4   Almost Always

5. Communicates measurable standards against which people will be evaluated

   Almost Never   0   1   2   3   4   Almost Always

6. Solicits divergence of thinking on issues

   Almost Never   0   1   2   3   4   Almost Always

7. Sends key people to seminars for developmental purposes

   Almost Never   0   1   2   3   4   Almost Always

8. Attracts and trains people necessary to perform functions that will be critical within the next three to five years

   Almost Never   0   1   2   3   4   Almost Always

9. Changes the organization to fit the people who are reluctant to transfer, retire, be promoted, etc. (rather than insisting on an organization that is designed to accomplish the work that is expected of it)

   Almost Never   0   1   2   3   4   Almost Always

10. Procrastinates in dealing with poor performers

    Almost Always   0   1   2   3   4   Almost Never

11. Encourages subordinates to express their ideas in written form on one to two pages

    Almost Never   0   1   2   3   4   Almost Always

12. Holds people accountable for technical levels of performance as well as dollars (e.g., speed, efficiency, rates, rejection)

    Almost Never   0   1   2   3   4   Almost Always

13. Is frequently seen in the work areas of the people who report to the manager as well as their people (e.g., "shows the flag")

    Almost Never   0   1   2   3   4   Almost Always

14. Shows sensitivity in implementing change with people

    Almost Never   0   1   2   3   4   Almost Always

15. Increases a feeling of belongingness in the departments for which he/she is responsible

    Almost Never   0   1   2   3   4   Almost Always

16. Encourages the elimination of a we-they attitude among salaried and hourly employees

    Almost Never   0   1   2   3   4   Almost Always

17. Conveys a high concern for safety

    Almost Never   0   1   2   3   4   Almost Always

18. Makes self accessible to people who report to him or her

    Almost Never   0   1   2   3   4   Almost Always

19. Delegates responsibility commensurate with the authority of people

    Almost Never   0   1   2   3   4   Almost Always

20. Holds the key people accountable for motivating and training their people

    Almost Never   0   1   2   3   4   Almost Always

    Total Score = _____

Summary Comments

1. What is ___ doing that you believe is effective and you would like to see him/her continue doing?

2. What would you like to see ___ start doing, stop doing, or do differently?

Please record observations of critical incidents to support your ratings.

References

Ackerman v. *Western Electric Co., Inc.,* 1988. 860 F2d 1514.

Adams, J., Rice, R.W., & Instone, A., 1984. Follower attitudes toward women and judgements concerning performance by female and male leaders. *Academy of Management Journal, 27,* 636–643.

Albermarle Paper Company v. *Moody,* 1975. U.S. Supreme Court Nos. 74–389 and 74–428, 10 FEP Cases 1181.

Alexander, S., & Ruderman, M., August 1983. The influence of procedural and distributive justice on organizational behavior. Paper presented at the annual meeting of the American Psychological Association, Anaheim, CA.

Amiel, B., May 1991. Through the lenses of gender and ethnicity. *Maclean's,* p. 15.

Amir, Y., Kovarsky, Y., & Sharan, S., 1970. Peer nominations as a predictor of multistage promotions in a ramified organization. *Journal of Applied Psychology, 54,* 462–469.

Anastasi, A., 1976. *Psychological Testing.* New York: Macmillan.

Anderson, G.C., & Barnett, J.G., 1987. Characteristics of effective appraisal interviews. *Personnel Review, 16,* 18–25.

Andrews, I.R., & Henry, M.M., 1963. Management attitudes toward pay. *Industrial Relations, 3,* 29–39.

Ansonia Board of Education v. *Philbrook,* 1986. 42REP 359.

Arvey, R.D., & Faley, R.H., 1988. *Fairness in selecting employees.* Reading, MA: Addison-Wesley.

Ashford, S., 1989. Self assessments in organizations: A literature review and integration model. *Research in Organizational Behavior, 11,* 33–174.

Atkin, R.S., & Conlon, E.J., 1978. Behaviorally anchored rating scales: Some theoretical issues. *Academy of Management Review, 3,* 119–128.

Austin, J.T., & Villanova, P., 1992. The criterion problem: 1917–1992. *Journal of Applied Psychology, 77,* 836–874.

Bakke v. *Regents of the University of California,* 1978. 17 FEB.

Balkin, D.B., 1992. Managing employee separations with the reward system. *Academy of Management Executive, 6,* 64–71.

Bandura, A., 1977. *Social Learning Theory.* Englewood Cliffs, NJ: Prentice-Hall.

———, 1982. Self-efficacy mechanism in human agency. *American Psychologist, 37,* 122–147.

———, 1986. *Social Foundations of Thought and Action.* Englewood Cliffs, NJ: Prentice Hall.

———, 1988. Organizational applications of social cognitive theory. *Australian Journal of Management, 13,* 275–302.

———, & Schunk, D.H., 1981. Cultivating competence, self-efficacy and intrinsic interest through proximal self-motivation. *Journal of Personality and Social Psychology, 41,* 586–598.

———, Reese, C., & Adams, N.E., 1982. Microanalysis of action and fear arousal as a function of differential levels of perceived self-efficacy. *Journal of Personality and Social Psychology, 43,* 5–21.

Baron, R.A., 1988. Negative effects of destructive criticism: Impact on conflict, self-efficacy, and task performance. *Journal of Psychology, 73,* 199–207.

Barrett, G. V., & Kernan, M.C., 1987. Performance appraisal and terminations: A review of court decisions since *Brito* v. *Zia* with implications for personnel practices. *Personnel Psychology, 40,* 489–501.

Barrett, R.S., 1966. The influence of the supervisor's requirements on ratings. *Personnel Psychology, 19,* 375–387.

Bassett, G.A., & Meyer, H.H., 1968. Performance appraisal based on self-review. *Personnel Psychology, 21,* 421–430.

Bayroff, A.G., Haggerty, M.R., & Rundquist, E.A., 1954. Validity of ratings as related to rating techniques and conditions. *Personnel Psychology, 7,* 92–113.

Bem, D.J., 1972. Self-perception theory. In L. Berkowitz, ed., *Advances in Experimental Social Psychology.* New York: Academic Press.

Benson v. *Co-Op Atlantic,* 1985. 53 Nfld. & P.E.I.R. 210, 156 A.P.R. 210, 5S6.14723.

Benson, P.G., Buckley, M.R., & Hall, S., 1988. The impact of rating scale format on rater accuracy: An evaluation of the mixed standard scale. *Journal of Management, 14,* 415–423.

Bernardin, H.J., 1978. Effects of rater training on leniency and halo errors in student ratings of instructors. *Journal of Applied Psychology, 63,* 301–308.

————, 1980. Rater training: The state of confusion. Paper presented at the First Annual Symposium on Industrial-Organizational Psychology, Old Dominion University, Norfolk, Virginia.

————, & Beatty, R.W., 1984. *Performance appraisal: Assessing Human Behavior at Work.* Boston: Kent-Wadsworth.

————, & Beatty, R.W., Summer 1987. Can subordinate appraisals enhance managerial productivity? *Sloan Management Review,* pp. 63–73.

————, & Buckley, M.R., 1981. Strategies in rater training. *Academy of Management Review, 6,* 205–212.

————, & Pence, E.G., 1980. The effects of rater training: Creating new response sets and decreasing accuracy. *Journal of Applied Psychology, 65,* 60–66.

————, & Walter, C.S., 1977. Effects of rater training and diary-keeping on psychometric error in ratings. *Journal of Applied Psychology, 62,* 64–69.

————, Morgan, B.B., & Winne, P.S., 1980. Design and installation of a performance evaluation system in the Norfolk Police Department. *JSAS Catalogue of Selected Documents in Psychology,* 10, MS 2010.

Bersoff, D.N., 1988. Should subjective employment devices be scrutinized? It's elementary, my dear Ms. Watson. *American Psychologist, 43,* 1016–1018.

Bies, R.J., & Moag, J.S., 1986. Interactional justice: Communicating criteria of fairness. In R.J. Lewicki, B.H. Sheppard & M.H. Bazerman, eds., *Research on Negotiation in Organizations.* Greenwich, CT: JAI Press.

Blanz, F., & Ghiselli, E.E., 1972. The mixed standard scale: A new rating system. *Personnel Psychology, 25,* 185–199.

Blum, M.L, & Naylor, J.C., 1968. *Industrial Psychology: Its Theoretical and Social Foundations.* New York: Harper & Row.

Blumrosen, A.W., 1989. The 1989 supreme court ruling concerning employment discrimination and affirmative action: A minefield for employers and a gold mine for their lawyers. *Employee Relations Law Journal, 15,* 175–186.

Borman, W.C., 1975. Effects of instructions to avoid halo error on reliability and validity of performance evaluation ratings. *Journal of Applied Psychology, 60,* 556–560.

———, 1979. Format and training effects on rating accuracy and rater errors. *Journal of Applied Psychology, 64,* 410–421.

Boureslan v. *Aramco,* 1988. 857 F.2d 1014, 48 FEP 1 (5th Cir).

Bretz, R.D. Jr., & Milkovich, G.T., 1989. Performance appraisal in large organizations: Practice and research implications. (Working paper No. 89–17), Ithaca, NY: Cornell University, Center for Advanced Human Resource Studies (CAHRS).

Brief, A., 1980. Peer assessment revisited. A brief comment on Kane and Lawler. *Psychological Bulletin, 88,* 78–79.

Brito v. *Zia Company,* 1973. 478 F.2d. 1200.

Brogden, H.E., & Taylor, E.K., 1950. The dollar criterion: Applying the cost accounting concept to criterion construction. *Personnel Psychology, 3,* 135–154.

Burchett, S.R., & DeMeuse, K.P., 1985. Performance appraisal and the law. *Personnel, 62,* 29–37.

Burke, R.J., Weitzel, W., & Weir, T., 1978. Characteristics of effective employee performance review and development interviews: Replication and extension. *Personnel Psychology, 31,* 903–919.

Burnaska, R.J., 1976. The effects of behavior modeling training upon managers' behaviors and employees' perceptions. *Personnel Psychology, 29,* 329–335.

Burns, M.O., & Seligman, M.E.P., 1990. Explanatory style, helplessness & depression. In C.R. Snyder and D.R. Forsyths, eds., *Handbook of Social and Clinical Psychology.* New York: Pergamon Press.

Campbell, D.J., & Lee, C., 1988. Self-appraisal in performance evaluation: Development versus evaluation. *Academy of Management Journal, 13,* 302–314.

Campbell, J.P., 1977. The cutting edge of leadership: An overview. In J.G. Hunt & L.L. Larson, eds., *Leadership: The Cutting Edge.* Carbondale: Southern Illinois University Press.

———, Dunnette, M.D., Lawler, E.E., & Weick, K.E., 1970. *Managerial Behavior, Performance, and Effectiveness.* New York: McGraw-Hill.

Canadian Human Rights Act, 1978. Section 11, Canadian Human Rights Commission, Ottawa.

Casas v. *First American Bank,* 1983. 31 Fair Empl. Prac. Cas (BNA) 1479 (DDC).

Chalk v. *United States District Court,* 1988. 840, F.2d 701, 46 FEP 279 (9th Cir.).

Chamberlain v. *Bissell, Inc.,* 1982. D.C. Mich, 547 FSupp 1067.

Chaves v. *Thomas,* 1984. 35 Empl. Prac. Dec. P34,660.

Cleveland, J.N., & Landy, F.J., 1981. The influence of rater and ratee age on two performance judgements. *Personnel Psychology, 34,* 19–30.

——, Murphy, K.R., & Williams, R.E., 1989. Multiple uses of performance appraisal: Prevalence and correlates. *Journal of Applied Psychology, 74,* 130–135.

Coburn v. *Pan American World Airlines, Inc.,* 1982. CADC, 711 F2nd 339.

Cohen, R.L., 1985. Procedural justice and participation. *Human Relations, 38,* 643–663.

Cole v. *Dresser Canada Ltd.,* 1983. 4 C.C.E.L. 230 (Ont. H.C.), 5S6.14770.

Cooper, W.H., 1981. Conceptual similarity as a source of illusory halo in job performance ratings. *Journal of Applied Psychology, 66,* 302–307.

Cornell v. *Rogers Cablesystems Inc.,* 1987. 17 C.C.E.L. 232, 87 C.L.L.C. 14,054 (Ont. Dist. Ct.), 6S3.7741.

Cozan, L.W., 1955. Forced choice: Better than other rating methods? *Personnel, 36,* 80–83.

Cox, J.A., & Krumholtz, J.D., 1958. Racial bias in peer ratings of basic airmen. *Sociometry, 21,* 292–299.

Craft v. *Metromedia, Inc.,* 1985. 766 F.2d 1205, 38 FEP 404 (8th Cir.).

Cummings, L.L., & Schwab, D., 1973. *Performance in Organizations: Determinants and Appraisals.* Glenview, IL: Scott, Foresman.

Curtis, B., Smith, R.E., & Smoll, F.L., 1979. Scrutinizing the skipper: A study of leadership behaviors in the dugout. *Journal of Applied Psychology, 64,* 391–400.

Cygnar v. *Chicago,* 1989. 865 U.S.F.2d 827.

Daley, D.M., 1987. Performance appraisal and the creation of training and development expectations: A weak link in MBO-based appraisal systems. *Review of Public Personnel Administration, 8,* 1–10.

Deci, E.L., 1972. The effects of contingent and noncontingent rewards and controls on intrinsic motivation. *Organizational Behavior and Human Performance, 8,* 217–229.

DeJung, J.E., & Kaplan, H., 1962. Some differential effects of race of rater and ratee on early peer ratings of combat attitude. *Journal of Applied Psychology, 46,* 370–374.

Deming, W.E., 1986. *Out of the Crisis.* Cambridge: MIT Press.

DeNisi, A.S., & Mitchell, J.L., 1978. An analysis of peer ratings as predictors and criterion measures and a proposed new application. *Academy of Management Review, 3,* 369–374.

Dickerson v. *United States Steel Corp.,* 1978. 582 F.2d. 827, 17 FEP 1589 (3d Cir.).

Dickinson, T.L., & Glebocki, G.G., 1990. Modification in the format of the mixed standard scale. *Organizational Behavior and Human Decision Processes, 47,* 124–137.

———, & Zellinger, P.M., 1980. A comparison of the behaviorally anchored rating and mixed standard scale formats. *Journal of Applied Psychology, 65,* 147–154.

Diggs v. *Harris Hospital-Methodist Inc.,* 1988. CA5(Tex), 847 F2nd 270.

Dipboye, R.L., & de Pontbriand, R., 1981. Correlates of employee reactions to performance appraisals and appraisal systems. *Journal of Applied Psychology, 66,* 248–251.

Domingo v. *New England Fish Company,* 1977. 445 F. Supp. 421, W.D. Wash.

Dorfman, P.W., Stephan, W.G., & Loveland, J., 1986. Performance appraisal behaviors: Supervisors perceptions and subordinate reactions. *Personnel Psychology, 39,* 579–595.

Dossett, D.L., Latham, G.P., & Mitchell, T.R., 1979. The effects of assigned versus participatively set goals, KR, and individual differences when goal difficulty is held constant. *Journal of Applied Psychology, 64,* 291–298.

Dostoevsky, F., 1911. *The House of the Dead.* London: J.M. Dent.

Downs, S., Farr, R.M., & Colbeck, L., 1978. Self-appraisal: A convergence of selection and guidance. *Journal of Occupational Psychology, 51,* 271–278.

Drauden, G.M., & Peterson, W.G., 1977. Domain sampling approach to job analysis. *JSAS Catalogue of Selected Documents in Psychology,* 7:MS 1449.

Dreher, G.F., & Sackett, P.R., eds., 1983. *Perspectives on Employee Staffing and Selection.* Homewood, IL: Irwin.

Drucker, P., 1973. *Management: Tasks, Responsibilities, and Practices.* New York: Harper & Row.

Duarte, N.T., Goodson, J.R., & Klich, N.R., 1991. When time heals all ratings: The interactive effects of time in the supervisor-subordinate relationship on the accuracy of the performance appraisal. In J.L. Wall & L.R. Jauch, eds., *Academy of Management Best Paper Proceedings,* pp. 262–266.

Dunnette, M.D., 1976. Mish-mash, mush, and milestones in organizational psychology. In H. Meltzer & F.R. Wickert, eds., *Humanizing Organizational Behavior.* Springfield, IL.: Charles C. Thomas.

Dwyer, P., July 1989. The blow to affirmative action may not hurt that much. *Business Week,* pp. 61–63.

Eden, D., 1988. Pygmalion, goal setting, and expectancy: Compatible ways to boost productivity. *Academy of Management Review, 13,* 639–653.

———, & Ravid, G., 1982. Pygmalion v. self expectancies: Effects of instructor and self expectancy on trainee performance. *Organizational Behavior and Human Performance, 30,* 351–364.

———, & Shami, A.B., 1982. Pygmalion goes to boot camp: Expectancy, leadership, and trainee performance. *Journal of Applied Psychology, 67,* 194–199.

Eder, R.W., & Fedor, D.B., 1989. Priming performance self-evaluations: Moderating effects of rating purpose and judgement confidence. *Organizational Behavior & Human Decision Processes, 44,* 474–493.

Edwards, K.A., September 1976. Fair employment and performance appraisal: Legal requirements and practical guidelines. In D.L. DeVries, chm., Performance appraisal and feedback: Flies in the ointment. Symposium presented at the annual meeting of the American Psychological Association, Washington, D.C.

Equal Employment Opportunity Commission, 1978. Uniform Guidelines on Employee Selection. *Federal Register, 43,* 38290–38309.

———, 1979. Adoption of questions and answers to clarify and provide a common interpretation of the Uniform Guidelines on Employee Selection Procedures. *Federal Register, 44,* 11996–12009.

Equal Employment Opportunity Commission v. *Sandia Corp.,* 1980. CANM, 639 F2nd 600.

Erwin v. *Bank of Mississippi,* 1981. DCMiss, 512 FSupp 545.

Evans, M.G., 1970. The effects of supervisory behavior on the path-goal relationship. *Organizational Behavior and Human Performance, 5,* 277–298.

————, 1972. Leadership behaviors: Demographic factors and agreement between subordinate and self-descriptions. *Personnel Psychology, 25,* 649–653.

Everitt et al. v. *City of Marshall, Texas, et al.,* 1983. 703 F.2d 207 (5th Cir.); cert. den., 464 U.S. 894.

Eyres, P.S., 1989. Legally defensible performance appraisal systems. *Personnel Journal, 7,* 58–62.

Farh, J.L., Cannella, A., Jr., & Bedeian, A., 1991. The impact of purpose on rating quality and user acceptance. *Group and Organizational Studies, 16,* 367–386.

Farh, J.L., & Dobbins, G.H., 1989. Effects of self-esteem on leniency bias in self-reports of performance: A structural equation model analysis. *Personnel Psychology, 42,* 835–850.

————, & Werbel, J.D., 1986. Effects of purpose of the appraisal and expectation of validation on self-appraisal leniency. *Journal of Applied Psychology, 71,* 527–529.

————, Werbel, J.D., & Bedeian, A., 1988. An empirical investigation of self-appraisal-based performance evaluation. *Personnel Psychology, 41,* 141–156.

Fay, C.H., & Latham, G.P., 1982. Effects of training and rater scale on rating errors. *Personnel Psychology, 35,* 105–116.

Feild, H.S., & Holley, W.H., 1982. The relationship of performance appraisal system characteristics to verdicts in selected employment discrimination cases. *Academy of Management Journal, 25,* 392–406.

————, 1981. Beyond attribution theory: Cognitive processes in performance appraisal. *Journal of Applied Psychology, 66,* 127–148.

Festinger, L., 1954. A theory of social comparison processes. *Human Relations, 7,* 117–140.

Fiske, D.W., 1960. Variability among peer ratings in different situations. *Educational and Psychological Measurement, 20,* 283–292.

Flanagan, J.C., 1949. Critical requirements. A new approach to employee evaluation. *Personnel Psychology, 2,* 419–425.

————, 1954. The critical incident technique. *Psychological Bulletin, 51,* 327–358.

Folger, R., Konovsky, M.A., & Cropanzano, R., 1992. A due process metaphor for performance appraisal. In B.M. Staw & L.L. Cummings, eds., *Research in Organizational Behavior, 14,* 129–177.

Fowler, R.L., 1985. Testing for substantive significance in applied research by specifying non-zero effect null hypotheses. *Journal of Applied Psychology, 70,* 215–218.

Fox, S., & Dinur, Y., 1988. Validity of self-assessment: A field evaluation. *Personnel Psychology, 41,* 581–592.

————, Ben-Nahum, Z., & Yinon, Y., 1989. Perceived similarity and accuracy of peer ratings. *Journal of Applied Psychology, 74,* 781–786.

Frank, J., 1983. *Dostoevsky: Years of Ordeal.* Princeton, NJ: Princeton University Press.

Frayne, C.A., & Latham, G.P., 1987. Application of social learning theory to employee self-management of attendance. *Journal of Applied Psychology, 72,* 387–392.

French, W.L., Bell, C.H., Jr., & Zawacki, R., 1989. *Organization Development.* Plano, TX: Business Publications.

Friedman, B.A., & Cornelius, E.T., III., 1976. Effect of rater participation in scale construction on the psychometric characteristics of two rating scale formats. *Journal of Applied Psychology, 61,* 210–216.

Galbraith, J.R., 1977. *Organization Design.* Reading, MA: Addison-Wesley.

Ghiselli, E.E., 1956. Dimensional problems of criteria. *Journal of Applied Psychology, 40,* 1–4.

Gist, M., 1989. The influence of training method on self-efficacy and idea generation among managers. *Personnel Psychology, 42,* 787–805.

Glass v. *Petro-tex Chemical Corp.,* 1985. 757 F.2d 1554, 37 FEP972 (5th Cir.).

Goddard, R.W., 1989. Is your appraisal system headed for court? *Personnel Journal, 68,* 114–118.

Goldsten, I.L. & Sorcher, M., 1974. *Changing Supervisor Behavior.* Elmsford, NY: Pergamon Press.

Gomez-Mejia, L.R., 1988. Evaluating employee performance: Does the appraisal instrument make a difference? *Journal of Organizational Behavior Management, 9,* 155–172.

Gordon, L.V., & Medland, F.F., 1965. The cross-group stability of peer ratings of leadership potential. *Personnel Psychology, 18,* 173–177.

Grant v. *Gannett Co., Inc.,* 1982. DCDel, 538 FSupp 686.

Gray v. Electrolux Canada, 1986. 45 Man.R.(2d)82 (Q.B.) 6S3.7798.

Greenberg, J., 1982. Approaching equity and avoiding inequity in groups and organizations. In J. Greenberg & R.L. Cohen, eds., *Equity and Justice in Social Behavior.* New York: Academic Press, pp. 389–435.

————, 1986. Determinants of perceived fairness of performance evaluations. *Journal of Applied Psychology, 71,* 340–342.

————, 1987. Using diaries to promote procedural justice in performance appraisal. *Social Justice Research, 1,* 219–234.

————, 1988. Using explanations to manage impressions of performance appraisal fairness. In J.R. Greenberg & R. Bies (Chairs), Communicating fairness in organizations, symposium presented at the annual meeting of the Academy of Management, Anaheim, CA.

————, 1990. Looking fair vs. being fair: Managing impressions of organizational justice. In B.M. Staw & L.L. Cummings, eds., *Research in Organizational Behavior, 12,* 111–158.

————, & McCarty, L.L., August 1990. The interpersonal aspects of procedural justice: A new perspective on pay fairness. *Labor Law Journal,* Vol. 44, pp. 580–586.

Greenhaus, J.H., Parasuraman, S., & Wormley, W.M., 1990. Effects of race on organizational experience, job performance evaluations, and career outcomes. *Academy of Management Journal, 33,* 64–86.

Greenspan v. Automobile Club of Michigan, 22FEP 195, 1980.

Greller, M.M., 1975. Subordinate participation and reaction to the appraisal interview. *Journal of Applied Psychology, 60,* 544–549.

Griffeth, R.W., & Bedeian, A.G., 1989. Employee performance evaluations: Effects of ratee age, rater age, and ratee gender. *Journal of Organizational Behavior, 10,* 83–90.

Griggs v. Duke Power Company, 1971. 401 U.S., 3 EPD 8137.

Grunwald, H., & Duncan, R., February 4, 1980. An interview with Fidel Castro. *Time Magazine,* pp. 48–49.

Guion, R.J., 1961. Criterion measurement and personnel judgments. *Personnel Psychology, 14,* 141–149.

Guion, R.M., 1965. *Personnel testing.* New York: McGraw-Hill.

Hanges, P.J., Baverman, E.P., & Rentsch, J.R., 1991. Changes in raters' perceptions of subordinates: A catastrophe model. *Journal of Applied Psychology, 76,* 878–888.

Harackiewicz, J.M., & Larson, J.R., Jr., 1986. Managing motivation: The impact of supervisor feedback on subordinate task interest. *Journal of Personality and Social Psychology, 51,* 547–556.

Harris, M.M., & Schaubroeck, J., 1988. A meta-analysis of self-supervisor, self-peer, and peer-supervisor ratings. *Personnel Psychology, 41,* 43–62.

Hedge, J.W., & Kavanagh, M.J., 1988. Improving the accuracy of performance evaluations: Comparison of three methods of performance appraiser training. *Journal of Applied Psychology, 73,* 68–73.

Herzberg, F., 1968. One more time: How do you motivate employees? *Harvard Business Review,* Vol. 1, 53–62.

Hillery, J.M., & Wexley, K.N., 1974. Participation in appraisal interviews conducted in a training situation. *Journal of Applied Psychology, 59,* 168–171.

Hinrichs, J.R., 1978. *Practical Management of Productivity.* New York: Van Nostrand Reinhold.

Hoffman, C.C., Fredricks, A., & Doverspike, D., 1983. Another look at "Do behavioral observation scales measure observation?" Paper presented at the 91st annual meeting of the American Psychological Association, Anaheim, CA.

———, Nathan, B.R., & Holden, L.M., 1991. A comparison of validation criteria: Objective versus subjective performance measures and self-versus supervisor ratings. *Personnel Psychology, 44,* 601–619.

Hollander, E.P., 1954a. Buddy ratings: Military research and industrial implications. *Personnel Psychology, 7,* 385–393.

———, 1954b. Peer nominations on leadership as a predictor of the pass-fail criterion in naval air training. *Journal of Applied Psychology, 38,* 150–153.

———, 1957. The reliability of peer nominations under various conditions of administration. *Journal of Applied Psychology, 41,* 85–90.

———, 1965. Validity of peer nominations in predicting a distant performance criterion. *Journal of Applied Psychology, 49,* 434–438.

Howard v. *Miller Brewing Co.,* 1983. 31 FEP Cases 850 (N.D.N.Y.).

Hudson v. *Western Airlines, Inc.,* 1988. 851 F.2d 261, 47FEP 295 (9th Cir.).

Hughes, G.L., & Prien, E.P., 1986. An evaluation of alternative scoring methods for mixed standard scale. *Personnel Psychology, 39,* 839–847.

Hung, J.H., & Rosenthal, T.L., 1981. Therapeutic videotaped playback. In J.L. Fryeor and R. Flishan, eds., *Videotheraphy in Mental Health.* Springfield, IL: Charles C. Thomas, 5–46.

Hunter, J.E., Schmidt, F.L., & Jackson, G.B., 1982. *Meta-Analysis: Cumulating Research Findings Across Studies.* Beverly Hills: Sage.

Ibrahim v. *Association of Professional Engineers, Geologists and Geophysicists of Alberta,* 1985. 41 Alta. L.R. (2d), 126, 64A.R. 292 (Q.B.) 5S6.14736.

Imada, A.S., 1982. Social interaction, observation, and stereotypes as determinants of differentiation in peer ratings. *Organizational Behavior and Human Performance, 29,* 397–415.

Industrial-Organizational Psychology Division of the American Psychological Association, 1980. Principles for the validation and use of personnel procedures. Discussion Draft.

Ivancevich, J.M., Donnelly, J.H., & Lyon, H.L., 1970. A study of the impact of management by objectives on perceived need satisfaction. *Personnel Psychology, 23,* 139–151.

Jackson v. *Gulf Oil Corp.,* 1981. 23 Empl. Prac. Dec. P30,953 (S.D.Tex.) 648 F.2d 1340 (5h cir.).

Jako R.A., & Murphy, K.R., 1990. Distributional ratings, judgement decomposition, and their impact on interrater agreement and rating accuracy. *Journal of Applied Psychology, 75,* 500–505.

Jaques, E. *Requisite organization: The CEO's guide,* 1980. Arlington, VA: Carson Hall and Co.

James v. *Stockham Valves and Fittings Co.,* 1978. 559 F.2d. 310, cert. denied 434 U.S. 1034.

Jasany v. *United States Postal Service,* 1985. 755 F.2d 1244 (16th Cir).

Jenkins, G.D., & Taber, T.A., 1977. A Monte Carlo study of factors affecting three indices of composite scale reliability. *Journal of Applied Psychology, 62,* 392–398.

Johnson v. *Transportation Agency of Santa Clara County, CA.,* 1987. 480 U.S. 616–632.

Kafry, D., Jacobs, R., & Zedeck, S., 1979. Discriminability in multidimensional performance evaluations. *Applied Psychologist Measurement, 3,* 187–192.

Kandel, W.L., Winter 1988. Current developments in EEO. *Employee Relations, 13,* 520–529.

Kane, J.S., & Bernardin, H.J., 1982. Behavioral observation scales and the evaluation of performance appraisal effectiveness. *Personnel Psychology, 35,* 635–642.

———, & Lawler, E.E., III., 1978. Methods of peer assessment. *Psychological Bulletin, 85,* 555–586.

———, & Lawler, E.E., III., 1980. In defense of peer assessment. A rebuttal of Brief's critique. *Psychological Bulletin, 88,* 80–81.

Kanfer, F.H., 1980. Self-management methods. In F.H. Kanfer & A.P. Goldstein, eds., *Helping People Change: A Textbook of Methods.* New York: Pergamon Press.

Kanfer, R., Sawyer, T., Earley, P.C., & Lind, E.A., 1986. Participation in task evaluation procedures: The effects of influential opinion expression and knowledge of evaluative criteria on attitudes and performance. *Social Justice Research, 1,* 235–249.

Kaplan, R.E., Drath, W.H., & Kofodimus, J.R., 1987. High hurdles: The challenge of executive self-development. *The Academy of Management Executive, 1,* 195–206.

Karoly, P., & Kanfer, F.H., 1982. *Self-Management and Behavior Change: From Theory to Practice.* New York: Pergamon Press.

Kavanagh, M.J., MacKinney, A. C., & Wolins, L., 1971. Issues in managerial performance: Multitrait-multimethod analysis of ratings. *Psychological Bulletin, 75,* 34–49.

Kay, E., Meyer, H.H., & French, J.R.P., Jr., 1965. Effects of threat in a performance appraisal interview. *Journal of Applied Psychology, 49,* 311–317.

Kearney, W.J., 1979. Behaviorally anchored rating scales - MBO's missing ingredient. *Personnel Journal, 58,* 20–25.

Kilmann, R.H., & Herden, R.P., 1976. Towards a systematic methodology for evaluating the impact of intervention on organizations. *Academy of Management Review, 2,* 87–98.

Kirkland v. *New York Department of Correctional Services,* 1974. 7FEB700.

Komacki, J.L., & Desselles, M.L., in press. *Supervision Reexamined: The Role of Monitors and Consequences.* Boston: Allyn & Unwin.

Korman, A.K., 1968. The prediction of managerial performance: A review. *Personnel Psychology, 21,* 295–322.

Krackhardt, D., McKenna, J., Porter, L.W., & Steers, R.M., 1978. Goal setting, supervisory behavior, and employee turnover: A field experiment. Technical Report No. 17, Graduate School of Management, University of Oregon.

Kraft v. *Wine Rope Industries,* 1985. 30 ACWS (2d) 76.

Kraiger, K., & Ford, J.K., 1985. A meta-analysis of ratee race effects in performance ratings. *Journal of Applied Psychology, 70,* 56–65.

Kremer, J.F., 1990. Construct validity of multiple measures in teaching, research and service and reliability of peer ratings. *Journal of Educational Psychology, 82,* 213–218.

Krzystofiak, F., Cardy, R., & Newman, J., 1988. Implicit personality & performance appraisal: The influence of trait inferences on evaluations of behavior. *Journal of Applied Psychology, 73,* 515–521.

Kubany, A.J., 1957. Use of sociometric peer nominations in medical education research. *Journal of Applied Psychology, 41,* 389–394.

Landy, F.J., & Farr, J.L., 1980. Performance rating. *Psychological Bulletin, 87,* 72–107.

———, & Vasey, J., 1991. Job analysis: The composition of SME samples. *Personnel Psychology, 44,* 27–50.

———, Barnes, J.L., & Murphy, K.R., 1978. Correlates of perceived fairness and accuracy of performance evaluation. *Journal of Applied Psychology, 63,* 751–754.

———, Farr, J.L., Saal, F.E., & Freytag, W.R., 1976. Behaviorally anchored scales for rating the performance of police officers. *Journal of Applied Psychology, 61,* 750–758.

Lane, J., & Herriot, P., 1990. Self-ratings, supervisor ratings, positions, & performance. *Journal of Occupational Psychology, 63,* 77–88.

Larson, J.R., Lingle, J.H., & Scerbo, M.M., 1984. The impact of performance cues on leader-behavior ratings: The role of selective information availability and probabilistic response bias. *Organizational Behavior and Human Performance, 33,* 323–349.

Latham, G.P., 1969. The development of job performance criteria for pulpwood producers in the southeastern United States. Unpublished master's thesis, Georgia Institute of Technology.

———, 1986. Job performance and appraisal. In C.L. Cooper and I. Robertson, eds., *International Review of Industrial and Organizational Psychology.* Chichester: Wiley.

———, & Baldes, J.J., 1975. The "practical significance" of Locke's theory of goal setting. *Journal of Applied Psychology, 60,* 122–124.

———, & Dossett, D.L., 1978. Designing incentive plans for unionized employees: A comparison of continuous and variable ratio reinforcement schedules. *Personnel Psychology, 31,* 47–61.

———, & Frayne, C.A., 1989. Self-management training for increasing job attendance: A follow-up and a replication. *Journal of Applied Psychology, 74,* 415–416.

———, & Fry, L.W., 1988. Measuring and appraising employee performance. In S. Gael, ed., *The Job Analysis Handbook.* New York: Wiley.

———, & Kinne, S.B., 1974. Improving job performance through training in goal setting. *Journal of Applied Psychology, 59,* 187–191.

———, & Saari, L.M., 1979a. The importance of supportive relationships in goal setting. *Journal of Applied Psychology, 64,* 163–168.

———, & Saari, L.M., 1979b. The application of social learning theory to training supervisors through behavioral modeling. *Journal of Applied Psychology, 64,* 239–246.

———, & Saari, L.M., 1984. Do people do what they say? Further studies on the situational interview. *Journal of Applied Psychology, 69,* 569–573.

———, & Wexley, K.N., 1977. Behavioral observation scales for performance appraisal purposes. *Personnel Psychology, 30,* 255–268.

———, & Wexley, K.N., 1981. *Increasing Productivity Through Performance Appraisal.* Reading, MA.: Addison-Wesley.

———, & Yukl, G.A., 1975. A review of research on the application of goal setting in organization. *Academy of Management Journal, 18,* 824–845.

———, Erez, M., & Locke, E., 1988. Resolving scientific disputes by the joint design of crucial experiments by the antagonists: Application to the Erez-Latham dispute regarding participation in goal setting. *Journal of Applied Psychology, 73,* 753–772.

———, Fay, C.H., & Saari, L.M., 1979. The development of behavioral observation scales for appraising the performance of foremen. *Personnel Psychology, 32,* 299–311.

———, Fay, C., & Saari, L.M., 1980. BOS, BES and baloney: Raising Kane with Bernardin. *Personnel Psychology, 33,* 815–821.

———, Mitchell, T.R., & Dossett, D.L., 1978. The importance of participative goal setting and anticipated rewards on goal difficulty and job performance. *Journal of Applied Psychology, 63,* 170–171.

————, Pursell, E.D., & Wexley, K.N., 1974. *Predicting Logging Performance Through Behavioral Accounting.* Tacoma, Wash.: Human Resource Planning and Development, Weyerhaeuser Company.

————, Wexley, K.N., & Pursell, E.D., 1975. Training managers to minimize rating errors in the observation of behavior. *Journal of Applied Psychology, 60,* 550–555.

————, Wexley, K.N., & Rand, T.M., 1975. The relevance of behavioral criteria developed from the critical incident technique. *Canadian Journal of Behavioural Science, 7,* 349–358.

————, Winters, D.C., & Locke, E.A., in press. Cognitive and motivational effects of participation: A mediator study. *Journal of Organizational Behavior.*

————, Skarlicki, D., Irvine, D., & Siegel, J., 1993. The increasing importance of performance appraisals to employee effectiveness in organizational settings in North America. In C.L. Cooper & I.T. Robertson, eds., *International Review of Industrial and Organizational Psychology.* Chichester-Wiley.

Laumeyer, J., & Beebe, T., 1988. Employees and their appraisal. *Personnel Administrator, 33,* 76–80.

Lawler, E.E., III., 1967. The multitrait-multirater approach to measuring managerial job performance. *Journal of Applied Psychology, 51,* 369–381.

————, 1971. *Pay and Organizational Effectiveness: A Psychological View.* New York: McGraw-Hill.

————, & Mohrman, S.A., 1989. With HR help, all managers can practice high involvement management. *Personnel, 66,* 26–31.

————, Mohrman, A.M., & Resnick, S., Summer 1984. Performance appraisal revisited. *Organization Dynamics,* pp. 20–35.

Lawler, T.G., 1988. The objectives of performance appraisal—or "Where can we go from here?" *Nursing Management, 19,* 82–88.

Lawrence, P.R., & Lorsch, J.W., 1967. *Organization and Environment.* Homewood, IL: Irwin.

Lawrie, J.W., 1989. Your performance: Appraise it yourself! *Personnel, 66,* 21–23.

Lawshe, C.M., 1959. Statistical theory and practice in applied psychology. *Personnel Psychology, 22,* 117–124.

Lazer, R.I., & Wikstrom, W.S., 1977. *Appraising Managerial Performance: Current Practices and Future Directions.* New York: Conference Board.

Leonard, J.S., Winter 1989. The changing face of employees and employment regulation. *California Management Review,* pp. 29–38.

Leung, K., & Li, W., 1990. Psychological mechanisms of process-control effects. *Journal of Applied Psychology, 75,* 613–620.

Leventhal, G.S., 1976. Fairness in social relationships. In J.W. Thibaut, J.T. Spence, & R.C. Carson, eds., *Contemporary Topics in Social Psychology.* Morristown, NJ: General Learning Press, pp. 211–239.

———, Karuza, J. Jr., & Fry, W.R., 1980. Beyond fairness: A theory of allocation preferences. In G. Mikula, ed., *Justice and Social Interaction.* Bern, Switzerland: Huber.

Levine, E.L., Ash, R.A., & Bennett, N., 1980. Exploratory comparative study of four job analysis methods. *Journal of Applied Psychology, 65,* 524–535.

———, Ash, R.A., Hall, H., & Sistruck, F., 1983. Evaluation of job analysis methods by experienced job analysts. *Academy of Management Journal, 26,* 339–348.

Levine, J., & Butler, J., 1952. Lecture versus group discussion in changing behavior. *Journal of Applied Psychology, 36,* 29–33.

Levine, J.M., & Moreland, R.L., 1990. Progress in small group research. *Annual Review of Psychology, 41,* 585–634.

Levinson, D., 1987. Making employee performance evaluations work for you. *Nonprofit World, 5,* 28–30.

Likert, R., 1932. A technique for the measurement of attitudes. *Archives of Psychology, 140,* 44–53.

———, 1967. *The Human Organization.* New York: McGraw-Hill.

Lissak, R.I., 1967. Procedural fairness: How employees evaluate procedures. Unpublished doctoral dissertation, University of Illinois.

Lissitz, R.W., & Green, S.B., 1975. Effect of the number of scale points on reliability: A Monte Carlo approach. *Journal of Applied Psychology, 60,* 10–13.

Locher, A.H., & Teel, K.S., September 1988. Assessment: Appraisal trends. *Personnel Journal,* pp. 139–144.

Locke, E.A., 1968. Toward a theory of task motivation and incentives. *Organizational Behavior and Human Performance, 3,* 157–189.

———, 1976. The nature and causes of job satisfaction. In M. Dunnette, ed., *Handbook of Industrial and Organizational Psychology.* Chicago: Rand McNally.

————, & Latham, G.P., 1990. *A Theory of Goal Setting and Task Performance.* Englewood Cliffs, NJ: Prentice-Hall.

————, Frederick, E., Lee, C., & Bobko, P., 1984. Effect of self-efficacy, goals, and task strategies on task performance. *Journal of Applied Psychology, 69,* 241–251.

————, Kirkpatrick, S., Wheeler, J.K., Schneider, J., Niles, K., Goldstein, H., Welsh, K., & Chah, D., 1991. *The Essence of Leadership: The Four Keys to Leading Successfully.* New York: Lexington Books.

Loftus, E.F., 1983. Silence is not golden. *American Psychologist, 38,* 564–572.

Longnecker, C.O., & Gioia, D.A., 1992. The executive appraisal paradox. *Academy of Management Executive, 6,* 18–27.

————, Sims, H.R., Jr., & Gioia, D.A., 1987. Behind the mask: The politics of employee appraisal. *Academy of Management Executive, 1,* 183–193.

Love, K.G., 1981. Comparison of peer assessment methods: Reliability, validity, friendship bias, and user reaction. *Journal of Applied Psychology, 66,* 451–457.

Lykken, D.J., 1968. Statistical significance in psychological research. *Psychological Bulletin, 70,* 151–159.

Mabe, P.A., III., & West, S.G., 1982. Validity of self-evaluation of ability: A review and meta-analysis. *Journal of Applied Psychology, 67,* 280–296.

MacEachern v. *Nova Scotia (Attorney General),* 1987. 19 C.C.E.L. 16, 6S3.7719.

Maier, N.R.F., 1958. *The Appraisal Interview.* New York: Wiley.

Makihara, K., 1990. Who needs equality? *Time, 136,* Special Issue, p. 35.

Mallinger, M.A., & Cummings, T.G., 1986. Improving the value of performance appraisals. *Advanced Management Journal, 51,* 19–21.

Maloney, P.W., & Hinrichs, J.R., 1959. A new tool for supervisory self-development. *Personnel, 36,* 46–53.

Manners v. *Fraser Survey Docks Ltd.,* May 11, 1981. Unpublished DCSC.

Manz, C.C., & Sims, H.P., Jr., 1980. Self-management as a substitute for leadership: Social learning theory perspective. *Academy of Management Review, 7,* 195–204.

Markou v. *Water Refining Company Limited,* 1980. 2 ACWS (2d) 210.

Martin, D.C., Bartol, K.M., & Levine, M.J., 1986. The legal ramifications of performance appraisal. *Employee Relations Law Journal, 12,* 370–395.

Martin, S.L., & Klimoski, R.J., 1990. Use of verbal protocols to trace cognitions associated with self- and supervisor evaluations of performance. *Organizational Behavior and Human Decision Processes, 46,* 135–154.

Martinez v. El Paso County, 1983. CATex, 710 F2d 1102.

Mayfield, E.C., 1970. Management selection: Buddy nominations revisited. *Personnel Psychology, 23,* 377–391.

————, 1972. Value of peer nominations in predicting life insurance sales performance. *Journal of Applied Psychology, 56,* 319–323.

McCall, M.W., & DeVries, D.I., September 1976. Appraisal in context: Clashing with organizational realities. In D. DeVries, chm., Performance appraisal and feedback: Flies in the ointment. Symposium presented at the annual meeting of the American Psychological Association, Washington, D.C.

————, & Lombardo, M.M., 1983. Off the track: Why and how successful executives get derailed (Technical Report No. 9). Greensboro, NC: Center for Creative Leadership.

McCarther v. Camelot Inn of Little Rock, 1981. DCArk, 513 FSupp 355.

McCormick, E.J., 1979. *Job Analysis: Methods and Applications.* New York: AMACOM.

McEvoy, G.M., 1988. Evaluating the boss: Should subordinate appraisals of management be allowed? *Personnel Administrator, 33,* 115–120.

————, & Buller, P., 1987. User acceptance of peer appraisals in an industrial setting. *Personnel Psychology, 40,* 785–797.

————, Buller, P., & Roghaar, S.R., 1988. A jury of one's peers. *Personnel Administrator, 33,* 94–101.

McFarlane Shore, L., & Thornton, G.C., III., 1986. Effects of gender on self and supervisory ratings. *Academy of Management Journal, 29,* 115–129.

McKenna, D.D., & Golz, J.M., 1983. Do behavioral observation scales measure traits? Effects of memory availability on performance ratings. Paper presented at the 91st annual meeting of the American Psychological Association, Anaheim, CA.

McShane, S.L., 1989. Employee performance and wrongful dismissal. Presentation at Violating the Employment Relationship. Seminar for professional human resource managers. Vancouver, BC.

Meichenbaum, D., 1974. Self-instructional strategy training: A cognitive prothesis for the aged. *Human Development, 17,* 273–280.

———, 1977. *Cognitive Behavior Modification: An Integrative Approach.* New York: Plenum Press.

Meritor Savings Bank v. *Vinson,* 1986. 477 U.S. 57; 40 FEP 1822.

Metz v. *Transit Mix, Inc.,* 1987. 828 F.2d 1202, 44 FEP 1339, (7th Cir.).

Metz, E.J., 1989. Designing legally defensible performance appraisal systems. *Training and Development Journal, 42,* 47–51.

Meyer, H.H., Winter 1975. The pay-for-performance dilemma. *Organizational Dynamics, 3,* 39–50.

———, 1977. The annual performance review discussion: Making it constructive. *Personnel Journal, 56,* 508–511.

———, 1991. A solution to the performance appraisal enigma. *Academy of Management Executive, 5,* 68–75.

———, & Kay, E.A., 1964. Comparison of a work planning program with the annual performance appraisal interview approach. Behavioral Research Report No. ESR1 7, General Electric Company.

———, Kay, E., & French, J.R.P., Jr., 1965. Split roles in performance appraisal. *Harvard Business Review, 43,* 123–129.

Meyer, W.E., 1981. A process for evaluating senior management performance considering the environment in which that performance takes place. Internal Report, LTV Incorporated.

Milkovich, G.T., Glueck, W.F., Barth, R.T., & McShane, S.L., 1988. Employment planning. In *Canadian Personnel/Human Resource Management: A Diagnostic Approach.* Plano, TX: Business Publications Inc.

Miller, L.M., 1978. *Behavior Management: The New Science of Managing People at Work.* New York: Wiley.

———, 1974. Psychological testing and fair employment practices: A testing program that does not discriminate. *Personnel Psychology, 27,* 49–62.

Mills, P.K., 1983. Self management. *Academy of Management Review, 8,* 445–453.

Miner, J.B., 1974. Psychological testing and fair employment practices: A testing program that does not discriminate. *Personnel Psychology, 27,* 49–62.

Mintzberg, H., 1989. *Mintzberg on Management: Inside Our Strange World of Organizations.* New York: Free Press.

Mitchell, T.R., & Wood, R.E., 1980. Supervisor's responses to subordinate poor performance: A test of an attributional model. *Organizational Behavior and Human Performance, 25,* 123–138.

Mitnick, M.M., 1977. Equal employment opportunity and affirmative action: A managerial training guide. *Personnel Journal, 56,* 492–497, 529.

Mobley, W.H., 1974. The link between MBO and merit compensation. *Personnel Journal, 53,* 423–427.

————, 1982. Supervisor and employee race and sex effects on performance appraisals: A field study of adverse impact and generalizability. *Academy of Management Journal, 25,* 598–606.

Moody v. *Albermarle Paper Co.,* 1973. 474 F.2d. 134 (Ca-4), 5 EPD 8470.

Moses, J.L., & Byham, W.C., 1977. *Applying the Assessment Center Method.* New York: Pergamon Press.

Mount, M.K., & Thompson, D.E., 1987. Cognitive categorization and quality of performance ratings. *Journal of Applied Psychology, 72,* 240–246.

Mullins, C.W., & Kimborough, W.W., 1988. Group composition as a determinant of job analysis outcomes. *Journal of Applied Psychology, 73,* 657–664.

Mumford, M.D., 1983. Social comparison theory and the evaluation of peer evaluations: A review and some applied implications. *Personnel Psychology, 36,* 867–882.

Munchus, G., III., 1989. Personal legal liability of managers under employment discrimination law: Some historical case observations. *Academy of Management Executive, 3,* 246–248.

Murphy, K.R., 1991. Criterion issues in performance appraisal research: Behavioral accuracy versus classification accuracy. *Organizational Behavior and Human Decision Processes, 50,* 45–50.

————, Martin, C., & Garcia, M., 1982. Do behavioral observation scales measure observation? *Journal of Applied Psychology, 67,* 562–567.

Musicante, G.R., Pajer, R.G., & Goldstein, I.L., 1988. Design, implementation and evaluation of a behavioral observation scales–based appraisal system: Performance observation scales. Paper presented at the annual meeting of the Academy of Management. Anaheim, CA.

Nagle, B.F., 1953. Criterion development. *Personnel Psychology, 6,* 271–289.

Napier, N.K., & Latham, G.P., 1986. Outcome expectancies of people who conduct performance appraisals. *Personnel Psychology, 39,* 827–837.

Nathan B.R., & Alexander, R.A., 1985. The role of inferential accuracy in performance rating. *Academy of Management Review, 10,* 109–115.

————, & Cascio, W.F., 1986. Legal and technical standards for performance assessment. In R.A. Burk, ed., *Performance Assessment: Methods and Applications,* Baltimore: Johns Hopkins University Press, pp. 1–50.

————, & Lord, R.G., 1983. Cognitive categorization and dimensional schemata: A process approach to the study of halo in performance ratings. *Journal of Applied Psychology, 68,* 102–114.

————, Mohrman, A.H., Jr., & Milliman, J., 1991. Interpersonal relations as a context for the effects of appraisal interviews on performance and satisfaction: A longitudinal study. *Academy of Management Journal, 34,* 352–369.

Nemeroff, W.F., & Wexley, K.N., 1977. Relationships between performance appraisal interview outcomes by supervisors and subordinates. Paper presented at the annual meeting of the Academy of Management, Orlando, FL.

Nieva, V.F., & Gutek. B.A., 1980. Sex effects on evaluation. *Academy of Management Review, 5,* 267–276.

Norman, C.A., & Zawacki, R.A., 1991. Team appraisals—team approach. *Personnel Journal, 70,* 101–104.

O'Connor, E.J., Peters, L.H., Pooyan, A., Weekley, J., Frank, B., & Erenkrantz, B., 1984. Situational constraint effects on performance, affective reactions, and turnover. A field replication and extension. *Journal of Applied Psychology, 69,* 663–772.

Odiorne, G.S., 1970. *Training by Objectives: An Economic Approach to Management Training.* New York: Macmillan.

Osburn, H.G., & Manese, W.R., 1972. *How to Install and Validate Employee Selection Techniques.* Washington: American Petroleum Institute.

Otis, J., 1952. Whose criterion? Presidential address, Division 14, American Psychological Association. In W.W. Ronan & E.P. Prien, 1971, eds., *Perspectives on the Measurement of Human Performance.* New York: Appleton-Century-Crofts.

Paitich v. *Clarke Institute of Psychiatry,* 1988. 19 CCEL 105 (Ont H.C.J.).

Palmer Coking Coal Company v. *Director, O.W.C.P.,* 1983. 720 F.2d 1054 (9th Cir.).

Peters, L.H., O'Connor, E.J., Weekley, J., Pooyan, A., Frank, B. & Erenkrantz, B., 1984. Sex bias and managerial evaluation: A replication and extension. *Journal of Applied Psychology, 69,* 349–352.

Peters, T.J., & Waterman, R.H., Jr., 1982. *In Search of Excellence: Lessons from America's Best-Run Companies.* New York: Harper & Row.

Podsakoff, P.M., & Todor, W.D., 1985. Relationships between leader reward and punishment behavior and group processes and productivity. *Journal of Management, 11,* 55–73.

——, Todor, W.D., & Skov, R., 1982. Effects of leader contingent and non-contingent reward and punishment behaviors on subordinate performance and satisfaction. *Academy of Management Journal, 25,* 810–812.

Price Waterhouse v. *Hopkins,* 1989. 263 U.S. 321.

Prien, E.P., & Hughes, G.L., 1987. The effect of quality control revisions on mixed standard scale rating errors. *Personnel Psychology, 40,* 815–823.

Prince, J.B., & Lawler, E.E., 1986. Does salary discussion hurt the developmental performance appraisal? *Organizational Behavior and Human Decision Processes, 37,* 357–375.

Pulakos, E.D., & Wexley, K.N., 1983. The relationship among perceptual similarity, sex, and performance ratings in manager-subordinate dyads. *Academy of Management Journal, 26,* 129–139.

——, White, L.A., Oppler, S.H., & Borman, W.C., 1989. Examination of race and sex effects on performance ratings. *Journal of Applied Psychology, 74,* 770–780.

Pursell, E.D., Dossett, D.L., & Latham, G.P., 1980. Obtaining validated predictors by minimizing rating errors in the criterion. *Personnel Psychology, 33,* 91–96.

Rand Corporation, 1988. *Annual Report—The Institute for Civil Justice.* Santa Monica, CA: Rand.

Rand, T.M., & Wexley, K.N., 1975. A demonstration of the Byrne similarity hypothesis in simulated employment interviews. *Psychological Reports, 36,* 535–544.

Ratheon Co. v. *FEHC,* 1988. 46 FEP 1089 (Cal. Super. Ct.).

Redeker, J.R., 1986. The supreme court on affirmative action: Conflicting opinions. *Personnel, 63,* 8–14.

Reid v. *Russel Steel Ltd.,* 1981. 2 C.H.R.R. D/402.

Rios v. *Enterprise Association Steamfitters Local 638,* 1988. 860 F.2d 1168, 48 REP 433 (2d Cir.).

Roadman, H.E., 1964. An industrial use of peer ratings. *Journal of Applied Psychology, 48,* 211–214.

Roberts v. *Versatile Farm Equipment et al.,* 1987. 16 C.C.E.L. 9, 53 Sask. R.219 (Q.B.) 6S3.7792.

Robson v. *General Motors of Canada,* 1982. 37 O.R. (2nd) 229 (Co.Ct.), 3S3.55374.

Rogers, B.F., 1960. The current status of the United States Air Force Officer Effectiveness Report. Unpublished master's thesis, Florida State University.

Ronan, W.W. & Prien, E., 1971. *Perspectives on the Measurement of Human Performance.* New York: Appleton-Century-Crofts.

————, & Latham, G.P., 1974. The reliability and validity of the critical incident technique: A closer look. *Studies in Personnel Psychology, 6,* 53–64.

————, & Prien, E.P., 1966. *Toward a Criterion Theory: A Review and Analysis of Research and Opinion.* Greensboro, NC: The Richardson Foundation.

Roscoe v. *McGavin Foods Ltd.,* 1983. 2 C.C.E.L. 287 (B.C.S.C.) 4S4.55444.

Rothstein, H.R., & Chooi, M.C.M., August 1990. Evaluating the impact of behavioral performance appraisal procedures and feedback: An experimental analysis. Paper presented at the annual meeting of the Academy of Management, San Francisco.

Rowe v. *General Motors,* 1972. 4 FEP 445.

Ryan, T.A., & Smith, P.C., 1954. *Principles of Industrial Psychology.* New York: Ronald.

Saari, L.M., & Latham, G.P., 1980. The validity of trainer ratings in an organizational setting. Unpublished manuscript.

Sackett, P.R., & DuBois, C.L.Z., 1991. Rater-ratee effects on performance evaluation: The effects of work group representation on male-female and white-black differences in performance ratings. *Journal of Applied Psychology, 76,* 873–877.

————, DuBois, C.L.Z., & Wiggins Noe, A., 1991. Tokenism in performance evaluation: The effects of work group representation on male-female and white-black differences in performance ratings. *Journal of Applied Psychology, 76,* 263–267.

Schmidt, F.L., & Johnson, R.H., 1973. Effect of race on peer ratings in an industrial situation. *Journal of Applied Psychology, 57,* 237–241.

———, & Kaplan, L., 1971. Composite vs. multiple criteria: A review and resolution of the controversy. *Personnel Psychology, 24,* 419–434.

———, Hunter, J.E., Outerbridge, A.N., & Trattner, M.H., 1986. The economic impact of job selection methods on size, productivity, and payroll costs of the federal work force: An empirically based demonstration. *Personnel Psychology, 39,* 1–19.

Scholtes, P.R., 1987. An elaboration on Deming's teachings on performance appraisal. Madison, WI: Joiner Association.

Schwab, D.P., Heneman, H.G., & DeCotiis, T.A., 1975. Behaviorally anchored rating scales: A review of the literature. *Personnel Psychology, 28,* 549–562.

Scott v. *Domtar Sonoco Containers Inc.,* 1987. 20, C.C.E.L. 290 (Ont. Dist. Ct.) 6S3.7754.

Seiler, L.H., & Hough, R.L., 1970. Empirical comparisons of the Thurstone and Likert techniques. In G.F. Summers, ed., *Attitude Measurement.* Chicago: Rand McNally.

Siegel, L., 1982. Paired comparison evaluations of managerial effectiveness by peers and supervisors. *Personnel Psychology, 35,* 843–852.

Simpson, S., McCarrey, M., & Edwards, H.P., 1987. Relationship of supervisors' sex role stereotypes to performance evaluation of male and female subordinates in non-traditional jobs. *Canadian Journal of Administrative Science, 4,* 15–30.

Singh v. *Security and Investigation Services Ltd.,* May 31, 1977. Ontario Board of Inquiry, unreported.

Sisson, E.D., 1948. Forced choice: The new army rating. *Personnel Psychology, 1,* 365–381.

Skarlicki, D., Latham, G.P., & Whyte, G., 1993. Utility analysis: Recycling intractable problems. Working paper, University of Toronto.

Skinner, B.F., 1987. What ever happened to psychology as the science of behavior? *American Psychologist, 42,* 780–786.

Slater, P.E., 1958. Contrasting correlates of group size. *Sociometry, 21,* 129–139.

Slocum, J., & Sims, H., 1980. A typology for integrating technology, organization and job design. *Human Relations, 33,* 193–212.

Smith, P.C., 1976. Behaviors, results, and organizational effectiveness: The problem of criteria. In M.D. Dunnette, ed., *Handbook of Industrial and Organizational Psychology.* Chicago: Rand McNally.

Smith, P., & Kendall, L.M., 1963. Retranslation of expectations: An approach to the construction of unambiguous anchors for rating scales. *Journal of Applied Psychology, 47,* 149–155.

Smither, J.W., & Reilly, R.R., 1987. True intercorrelation among job components, time delay in rating, and rater intelligence as determinants of accuracy in performance ratings. *Organizational Behavior and Human Decision Processes, 40,* 369–391.

————, Barry, S.R., & Reilly, R.R., 1989. An investigation of the validity of expert true score estimates in appraisal research. *Journal of Applied Psychology, 74,* 143–151.

Somers, M.J., & Birnbaum, D., 1991. Assessing self-appraisal of job performance as an evaluation device: Are the poor results a function of method or methodology? *Human Relations, 44,* 1081–1091.

Spool, M., 1978. Training programs for observers of behavior: A review. *Personnel Psychology, 31,* 853–888.

Stein v. *B.C. Housing Management Commission,* Feb. 17, 1989. Unpublished BCSC.

Stockford, L., & Bissell, H.W., 1949. Factors involved in establishing a management-rating scale. *Personnel, 26,* 94–116.

Steers, R.M., & Lee, T.W., 1983. Facilitating effective performance appraisals: The role of employee commitment and organizational climate. In F. Landy, S. Zedeck, & J. Cleveland, eds., *Performance Measurement and Theory.* Hillsdale, NJ: Lawrence Erlbaum Associates.

Tabone v. *Midas Canada Inc.,* 1986. 46 Alta. L.R. (2d) 238, 72 A.R. 297 (Q.B.) 6S3.7770.

Teel, K.S., 1978. Self-appraisal revisited. *Personnel Journal, 57,* 364–367.

Thompson, D.E., & Thompson, T.A., 1982. Court standards for job analysis in test validation. *Personnel Psychology, 35,* 865–874.

Thorndike, R.L., 1949. *Personnel Selection: Test and Measurement.* New York: Wiley.

Thurstone, L.L., 1928. Attitudes can be measured. *American Journal of Sociology, 33,* 529–554.

Tice, L.E., 1989. *A Better World A Better You*. Englewood Cliffs, NJ: Prentice-Hall.

Toops, M.A., 1944. The criterion. *Educational and Psychological Measurement, 4*, 271–297.

Trattner, M.H., 1963. Comparison of three methods for assembling aptitude test batteries. *Personnel Psychology, 16*, 221–232.

Tremblett v. *Aardvark Pest Control, Ltd.,* 16 C.C.E.L. 306 (Ont. Dist. Ct.) 6S3.7826.

Trempe, J., Rigny, A.J., & Haccoun, R., 1985. Subordinate satisfaction with male and female managers: Role of perceived supervisory influence. *Journal of Applied Psychology, 70*, 44–47.

Trotter v. *Chesley Town,* 1990. T.L.W. 944-035 (Ontario District Court).

Tuttle, T.C., 1983. Organizational productivity: A challenge for psychologists. *American Psychologist, 38*, 479–486.

Tyler, T.R., 1989. The psychology of procedural justice: A test of the group-value model. *Journal of Personality and Social Psychology, 57*, 830–838.

———, & Bies, R.J., 1989. Beyond formal procedures: The interpersonal context of procedural justice. In J. Carroll, ed., *Advances in Applied Social Psychology: Business Settings*. Hillsdale, NJ: Lawrence Earlbaum & Associates.

———, & Caine, A., 1981. The role of distributive and procedural fairness in the enforcement of formal leaders. *Journal of Personality and Social Psychology, 41*, 643–655.

———, & Folger, R., 1980. Distributional and procedural aspects of satisfaction with citizen-police encounters. *Basic and Applied Social Psychology, 1*, 281–292.

Tziner, A., & Kopelman, R., 1988. Effects of rating format on goal-setting dimensions: A field experiment. *Journal of Applied Psychology, 73*, 323–326.

———, & Latham, G.P., 1989. The effects of appraisal instrument, feedback and goal setting on worker satisfaction and commitment. *Journal of Organizational Behavior, 10*, 145–153.

———, Kopelman, R., & Livneh, N., 1992. Effects of performance appraisal format on perceived goal characteristics, appraisal process satisfaction, and changes in rated job performance: A field experiment. Paper presented at the Annual Meeting of the Academy of Management, Las Vegas.

United States v. *City of Chicago,* 1976. 8 EPD.

United States v. *Paradise,* 1987. 43 FEP 1.

United States v. *Paradise,* 1984. No. 85-999, slip op (U.S. February 25).

Vorvis v. *Insurance Corporation of British Columbia,* 1984. 9DLR (4th) 40 (C.A.).

Vroom, V.H., & Maier, N.R.F., 1961. Industrial social psychology. *Annual Review of Psychology, 12,* 413–446.

Wade v. *Mississippi Cooperative Extension Service,* 1974. 372 F. Supp. 126, 7 EPD 9186.

Waite v. *LaRonge Child Care Co-operative,* 1985. 40 Sask. R. 260 (Q.B.) 5S6.14795.

Waldman, D.A., & Avolio, B.J., 1991. Race effects in performance evaluations: Controlling for ability, education, and experience. *Journal of Applied Psychology, 76,* 897–901.

Wallace v. *Toronto Dominion Bank,* 1981. 41 O.R.(2nd.) 161, 145 D.L.R. (3rd.) 431, 83 C.L.L.C. 14,031 (C.A.) 4S4.55362.

Wallace, S.R., 1965. Criteria for what? *American Psychologist, 20,* 411–417.

Wanous, J.P., 1989. Installing a realistic job preview: Ten tough choices. *Personnel Psychology, 42,* 117–134.

————, 1992. *Recruitment, Selection, Orientation and Socialization of Newcomers.* Reading, MA: Addison-Wesley.

Ward's Cove v. *Antonio,* 1989. 57 U.S.L.W. 4583.

Warmke, D.L., & Billings, R.S., 1979. Comparison of training methods for improving the psychometric quality of experimental and administrative performance ratings. *Journal of Applied Psychology, 64,* 124–131.

Waters, L.K., & Waters, C.W., 1970. Peer nominations as predictors of short term sales performance. *Journal of Applied Psychology, 54,* 42–44.

Watson v. *Fort Worth Bank and Trust Company,* 1988. 487 U.S. 108.

Wayne, S.J., & Ferris, G.R., 1990. Influence tactics, affect and exchange quality in supervisor-subordinate interactions: A laboratory experiment and field study. *Journal of Applied Psychology, 75,* 487–499.

Weiss, D.H., May 1988. The legal side of performance appraisals. *Management Solutions,* 27–31.

Weitz, J., 1958. Selecting supervisors with peer ratings. *Personnel Psychology, 11,* 25–35.

Wendelken, A.J., & Inn, A., 1981. Nonperformance influences on performance evaluations: A laboratory phenomenon. *Journal of Applied Psychology, 66,* 149–158.

Wernimont, P.R., & Campbell, J.P., 1968. Signs, samples, and criteria. *Journal of Applied Psychology, 52,* 372–376.

Wexley, K.N., & Latham, G.P., 1991. *Developing and Training Human Resources in Organizations.* New York: HarperCollins.

———, & Nemeroff, W.F., 1974. Effects of racial prejudice, race of applicant, and biographical similarity on interviewer evaluations of job applicants. *Journal of Social and Behavioral Sciences, 20,* 66–78.

———, & Pulakos, E.D., 1982. Sex effects on performance ratings in manager-subordinate dyads: A field study. *Journal of Applied Psychology, 67,* 433–439.

———, & Silverman, S.V., 1993. *Working Scared: Achieving Success in Trying Times.* San Francisco: Jossey-Bass.

———, & Yukl, G.A., 1977. *Organizational Behavior and Personnel Psychology.* Homewood, IL: Irwin.

———, Sanders, R.E., & Yukl, G.A., 1973. Training interviewers to eliminate contrast effects in employment interviews. *Journal of Applied Psychology, 57,* 233–236.

———, Singh, J.P., & Yukl, G.A., 1973. Subordinate personality as a moderator of the effects of participation in three types of appraisal interviews. *Journal of Applied Psychology, 58,* 54–59.

———, Yukl, G.A., Kovacs, S.Z., & Sanders, R.E., 1972. Importance of contrast effects in employment interviews. *Journal of Applied Psychology, 56,* 45–48.

Wherry, R.J., & Bartlett, C.J., 1982. The control of bias in ratings: A theory of rating. *Personnel Psychology, 35,* 521–525.

———, & Fryer, H., 1949. Buddy ratings: Popularity contest or leadership criteria? *Personnel Psychology, 2,* 147–159.

White, J., 1982. *Rejection.* Reading, MA: Addison-Wesley.

Wiersma, U., & Latham, G.P., 1986. The practicality of behavioral observation scales, behavioral expectation scales, and trait scales. *Personnel Psychology, 39,* 619–628.

————, van den Berg, P., & Latham, G.P., July 1992. Dutch reactions to behavioral observation, behavioral expectation, and trait scales. Paper presented at the Third International Conference on Personnel and Human Resources Management. Hertfordshire, England.

Williams, S.E., & Leavitt, H.J., 1947. Group opinion as a predictor of military leadership. *Journal of Consulting Psychology, 11,* 283–291.

Wood, R.E., & Bandura, A., 1985. Impact of conceptions of ability on self-regulatory mechanisms and complex decision making. *Journal of Personality and Social Psychology, 5,* 805–814.

Wright, P.M., & Wexley, K.N., May 1985. How to choose the kind of job analysis you really need. *Personnel,* 51–55.

Wygant v. *Jackson Board of Education,* 1986. 476 U.S. 267.

Yukl, G.A., & Latham, G.P., 1975. Consequences of reinforcement schedules and incentive magnitudes for employee performance: Problems encountered in an industrial setting. *Journal of Applied Psychology, 60,* 294–298.

Zaleznik, A., 1989. *The Managerial Mystique.* New York: Harper & Row.

Index